D1549853

THE HAUNT OF MISERY

THE HAUNT
OF MISERY
Critical essays in social work and helping

Edited by
CHRIS ROJEK,
GERALDINE PEACOCK,
and STEWART COLLINS

ROUTLEDGE
London and New York

First published in 1989 by Routledge
11 New Fetter Lane, London, EC4P 4EE.

© 1989 Routledge

Typeset by Gilfillan Ltd, Mitcham, Surrey.
Printed and bound in Great Britain by
Mackays of Chatham PLC, Kent

British Library Cataloguing in Publication Data
The haunt of misery : critical essays in social work and helping.
    1. Great Britain. Welfare work
    I. Rojek, Chris
    II. Peacock, Geraldine
    III. Collins, Stewart
    361.3'0941

ISBN 0-415-01744-0

Contents

Contributors

Roger Ballard, Lecturer in Social Work, Department of Psychology, University of Leeds

Stewart Collins, Senior Lecturer in Social Work, The Queen's College, Glasgow

Patricia Kearney, Social Worker, University College Drug Dependency Unit, London

Mary Marshall, Director, Age Concern Scotland, Edinburgh

Geraldine Peacock, Deputy Director, London Boroughs' Training Committee

Geoffrey Pearson, Professor of Social Work, Middlesex Polytechnic

Chris Rojek, Senior Editor in Sociology, Routledge

Mike Stein, Lecturer in Applied Social Studies and Dr Barnardo's Research Fellow, University of Leeds

Editors' note

Readers with a nose for nepotism may wonder at the connection between the imprint of the book and the current employment status of one of the editors. Such readers should know that the book was contracted, together with its companion volume, *Social Work and Received Ideas*, when all three editors worked as full-time lecturers at The Queen's College, Glasgow. Furthermore, the original publisher was to be Tavistock Publications, not Routledge. However, along the way, the market which dispersed the authors around the country also intervened to bring about the merger of Tavistock into Routledge.

Such is the manner of the world and times in which we live.

Introduc
'The immense hau

'The immense haunt of misery' is Engels' phrase. It crops up in the 'Preface' to the English edition of his book, *The Condition of the Working Class in England* (Engels 1892). The phrase refers to the poor of London's East End. Engels saw in them the humiliating misery caused by class inequality and exploitation. Yet, as a dialectical thinker, he also saw the latent power of the poor to overthrow the system that enslaves them. Indeed, the 'Preface' comments favourably on the 'New Unionism' of unskilled workers in the 1880s as a sign of what collective organisation and action can achieve.

In reformulating Engels' phrase for the title of this book we do not mean to suggest that the working class in Britain is in a revolutionary situation. Far from it. Antagonism against capitalism is real and widespread. But one can no longer share Engels' conviction that class is the only or the most salient dimension of opposition. In the last twenty-five years, movements based on gender, race, and subculture (e.g., ecology groups, CND, youth groups, etc.), have emerged which lack a distinctive or consistent class character.

These developments have far-reaching implications for social work in general, and radical social work in particular. Jones may be right to declare that 'in the main the clients of social work are working class and poor' (Jones 1983: 12). But he is wrong to appear to be so final in his statement. Within the social categories of 'working class' and 'poor', important status and subcultural divisions and variations exist. Unless we recognise their confused and conflicting implications we will fall prey to unrealistic expectations regarding class organisation and action. What is more, status and subcultural distinctions and variations are not confined to social classes. Within the social categories of gender and race important sectional divisions exist, which make the unqualified use of terms like 'gender' and 'race' as the founda-

1

revolutionary politics highly problematic.
k and Received Ideas (Rojek, Peacock, and Collins
ch is the companion volume to this set of critical
we argued that social work is in a profound state of crisis.
is is hardly an exceptional argument. Indeed, in critical circles
surrounding social work it might almost be said to be the conventional wisdom. Others have emphasised the role of class inequality, cuts in state funding and the growing influence of red tape and professionalism in explaining the crisis (see, for example, Bolger *et al.* 1981; Corrigan and Leonard 1978; Galper 1975; and Richan and Mendelsohn 1973). For our own part, we see these factors as only parts of the story. In *Social Work and Received Ideas* we argued that the roots of the crisis lie in the failure of the received ideas and language of social work to express felt need. The traditional social-work values of self-realisation, respect for clients and non-judgementalism are host to a variety of contradictions. As Wilkes (1985: 50) says of self-realisation:

> The BASW Code of Ethics recognises 'the value and dignity of every human being' and accepts 'the responsibility to encourage and facilitate the self realisation of the individual person with due regard to others'. At the same time social work education teaches methods that are decidedly directive in that they are based on theories purporting to explain human behaviour with a view to improving it.

Similarly, Dale and Foster (1986: 96) attack social workers influenced by psycho-dynamic approaches for not recognising 'that the problems faced by their individual female clients might have been more related to their positions in society than to their individual psyches'.

As for radical approaches, notably Marxism and feminism, the assumption of collectivism which they make begins to look more and more like a presumption. The problem here is not so much the proposition that oppressed collections of people, such as the working class and women, have real interests in changing society. Rather, it is the assumption that these interests are recognised in a uniform and binding way. Status and subcultural divisions between these collections of people have turned out to be far more diverse and resilient than was imagined in social works' radical *temps perdu* back in the 1960s and seventies. In addition, Marxism and feminism have been criticised for nursing a latent authoritarianism which belies their spirit of emancipation. For example, Yelloly (1987: 19) admonishes Marxist social workers for assuming that 'there is a "right" construction and the social worker knows what it is; no room here for woolly-minded attempts to "start where the family is" or to enter into their world of meanings, constructions and struggles'.

Not all of the contributors to this book share the analysis set out in *Social Work and Received Ideas*. However, what is common to all is a critical concern with the evident failure of social work in meeting, let alone satisfying, the felt needs of many clients. Geoffrey Pearson begins the collection with a typically refreshing and incisive piece. He argues that the mainspring behind the received ideas and practices of social work in the postwar period has been the assumption of full employment. Social work has pursued a 'rehabilitative ideal' which associates normal citizenship with property ownership and regular paid employment. Even during the time of full employment this position was unconvincing, for it marginalised the employment status of women. However, in the last decade, full employment has been transformed into a memory, leaving the rehabilitative ideal high and dry. Pearson dissects the mythology of unemployment in modern Britain and lays bare the personal and social consequences of being without work. The chapter also includes a memorable commentary on the invalid hopes generated in social work's 'radical hour' during the 1960s and seventies.

An important theme in Pearson's chapter is that social workers were not prepared for the problems caused by large-scale unemployment. The theme of lack of preparedness is continued in the second chapter. Geraldine Peacock examines the reaction to the AIDS crisis. She argues that the social problems caused by AIDS and HIV infection were used by some sections of public opinion to mobilise thinly veiled moral prejudices against homosexuals, drug users, ethnic minorities, and the permissive society. Public alarm was increased by the heavy-handed publicity used in the first stages of the government information campaign. Positive responses to people with AIDS and HIV infection were basically defined in medical terms – namely, finding the 'miracle' cure for the 'killer' disease. The positive potential of social work in providing counselling support and alleviating distress was almost wholly neglected. The chapter examines some of the initiatives made by social workers and voluntary organisations, like the Terrence Higgins Trust, to deal effectively and sensitively with the crisis. Peacock's chapter can be read as an important contribution to the growing literature on social work and AIDS and HIV infection. However, it is also a richly detailed case study in poor liaison among government agencies, doctors, social workers, and the media. Peacock shows how the public creation of received wisdom can obstruct the capacity of social work for effective help.

The question of the obstructive consequences of received wisdom is further examined in Chapter 3. Patricia Kearney considers social work and drug use. She identifies a failure of social workers to respond adequately. Social workers share many of the false received ideas on drug use which are entertained by the public. Kearney pays close attention to the powerful stereotypes of the drug user which abound in public life. She shows how these act as a barrier to effective social work. The problem is compounded by the organisation of work with drug users. Kearney maintains that the use of specialist workers isolates drug issues from generic social workers. False received ideas are therefore reinforced. The chapter concludes with a series of proposals designed to achieve a more positive response from social workers to the question of drug use.

An important recent trend in social work has been the growth of support for greater consumer involvement in social work. In Chapter 4 Stewart Collins and Mike Stein provide an overview of the strengths and weaknesses of the various initiatives in client participation in Britain. They consider the promise of participation in Patch, Decentralisation and Community Oriented Social Work. They continue by examining the impact of client collectives in social work. Collins and Stein argue that collectives can act as important forums for consciousness raising and mutual support. However, they also fully convey the practical difficulties caused by marginalisation in making collectives function effectively. Collins and Stein conclude that productive liaison between collectives and social work requires social workers to be sensitive to the integrity and autonomy of collectives. The authors include an extended discussion of the National Association of Young People in Care in order to illustrate the challenges and dilemmas posed by collective organisation.

Most commentators on planning for demand in social work and the social services in the years up to the year 2000 and beyond agree that care for the elderly will figure as a major growth area. However, as Mary Marshall points out in the fifth chapter of the book, the field of social work with elderly people is grossly underdeveloped. Moreover, many social workers and members of the public are prey to a web of unexamined assumptions and false received ideas on the needs of the elderly. In this informed and valuable commentary, Marshall dispels the myth that old age is a foreign country. Old people may have special needs with respect to their health or their experience of loss; but for the rest, their needs resemble those of any adult person. In the closing section of her chapter, Marshall uses this observation to criticise dominant systems of care for the elderly in long-stay hospitals and residential care settings. She argues that these systems play an important part in perpetuating damaging received ideas about the desires and needs of the elderly.

Britain is a multi-racial society. Yet the received ideas which govern social consciousness and social policy are dominated by the values of male, white, middle-class society. In Chapter 6 Roger Ballard considers the position of the black client in the white-dominated world of British social work. He argues that demographic and social forces have combined in the 1970s and eighties to make black clients feature as a larger proportion of inner city caseloads. At the same time, Ballard contends that social workers continue to labour under false assumptions regarding the cultural requirements and flexibility of ethnic minorities. He argues that the good intentions of Local Authority Racial Awareness Training programmes have often gone awry because of their political and sociological naïvety. Ballard shows clearly that racism is deeply embedded in white culture. Combating it requires social workers to do more than develop a knowledge base of the culture and lifestyle of ethnic minorities. It requires them to confront the unintentional ways in which social workers perpetuate racist values through their taken-for-granted thoughts, words, and actions.

Helping clients is a co-operative venture which involves social workers in close liaison with other specialist personnel. In the penultimate chapter of the book Stewart Collins explores relations between social workers and one specialist group of helpers: psychiatrists. He argues that social workers and psychiatrists regularly fail to see eye to eye. He analyses this in terms of the contrasting patterns of recruitment, different training processes and unequal social status between the two professions. Collins suggests that points of divergence between social workers and psychiatrists impede client care. The chapter fastens upon examples from the language of social work and psychiatry to illustrate how meanings collide and fragment in use. Collins also shows how negative received ideas about what are called 'mental health problems' are passed on through the linguistic and training inheritance of social workers.

The final chapter returns to the theme of power, participation, and planning in social work which was raised in Chapter 4. In it Chris Rojek considers the potential of self-management in social work. Rojek contends that the present hierarchical system of management is inefficient. In particular, the knowledge and skills of basic grade workers, ancillary staff and client groups are either used badly or ignored. Rojek relates the level of discontent among social workers, which is currently very high, to the dominant system of management. He employs comparative material from the Yugoslav experience of self-management to outline a model of self-management for social work in Britain. Rojek concludes that it would be foolish to see self-management as a cure-all philosophy. However, it does have the potential to increase collective responsibility and produce more relevant systems of social work.

Like all books, *The Haunt of Misery* is a product of time and place. The plan was conceived when all three of us worked as full-time lecturers on the three-year CQSW course for mature students with family commitments and the one-year CQSW course for postgraduate students at the Queen's College, Glasgow. This was between 1982 and 1986 – a time which spanned the report of the Barclay Committee (1982) which included proposals for fundamental reorganisation in social services, and the first meetings of social work educators to hammer out a new national qualifying course for students.

The essays were commissioned, written, and delivered between 1986 and 1988. Time will tell, but we believe that these will prove to be notorious years in the history of social work in Britain. In 1986 the Social Security Act was passed. The Act makes provision for the most sweeping changes in the system of benefits since the 1940s. April 1988 witnessed the application of these changes, which have far-reaching implications for the social-work role in dealing with claimants.

The years 1986 to 1988 are also memorable for the spate of public inquiries into the alleged failures of social workers in dealing with cases of child abuse. The report on the death of Tyra Henry (Lambeth Borough Council Sedley Report 1987), indicated that more efficient planning and liaison among social workers was needed, while the Carlile inquiry (Greenwich Borough Town Hall 1987) into the death of Kimberley Carlile concluded that her death at the hands of her stepfather could have been avoided. It found Greenwich social workers and health visitors to be negligent in monitoring the case. Public disquiet and scrutiny regarding the role of social work has intensified. As we write this introduction, the report of the Cleveland Inquiry and the publication of the Wagner and Griffiths reports are impending. All three are purported to have dramatic implications for the future of social work.

The planning and preparation of the book therefore coincided with one of the most disturbing and revisionist times in the history of British social work. Unquestionably, this reflects the expansion of a general moral and political climate in the 1980s of disenchantment with the philosophy of state assistance. The so-called 'enterprise culture' of the new right has placed more emphasis upon individual resourcefulness and voluntary care in the management of need. Translated into public policy, this has been expressed in official tolerance for unemployment figures of three million, the deterioration of public health and education services, and the reduction, in real terms, of money spent on personal social services. Not surprisingly, the gap in inequality between the richest and poorest sections of society has increased. The bottom 40 per cent of households witnessed a fall in their share of total household income from 8.7 per cent in 1981 to 6.4 per cent in 1983. The top fifth increased their share from 46.4 to 48.6 per cent. In terms of wealth, including pension rights, the share of the top 10 per cent of the population rose over the same period from 34 to 35 per cent. The number of families on or below the supplementary benefit line rose by 1.5 million from 3.9 million in 1979 to 5.5 million in 1983 (*Social Trends* 17 1987). Expressed in real terms, most welfare claimants are worse off in terms of income entitlement and quality of service than they were ten years ago. Furthermore, the provision of the Social Fund and Income Support arrangements under the terms of the 1986 Social Security Act look set to intensify this trend. The DHSS estimates that only 35 per cent of claimants will lose as a result of the changes. MacPherson and Svenson (1988), of the Benefits Research Unit at Nottingham University, estimate that the true figure is nearly 60 per cent of claimants. For some groups this figure will be higher. Thus, MacPherson and Svenson calculate that 81 per cent of couples with children, 74 per cent of single parents, and 90 per cent of pensioner couples will lose from the reforms.

At the same time the enterprise culture pumps out the message that the poor must pull themselves up by their own bootstraps. Self-help is the order of the day. The long-term unemployed, those who live on council estates, or who 'chose' to remain in areas of high unemployment are dismissed as failures. Since the enterprise culture is thoroughly materialistic, it devalues all forms of knowledge and expertise which do not carry an unreflective commitment to wealth creation. Hence, the slow attrition of public funds to the National Health Service, the personal social services and the vicious attacks on education, especially the provision of higher education in the humanities and social sciences. Hence too, the worship of the entrepreneur as the true practical social worker. For, as the culture has it, only the entrepreneur can create real jobs, and real jobs are seen as the true means of welfare for the poor.

If we lived in a society where everyone had equal opportunity, the enterprise culture would be more tenable. However, this is not the case. British society is marked by deep class inequality, sexism, and racism. The conceits of the enterprise culture have done little to diminish the exploitation and oppression of low-paid workers, women, and ethnic minorities. Indeed, the figures on inequality that we mentioned above suggest that relative deprivation in the poorest sections of society has increased since the end of the seventies. The principal beneficiaries of the so-called 'Thatcher revolution' have, unequivocally, been the rich. They have gained through the stock-market boom, cuts in income taxes, larger than average increases in gross pay, and major concessions on capital taxes, notably on Capital Gains Tax and Capital Transfer Tax.

The critical essays in this book explore some of the main problems facing social workers in a society which has become more candid in its exhibition of materialism and possessive individualism. They consider the flaws in the official philosophy of welfare management which, to adapt Adorno's (1973: 67) memorable phrase, displays 'self-righteous humanity in the midst of general inhumanity'. 'Misery' is a relative term. Our book will have failed if it leaves the reader with the presiding impression that conditions for clients and social workers are everywhere steadily deteriorating. In planning the book and commissioning the contributors, we sought to develop a more complicated, ambivalent picture. The management of welfare involves *struggle*. From adversity comes challenge; force promotes resistance; action breeds reaction — these are the themes that we aimed to emblazon in the book. We see social work as an axis of control and opposition in society. The essays in this book show that its capitulation to the values of the enterprise culture is uneven, calculating, and conditional.

Chris Rojek
Geraldine Peacock
Stewart Collins

London and Glasgow, 1988

References

Adorno, T. (1973) *The Jargon of Authenticity*, London: Routledge & Kegan Paul.

Barclay Committee Report (1982) *Social Workers, Their Roles and Tasks*, London: Bedford Square Press.

Bolger, S., Corrigan, P., and Frost, N. (1981) *Towards Socialist Welfare Work*, London: Macmillan.

Corrigan, P. and Leonard, P. (1978) *Social Work Practice under Capitalism*, London: Macmillan.

Dale, J. and Foster, P. (1986) *Feminists and the Welfare State*, London: Routledge & Kegan Paul.

Engels, F. (1892) *The Condition of the Working Class in England*, Moscow: Progress Publishers (1973 edn).

Galper, J. (1975) *The Politics of Social Service*, Englewood Cliffs, NJ: Prentice-Hall.

Greenwich Borough Town Hall (1987) *A Child in Mind: Protection of Children in a Responsible Society*, London.

Jones, C. (1983) *State Social Work and the Working Class*, London: Macmillan.

Lambeth Borough Council Sedley Report (1987) *Whose Child?*, London: Lambeth Borough Council.

MacPherson, S. and Svenson, M. (1988) 'Attrition benefits', The Guardian, 24 Feb.

Richan, C. and Mendelsohn, F.R. (1973), *Social Work: the Unloved Profession*, New York: Franklin Watts.

Rojek, C., Peacock, G., and Collins, S. (1988) *Social Work and Received Ideas*, London: Routledge.

Social Trends 17 (1987) London: HMSO.

Wilkes, R. (1985) 'Social work: what kind of profession?', in D. Watson (ed.), *A Code of Ethics for Social Work: the Second Step*, London: Routledge & Kegan Paul.

Yelloly, M. (1987) 'Why the theory couldn't become practice', *Community Care*, 29 Jan. 18–19, p. 19.

1

Women and men without work: The political economy is personal

Geoffrey Pearson

The return of mass unemployment upsets so many of the assumptions of the postwar welfare state, including the domain of social work. This is not only a matter of fiscal policy, in terms of how the welfare state would be financed through national insurance and taxation. The assumption of full employment also reached deep into everyday life, in that it determined what ordinary men and women might aspire to in terms of 'success' in their lives. It defined the aspiration to a decent job with a decent wage, a decent home, and a decent future for oneself and one's children as not only an achievable goal, but also as what life was really all about. This was 'normality', and those who could not (or who would not) fit in with this state of affairs were the 'deviants', the 'misfits', the 'drop-outs', and the 'inadequates' who were the business of social workers. The aim of social work, stated in its fundamentals, was then that of 'rehabilitation'.

Quite clearly, these definitions of a 'normal' citizen and 'normal' life aspirations have been disrupted by the return of mass unemployment. This, in turn, affects the aims of social work and the kinds of work which social workers are expected to do. A recent survey for the Health Education Council showed a number of ways in which unemployment was proving to be a disturbing influence for social workers, health visitors, and other related professionals (see Popay, Dhooge, and Shipman 1986). Mass unemployment meant for social workers, for example, that they were increasingly being brought into contact with many more 'normal' people than formerly – people, that is, who had been thrust into a variety of personal, social, and material difficulties as a direct consequence of unemployment, and who would not otherwise have been brought into contact with social workers. Increasing numbers of requests for help involved straightforward, but nevertheless often intractable, financial difficulties.

Larger numbers of young people who had been made homeless were requesting social work help. Frequently, it was not clear what social workers could be expected to do about these kinds of problems, and social workers seemed to be suffering from a sense of bewilderment. The burden of what I have to say is an attempt to clarify what this bewilderment is about, while also suggesting some possible lines of action.

Social work ideology and the 'rehabilitative ideal'

It is first necessary to recognise that social workers are often bewildered by the problems of unemployment for perfectly good reasons, because, just as mass unemployment undermines the expectations of what might count as a 'successful' life for so many people, equally social work's own accustomed attitude as to what might count as 'success' is thrown into disarray. The bedrock of social work's received ideas in the postwar era, which I will call the 'rehabilitative ideal', rested upon the assumptions of a full employment policy. People do not become the clients of social workers unless they are regarded as troublesome in some way, and one important source of trouble was the inability of a person to be self-reliant which would imply their capacity to maintain at least a foothold in the labour market.

The implicit goal within the 'rehabilitative ideal', which was to return clients to the labour market, could be sensed across a range of activities. The successful rehabilitation of mental patients, for example, could often be most easily tested against whether they were able to sustain a job. Indeed, sometimes this was the explicit formulation of the problem, whereby the rehabilitative task would be accomplished through combinations of social work assistance, occupational therapy, and sheltered employment schemes (see Heimler 1967). Work with the disabled, equally, often focused on the attempt to reintegrate people into the labour market – either as fully competitive workers, or through a variety of graded employment projects such as training centres, specially equipped workshops such as those for the blind, or 'Remploy'. In 'child-care' work also, the underlying problem would often prove to be family poverty which might have come about through haphazard work disciplines – although in the so-called 're-discovery of poverty' in the 1960s, one of the most important discoveries was that a significant proportion of poor people were in full-time employment, so that the actual problem was low wages (see Abel-Smith and Townsend 1967).

The aim of securing training opportunities and waged employment even for those of extremely limited ability, such as the mentally handicapped, was also often an achievable goal – whereas today it would more often be unthinkable for social workers to entertain such ideas. Indeed, it might be seen as no more than a cruel deception in the face of the actually existing limitations imposed by the conditions of mass unemployment.

The test of the 'rehabilitative ideal' was never more sure, however, than in work directed towards the 're-settlement' of offenders. If the devil made work for idle hands, then a 'steady job' was the most effective guarantee to remove someone from the temptation to commit further crime. This was explicitly stated in the Probation Rules, which required the probationer to 'lead an industrious life' through 'suitable and regular employment' (Home Office 1965). Moreover, this requirement stood in the shadow of a formidable historical legacy, going back to the origins of the system of penitentiaries and reformatory institutions in the late eighteenth and nineteenth centuries, whereby the place of enforced labour as an instrument of penal discipline and character reform had been central to the development of the modern state apparatus – whether in the form of 'hard labour' and penal servitude, the skills training and apprenticeship schemes of the Borstal system, or the symbolic physical labour of the tread-wheel and hand-crank (see Ignatieff 1978; Rusche and Kirchheimer 1939; Foucault 1977; Bentham 1791). Given the long service and pervasive influence of these penal philosophies, the consequences of high unemployment have been to disturb not only the work of probation officers, but also the assumptions underlying sentencing policies of the courts where employment status had been conventionally a major consideration (see Crow and Simon 1987).

The history of labour disciplines in the development of welfare services could, of course, be developed in considerable detail to encompass the traditions of the Poor Law and the workhouse, the Charity Organisation Society's notions of self-reliance, industrial schools for neglected children, General Booth's Salvationist schemes of spiritual reclamation, or the 'labour colonies' which preoccupied philanthropists such as Canon Barnett in the late nineteenth century as the necessary means for dealing with the 'residuum' of the poor (see Booth 1890; Stedman Jones 1971; Garland 1985). Nevertheless, it is sufficient to recognise that, although the development of the modern welfare state has often been understood as involving a sharp departure from these earlier traditions, we can see that the centrality of labour as an organ-

ising principle of interventions into the lives of the poor continued within the postwar social work ideology of the 'rehabilitative
ideal'. So that across a whole range of social work activities –
with the mentally ill, the physically disabled, the mentally handicapped, 'problem families', and offenders – the notion that the
client should regain a 'steady' employment record could be
regarded as a test of social work success, as well as a major justification for social work itself. And it was these tests and justifica-
tions, with their formidable historical lineage, which quite simply
became redundant with the return of mass unemployment.

The problem of gender: women, work, and the family

Here we must stand back for a moment, in order to reflect upon
the fact that it is not only that these assumptions have collapsed
in upon themselves in so many of our industrial towns and cities.
There is also a problem that the 'client' in these redundant social
work discourses was always assumed to be a man. And with this,
there was the attendant assumption that men were the sole
bread-winners in families, or in the case of single men that they
should be self-supporting. In the Beveridge formulation of the
postwar welfare state, it was a root assumption that women – who
at that critical moment of the war effort in 1942 were firmly
located as workers in the public services, aircraft factories, and
other war industries – would be economically dependent upon
men on the resumption of normality. Man and wife were regarded by Beveridge (1942: 49-50) 'as a team' for the purposes of
national insurance, with the further assumption that 'during
marriage most women will not be gainfully employed' except on
an 'intermittent' basis. The 'attitude of the housewife to gainful
employment outside the home is not and should not be the same
as that of the single woman. She has other duties . . . ' (ibid.: 52;
see Wilson 1977: 149-54).

As for 'single women', with or without children, these had
been traditionally defined as problems by their very status: 'problem mums' and 'neurotic spinsters'; 'blue stockings' and
'prudes'; women somehow dangerous by their very independence (see Jeffreys 1986). And nor was it only the single or
unmarried status of women which was regarded as problematic,
in that the entire basis of women's relations to the external world
of work was highly questionable. Under the extremities of war, it
had been grudgingly conceded that women must constitute a
major part of the workforce, involving the relaxation of conven-

14

tional attitudes and the provision of necessary child-care facilities as appendages to the war effort. By a variety of propaganda means and slogans women were coaxed out of the home – 'Women of Britain, Come into the Factories', 'Come and Help with the Victory Harvest', 'You are Needed in the Fields!' – even though, as the research of Denise Riley has shown, this was never intended as more than a temporary arrangement (see Riley 1979, 1981, and 1983). So that after the final victory harvest had been gathered in, the last rivet secured to the aircraft wing, and when the men were returned from the front – then the factory nurseries would be rapidly abandoned, and women's role would again be to preside over the family and home. An intriguing reflection of this 'temporary' state of affairs can be glimpsed in Stanley Spencer's paintings, *Shipbuilding on the Clyde*, which had been commissioned by the War Artists Advisory Committee in 1940. Although Spencer's sketches and studies for this commission included those of women welders in the shipyards, whether by design or default none of these were included in the completed pictures. We can only speculate by what mental processes the skills and labours of women workers had been rendered invisible in the finished product, thereby flawed as a historical record for all its impressive visual power (Arts Council, 1981).

In a legacy inherited from the early Victorians for whom the working mother was 'an unnatural condition' and 'a stigma upon the social state', the problem of the 'independent' woman would return time and time again – particularly when the question of juvenile crime was on the agenda (see Hill 1853: 39; Pearson 1983a). During the First World War, a perceived upsurge in juvenile delinquency which was said to have 'spread through the country like a plague' had been blamed on the wartime work of their mothers – 'some whose heads have been turned', it was said, 'by their new-found economic independence' (Leeson 1917: pp. 15 and 25). And then again after the Second World War, working mothers continued to be blamed for the rampage of 'latch-key kids', truants, vandals, and 'teddy boys'. As T. R. Fyvel described it:

The *general* exodus of married women, many of them mothers, into outside work, in itself helped to create a new social atmosphere, a new *general* way of family life, whereby 'home' for many boys and girls becomes less important in their lives, and the companionship and rules of the irresponsible gang therefore become more important.

(Fyvel 1963: 129)

There was in fact nothing particularly novel about these assertions, which had already been entirely familiar to Victorian
England. Even so, in the aftermath of war there were new arguments and concepts to conjure with such as John Bowlby's
'maternal deprivation', popularised by Fyvel as a lack of security
resulting from 'the mass movement of married women into outside work' which resulted in youngsters who grew up 'emotionally adrift' and 'whose delinquency can be described as a desperate
"stealing for love"'. We might think of this new kind of emphasis
on the psychological estrangements resulting from a mother's
absence from the home as a crucial moment in the consolidation
of the postwar mentality (see Pearson 1978: 150-2; Mitchell 1975:
227-8; Riley 1983).

The proper relationship between a woman, work, and the family as it was understood in the immediate postwar years was tightly confined. If she were a working-class girl, then upon leaving
school she should immediately enter into some kind of menial
employment, such as a shop assistant or factory hand. She
should then 'settle down' through courtship and marriage, but
not too quickly because early marriage itself was a source of great
social anxiety, into a properly regulated family life with a proper
quotient of children. When these were sufficiently grown up,
then she might return to another of those menial jobs reserved
for more mature working-class women – such as a cleaning-
woman in an office or factory, a 'dinner lady' serving in the
school canteen, a low-status ancillary post nursing the sick and
the elderly, or washing other people's laundry. Fyvel, again, oblig-
ingly summarised the prevailing assumptions:

> One can see quite a convenient pattern: a young married
> woman of today will go on working for the first years after
> marriage; she will then stop while she has children and they
> are small, and only as they reach school age and the state
> takes over will she go back to outside work.
>
> (Fyvel 1963: 128-9)

It should not go unnoticed, of course, that these restrictions
on the relationship between women, work, and the family were
not intended to have universal applicability. They were not
intended to constrain women of more affluent means, for example, who might employ nannies when their children were young
and then turn them over to privately run residential schools (the
so-called 'public' schools and 'prep' schools) for the remainder
of their education, so that the notion of a 'family ' or a 'home'

of which the 'latch-key' child was seen to be so sadly deprived simply had no relevance. Indeed, what we encounter in social work's 'rehabilitative ideal' is both a gender-specific and class-based set of discourses – one, moreover which, although it has been rendered obsolete in the context of mass unemployment, was even before that peculiarly ill-suited to so much of social work activity which actually involves working with women in a variety of caring roles. The cornerstone of the 'rehabilitative ideal' implied a fundamentally masculine assumption of returning clients to economic independence through the labour market. For women, on the other hand, where independence was not valued and even feared, it was marriage which was assumed to be the primary good. Marriage and employment, however, were mutually exclusive categories – except for strictly regulated phases in the life cycle. Thus we can see that when the structure of the 'rehabilitative ideal' is teased apart, even before the steep economic recession of the early 1980s had worked its damage, it was already riddled with contradiction and difficulty: difficulties which reached from the commanding heights of its masculine assumptions, to its bedraggled empirical roots.

World upside down: social work's 'radical' hour

Next we must consider, however briefly, the critique of the 'rehabilitative ideal' as it had been developed within the 'radical social work' movement, requiring a further shift of attention. Because it was not so much the gender confusions at the heart of the 'rehabilitative ideal' which attracted the fire of social work's radical critics of the late 1960s and 1970s, as its tendency to individualise and de-politicise social and economic problems such as poverty and social inequality.

Casework ideology, which had been the dominant expression of the rehabilitative ideal in the 1950s and 1960s, understood poverty and unemployment as an expression of personal inadequacy. 'Radical social work', on the other hand, saw this stance as a refusal to engage with the structural roots of social inequality. It was indisputable that under a full employment policy the ranks of the unemployed would include a disproportionate number of people who, by reason of physical illness or disabilities, mental illness, or mental handicap, were marginal to the labour market (see Hakim 1982). Nevertheless, within the heart of the 'affluent' 1960s, Britain's poverty problem had been recently 're-discovered'; and within this re-discovery it was found that one-third of those living at or near poverty levels were in full-time employment (Abel-Smith and Townsend 1967). This revelation indicated as well as anything could the bankruptcy of the idea that 'inadequacy' was at the root of family poverty, and it was seized upon as one of the emblems of the new 'radicalism' which emerged within social work in the late 1960s and early 1970s.

The issue was bluntly summarised in the first issue of *Case Con*, the magazine launched in Britain in 1970 to promote what it called 'revolutionary social work', in a knockabout critique of casework ideology which was carried on its front page in the form of a box cartoon. Here there was portrayed a cruel parody of a television game-show – 'Hello, good evening and welcome to "CAN-U-COPE", the Star Spangled Social Work Show featuring some of Britain's most deprived and inarticulate PROBLEM FAMILIES!!!' – in which the contestants were poor people and claimants who were required to talk to the camera for thirty seconds about their problems and worries without mentioning the words 'housing', 'money', or 'protest'. The leering impresario of this show, King Konn, thus set about to torment the first contestant, 'Mrs Inad' who proved quite incapable of talking about intra-psychic pain and the defects in her personality which Mr Konn identified as the source of her difficulties, and was soon bowled out. 'Defects?' asked Mrs Inad, 'I just need some money!!! Ooops . . . '

The lesson was clear: and nor was it only reflected in the 'student rag' traditions of *Case Con* and the other vaguely anarchistic manifestations of social work's 'radical' hour. There was also supporting evidence that clients' material difficulties were interpreted by social caseworkers as less significant than psychological problems in the empirical research conducted by Mayer and Timms, which appeared as *The Client Speaks*, and which had a profound impact on social work thinking (Mayer and Timms 1970). The argument also cohered with the emerging preoccupations of 'labelling theory', particularly well-exemplified by Thomas Scheff's study of how welfare clients were often powerless in the face of professional ideologies which shaped and determined what should be understood as the true 'reality' of their lives (Scheff 1968). The 'social construction of reality' was to become another slogan of the new radicalism, intended to indicate how professional power diverted attention away from material definitions of welfare problems. And it was in this context that the traditions of Freudian thought which had exercised such an influence upon the intellectual culture of postwar social work were to be dismissed and forgotten for an entire generation (see Pearson, Yelloly, and Treseder 1988).

However, social work's 'radicalism' did not only reassert the importance of the material and structural actualities of poverty and social inequality. It also went further than that and condemned out of hand all attempts to ameliorate the effects of poverty, such as casework or counselling, guidance on the management of scarce finances, or the encouragement of steady employment routines. These were judged to be a 'cool out' or a 'con', measures by which working-class anger was 'bought off' and 'defused', so that clients were adjusted to the system rather than being encouraged to vent their anger against it. This was, of course, a reflection of the most crude form of functionalism imaginable whereby the welfare state was understood as no more than a 'safety-valve' which protected the social system against the otherwise inevitable revolution. And yet, it was also a view which gained succour from the more subtle theorising of Herbert Marcuse, with his notion of 'repressive tolerance'. Social workers in this light became the 'soft cops' of the social control apparatus, guiding their impoverished clientele away from the true path of political necessity into the obscure labyrinths of psychological well-being. Casework, on this account, was what the Charity Organisation Society had said it was in the 1920s: the final bastion against Bolshevism.

It is rather obvious that this was a somewhat grandiose view of social work's capacity to sustain capitalism single-handedly against the revolutionary masses, although it was not obvious at the time. Social work's 'radicalism' was swept along with the current of the 'counter-culture' and the 'New Left' which was at one and the same time profoundly disillusioned with the historical prospects of European and North American civilisation, while also entertaining flighty visions of human emancipation. Indeed, this radicalism was torn by its own inner contradictions. Most significantly, its emphasis upon political materialism stood in an awkward relationship to the profoundly subjectivist and libertarian assumptions of its counter-cultural Utopianism. On the one hand, the poor should be encouraged to refuse the embrace of the 'caring professions'. But at the same time, 'All you need is love . . . . '

If love was to gain the upper hand in 'hippie' philosophies of where 'real' freedom was to be found for those disillusioned middle-class runaways from the affluent society who embraced the counter-cultural dream, it was a love which dared not speak its name in the dealings between radicalised social workers and their poor clientele. For radical social work, as I have already indicated, all attempts to ameliorate the effects of social inequali-

ty or to soften the blow of poverty were to be condemned as a
'con'. So that while the counter-culture came to be associated
with a vigorous 'personal politics', in the form of a politics of cultural diversity which addressed a number of 'underdog' causes
such as the rights of mental patients and homosexual liberties, it
had surprisingly little to offer in the way of a politics of material
deprivation. There were occasional gestures, and no doubt sometimes even small gains, in the sphere of 'community action'. The
'squatting' movement also, although confined almost entirely to
London, protected significant numbers of young people and students against homelessness; whereas the 'claimants union' movement, another manifestation of this period, stuttered to a halt
after a short period of agitation, its fragile energies already
exhausted before the emergence of the world recession (see
Rose 1974).

Nevertheless, what holds the attention more powerfully was
that social work's 'radicalism', with its fitful hold on a materialist
politics, simply failed to recognise the likely impact of the emerging crisis of the world economy. Indeed, what must now seem
quite astonishing was that unemployment simply did not register
as an issue, in spite of the fact that even in the early 1970s there
were worrying indications of rapidly advancing youth unemployment, especially among young black people (see Community
Relations Commission 1974). This lack of attention to the material world had also been reflected in the dominant emphasis of
'radical' deviancy theory and the 'misfit sociologies', where it
had been 'expressive' deviance and 'victimless' crimes such as
drug use and sexual deviation, rather than mainstream property
crime which had formed the central preoccupation (see Liazos
1972; Pearson 1975a). If casework ideology was criticised within
the 'radical' agenda for its neglect of material difficulties, this
proved to be a lonely island within a sea of de-materialised
counter-cultural concerns.

Even so, the problem of the 'radical' critique went even deeper
than that. Unemployment was not merely ignored within these
discourses, it was actively promoted as a 'progressive' and 'liberat-
ing' lifestyle. So that when the question of unemployment did
manage to sneak onto the counter-cultural agenda, it appeared
not as a social problem involving large areas of human difficulty,
but decked out in a hippie hat and a fashionably ragged Afghan
coat, smoking a joint, and exhorting those unfortunate enough
to be locked into the world of work to 'Turn On, Tune In, Drop
Out'. Fred Davis's distinctively West Coast late-sixties argument,
'Why all of us may be hippies some day', stated one version of

this heroic appreciation of unemployment. The hippie refusal of work signified a necessary, trail-blazing cultural exploration of the future – a future 'post-industrial' society where the revolution in production technologies and computers would render human labour unnecessary. Cautious in certain respects, Davis's appraisal of the political implication of the hippies nevertheless set out to rescue them from the obscurity of impoverished Haight Ashbury squats, 'collectives', and disorganised 'happenings' into a significant historical agenda. They were 'rehearsing *in vivo* a number of possible cultural solutions to central life problems posed by the emerging society of the future' where 'certain incipient problems of identity, work and leisure . . . loom ominously [in] Western industrial society' (Davis 1967: 12).

A stronger version of this argument is often inferred from Herbert Marcuse's writings, particularly those which became influential in the late 1960s and early 1970s (1968, 1972). Here the 'Great Refusal' of middle-class affluent lifestyles by the rebellious younger generation implied a new form of opposition to the 'comfortable, smooth, reasonable, democratic unfreedom [that] prevails in advanced industrial civilisation, a token of technical progress' (Marcuse 1968: 19). In the aesthetic fragmentation of modern art, Marcuse divined the emergence of a 'new sensibility' opposing the dominant moral and economic order, no less than in the childlike and playful surrealist antics of 'flower-power' and the 'yippies' which freely mixed sensuality, politics, and a reversal of what was defined as 'straight' and 'clean' in a polymorphous revel of subversion.

> The aesthetic morality is the opposition of puritanism. It does not insist on a daily bath or shower for people whose cleaning practice involve systematic torture, slaughtering, poisoning; nor does it insist on clean clothes for men who are professionally engaged in dirty deals. But it does insist on cleaning the earth from the very material garbage produced by the spirit of capitalism, and from this spirit itself. And it insists on freedom as a biological necessity; being physically incapable of tolerating any repression other than that required for the protection and amelioration of life.
>
> (Marcuse 1972: 35-6)

At one level, Marcuse's arguments were a continuation of the programme of the Frankfurt School of critical theory to secure a biological basis for human emancipation (see Jay 1973; Pearson 1975a). But these were also arguments which had come into their own in the context of the politics of the 'New Left' and the 'counter-culture'. In an astute appraisal of the student radical movement of the United States, Alvin Gouldner had summarised its aspirations in the following terms:

> Far from being 'materialists', these students are often delib-
> erately 'utopian' and activistically idealistic. The value
> emphases of the new student radicals centre on equality
> and freedom, but they do not stop there. They also include
> disgust at affluence without dignity; desire for beauty as well
> as democracy; belief in creativity rather than consensus;
> wish for community and communal values, and vehement
> rejection of depersonalised bureaucracy; desire to build a
> 'counter society' with 'parallel institutions' and not simply
> to be integrated into and be accepted by the dominant
> institutions; hostility to what is conceived of as the dehu-
> manisation and alienation of cash-nexus society; prefer-
> ence for individuated, intensely felt, and self-generated
> interpersonal style, including fuller sexual expression and
> experimentation. They want what they think of as warm
> human relations and a kind of 'inventive sensuality', rather
> than the rational discipline of either the independent pro-
> fessions or the bureaucratic establishments.
>
> (Gouldner 1971: 399-400)

This movement in North America had originally emerged from the training ground of the black civil-rights struggle, sub-sequently consolidated in the growing opposition to the war in Vietnam. Its support for Third World anti-imperialist struggles and those of the welfare poor in the USA did not, however, mean that what Gouldner described as 'stomach questions' were central to its agenda. This new radicalism had effectively broken from a politics which defined poverty as a major site of struggle for freedom and equality, to one which identified the detritus of 'affluence' as a larger constraint upon human possi-bility. Regarded by Gouldner, quite rightly, as 'a genuinely new social movement', which had 'jettisoned some of the most basic ground rules of the older liberal-left politics', his assess-ment was that 'it promises to be of abiding significance' (ibid.: 400).

With historical hindsight, we can see that in this final judge-ment Alvin Gouldner proved to be quite wrong in certain respects, although not in others. The new ecological politics of the 'Greens', which had undoubtedly found its initial inspirations within this counter-cultural 'New Left', is perhaps the most obvious and significant justification of Gouldner's assessment of the future viability of this form and style of politics. More recently, social theorists such as Alain Touraine, Manuel Castells, and Alberto Melucci have also suggested that a wider range and style of political involvements – embracing not only the ecological movement, but also the new feminism, youth movements, peace movements, and anti-nuclear movements, as well as a variety of 'grass-roots' urban movements – indicate a major new departure in the politics of western liberal democracies (see Touraine 1981 and 1983; Castells 1983; Melucci, 1980). The work of these 'social movement' theorists has also been applied to an understanding of the changing forms and contexts of 'race politics' and black people's struggles in contemporary Britain (Gilroy 1987).

Even so, in Britain where the impetus of late 1960s and 1970s radicalism was formed centrally around welfare concerns, here Gouldner's assessment is far less convincing. As the older liberal-left politics was forced onto the defence by the emerging world recession and the ideological onslaught of the 'New Right', counter-cultural Utopianism rapidly became an irrelevance to welfare concerns. Indeed, in the light of what I have said about the fundamental ambiguities within this 'radicalism' about its own assessments of poverty and social inequality, it should hardly come as a surprise to find that social work's 'radicalism' had very little to say about the emerging crisis of the welfare state. Its approach to the question of unemployment could hardly do other than founder on the multiple contradiction around its understanding of the nature of freedom and conformity, where compliance to the work ethic and employment status were seen as major constraints upon human possibility. Within a few years, all that would remain of the counter-cultural opposition to the idea that 'work' should be the defining qualities of life would be those older and more explicitly anarchistic formulations of the 'refusal' of work, together with visionary 'post-industrial' Marxism espoused by André Gorz (see Echanges et Mouvement 1979; Gorz 1982 and 1985). Indeed, the frailty of this position as a practical system of defence for the most vulnerable sections of society within the emerging contexts of mass unemployment can be judged against the rapidity with which the romanticised slogans of a 'refusal' of work were jettisoned in favour of the 'Right to Work' campaign.

The personal and social consequences of unemployment

What is then needed is a reconstruction of an understanding of unemployment and its consequences which is adequate to the practical needs of the defenceless and the weak. One central recognition to emerge from a review of the underpinning assumptions of social work's 'radical' hour is that it was quite incapable of providing anything which could effectively replace the 'rehabilitative ideal', which itself had become redundant – not because of the radical critique, however, but as a consequence of the altered political economy of the west.

One major difficulty as I have described it is that the romanticised, even heroic and essentially anarchist approaches to unemployment which formed a major part of the ground-swell of counter-cultural 'radicalism' were oblivious to the painful human difficulties occasioned by unemployment and poverty. What was missing was the recognition that social inequality is something to be endured for millions of people in Britain alone. Unemployment is not merely, in some disembodied sense a potential force for 'revolutionary' change in society. Nor, in an equally disembodied although opposed politics, merely a statistic in a government statement, to be hidden under the carpet in 'training schemes' which lead nowhere, to be further concealed in the repeated laundering and manipulation of the statistics themselves through reductions of entitlement to claim benefit, the steady removal of an obligation to register as unemployed, and the switching of status from unemployed to 'sick'. In all their different forms, these responses involve a dehumanised approach to unemployment and unemployed people. And social work's earlier 'radicalism' cannot exempt itself from this judgement. Because even when unemployment was not in itself celebrated as a route to 'freedom', as in the more exaggerated and romantic 'refusal of work' theses, then the idea that social workers might work alongside poor people to help to ameliorate their difficulties was also anathema as a 'cool-out' and a 'con'.

One outcome of social work's radical hour where this critical judgement might be faulted was the renewed emphasis upon the importance of welfare rights advocacy. Here the radical leaning towards political materialism could be given full expression, without any of the guilty feelings that welfare clients were merely being accommodated to the system. Even so, it risked its own dehumanisation of the object of welfare since the refusal by 'radical' social work to develop a personalised approach towards counselling the poor (that is, a psychology of human need) implied that clients existed only as a disembodied collection of 'rights' as defined by statute and regulation (see Pearson 1975a: 135). Moreover, where welfare rights were being subjected to repeated restrictions and limitations, the scope for advocacy was equally limited: 'Radical bandwagons such as "welfare rights" might even be a premonition of things to come . . . helping clients to get their rights when they have no rights' (Pearson 1975b: 44).

The limited gains possible through welfare rights advocacy can nevertheless offer tangible assistance to the poor. They cannot, however, provide an adequate framework to guide our actions where the human difficulties of poverty and unemployment can be shown to amount to more than merely financial deficiency. What is required is a philosophy which places the human subject, and not the cash-nexus, as central to our understanding and practice of welfare. Neither the 'rehabilitative ideal' which implied such a humanism but is now redundant, nor the 'radical' alternative which took such a complacent view of unemployment, can offer any obvious directions. Where, then, to turn?

If our actions are to be guided at all, then a highly significant resource is in the research tradition on the personal and social consequences of unemployment which was first gathered together during the slump of the 1930s, and which is now being consolidated in a renewed tradition of applied social research in the 1980s (see Jahoda *et al.* 1972; Jahoda 1982 and 1987; Bakke 1933 and 1960; Pilgrim Trust 1938; Allen *et al.* 1986; Fryer and Ullah 1987; Warr 1984; Kasl *et al.* 1975). The observable consequences of unemployment involve a range of major life difficulties other than financial problems. These include an increased likelihood of poor physical health, mental health problems and an increase in the suicide rate, and a higher mortality rate (see British Medical Association 1987; Hakim 1982; Whitehead 1987). Research on the prevalence of depression among women has also shown that one of the factors associated with the increased likelihood that a woman will suffer from a depressive condition is the absence of paid employment outside the home (Brown and Harris 1978; Brown 1978). On the available evidence it is also now indisputable, in spite of considerable and continuing political dispute, that unemployment leads to a higher crime rate and also to a higher prison population (see Hakim 1982; Downes 1983; Box 1987). Furthermore, the people most likely to suffer from victimisation by crime and violence are those who live in the poorest neighbourhoods, which suffer from a wide range of economic and social disadvantage (see Hough and Mayhew 1985;

Pearson 1988a). Recent surveys of illicit drug misuse, both in terms of national trends and more localised studies, have also shown a relationship between unemployment and drug misuse – and more particularly heroin misuse, something which could have been predicted from the urban ghetto experiences of North America during their own heroin epidemics of the 1960s and 1970s (see Peck and Plant 1986; Parker *et al.* 1986; Pearson *et al.* 1986; Pearson 1987a and 1987b; Feldman 1968; Chein *et al.* 1964; Johnson *et al.* 1985).

Although the demonstrable range of the consequences of unemployment is undoubtedly impressive, the mechanisms by which they work are not always well understood. Some of these problems might flow directly from poverty and poor diet. Others may be stress-induced, whereas the relationships between problems such as drug misuse and unemployment are both complex and sometimes puzzling, involving a range of connections which include economic exchange, lifestyle, and the workings of the housing market (see Pearson 1987b).

One can begin to sense some of the reasons for the bewilderment of social workers not only in the range of difficulties which mass unemployment brings in its wake, but also because social work intervention can only hope to have a very limited impact (if any impact at all) on problems such as low income, ill health, or inadequate housing. However, where social workers might aim to offer services which are relevant to unemployed people and their families is in relation to problems which could seem less tangible (and even less important) concerning lifestyle, identity, and morale.

Unemployed people will often experience bewildering and damaging shifts of emotion – despair, anger, loss, fear – as well as the material hardships of poverty. And it is here, in a reconstructed humanist appraisal of poverty and unemployment, that I wish to suggest that social workers might be well placed to offer effective and relevant forms of help to the unemployed.

Of course, this is to join swords once more with the inheritance of 'radical social work' where a major argument (in its materialist guise) was precisely that social workers who attended to the emotional contents of poor people's lives were merely deflecting them from the structural actualities of poverty and the necessity of political struggle. Without wishing to diminish in any way the importance of the material deprivations of unemployment, however, I intend to sketch out the grounds on which social workers might offer certain forms of guidance and counselling to the unemployed – organised around questions of how

to fashion a meaningful and effective identity, and how to minimise the effects of unemployment which otherwise threaten to
wreak havoc in people's lives. This implies an agenda for social
work which involves a break with both the 'rehabilitative ideal'
and also the imperatives of the 'radical' inheritance within social
work.

It is a commonplace of public debate in contemporary Britain
to say that if unemployment is not reduced, then there will be
more riots, violence, and vandalism. And while this is undoubtedly true, it does nevertheless detract from the more obvious feature of the lifestyle of the unemployed, which is not that it breeds
restlessness and riot, but that it leads to apathy and despair. This
was true in the inter-war years of the slump, just as it is today.
Which is not to say that there were not riots in the 1920s and
1930s, because in spite of all our forgetfulness about the 'good
old days', there were riots (see Pearson 1983a and 1987c;
Hannington 1973; Stevenson and Cook 1979). Even so, the typical day in the life of the unemployed does not involve rising at
the crack of dawn and plotting how to overthrow the state.
Rather, it will mean staying in bed until late in the day where it is
warmer, food intake is reduced, and clothes do not wear out so
easily.

In helping to understand and act upon these experiences, a
vital resource is what is best described as the 'social psychology'
of unemployment which must draw heavily upon the work of
Marie Jahoda, both in the 1930s and the present day, which has
justifiably proved so influential (see Jahoda *et al.* 1972; Jahoda
1982 and 1987). The key contribution of Jahoda's work is that
concepts of 'morale' and 'apathy' are broken down and clarified.
The shifting alteration of mood and cognition is placed within a
recognisable 'cycle of adjustment' to life on the dole. The
enforced withdrawal of unemployed people from wider social
involvements is placed centrally within her understanding of
their weakened capacities. Above all, perhaps, Jahoda has not
offered a rose-tinted view of employment status to be contrasted
uninvitingly against life on the 'scrap heap'; but a humanism
which understands that, just as self-worth and self-identity are
found and fashioned through the dominant form of employment
status in our society, the actually existing forms and routines of
employment are in themselves sometimes damaging and restric-
tive of human possibility.

Marie Jahoda's work in this area of research began with her
1930s study of *Marienthal*, an Austrian cotton town where the
consequences of the slump were particularly serious (Jahoda

et al. 1972). Marienthal had been virtually closed down by the recession, and it was Jahoda's overall finding that people retreated from virtually every sphere of public life. Their involvement in political and social clubs, their use of public libraries, the likelihood that someone would read a newspaper: these all declined markedly. With the initial onset of the recession people's health might even have improved, because of the wretched conditions of fibre pollution in the air of the cotton mills. But as family budgets tightened appreciably and household reserves had been exhausted, health began to decline. People even walked more slowly as they went about their non-existent business.

It was the disruption of time-routines and time-structures which Jahoda's work identified as a major area of difficulty for unemployed people – or, rather, unemployed men. Because again, as Jahoda's own work demonstrated so powerfully, the experience of 'unemployment' was quite different for women and men. For men it meant being 'idle' and 'workless', whereas for women it meant another form of 'work', unpaid domestic labour which might already have been a major part of their work both in external paid employment, as well as through 'housework', 'cooking', 'cleaning', 'child care', and other forms of human labour not counted in patriarchal definitions of the problem of unemployment. It is equally true, nevertheless, that a disproportionate number of poor people in contemporary Britain are women, and that it is not unreasonable to talk about the 'feminisation of poverty' (see Townsend 1987).

Women may be poorer than men, but even so the experience of unemployment for women is not one of being 'workless'. Christine Griffin's research on unemployment among young women has reinforced this understanding, demonstrating that it is not limited in its application to women who are 'housewives'. It is equally true that for young women, including unemployed school-leavers, unemployment often means that they must shoulder a major responsibility for a variety of domestic tasks (see Griffin 1985a and 1985b). This is much less true where unemployed men are concerned, and in spite of some indications that they will make a larger contribution to household work, the sexual division of domestic labour remains essentially intact. As Hilary Graham describes it: 'While unemployed men take on more chores, they not necessarily share responsibility. They help out and lend a hand, but the job remains the woman's' (Graham 1984: 61). Indeed, according to one recent research study by Lorna McKee and Colin Bell with the beguiling title 'His Unemployment, Her Problem', male unemployment was commonly associated with even an increasing rigidity of male and female roles within the family. For both women and men, the notion of the male 'bread winner' was found to be a deep-rooted preoccupation, with the feeling that unemployment was a serious injury to masculine pride – whereas for women, the problem was how to 'manage' on a reduced family income (McKee and Bell 1986).

This recognition of a sexual division of 'work' and the experience of unemployment has important implications for any attempt to reconstruct an adequate practical understanding of unemployment and its consequences, for both men and women. It might even make more sense to begin with women's experience of unemployment rather than men's. The work which must continue within an unemployed family, in order to reproduce bodily and mental health and to maintain effective domestic hygiene, is the vital means by which unemployed people can and must defend themselves against the most damaging effects of unemployment. To describe this necessary condition for the continuation of domestic household arrangements as 'idleness' is completely off the mark. Indeed, where financial resources are reduced within the domestic economy, then more physical labour (and not less) will be necessary to sustain health and well-being.

One way of approaching this sexual division of labour within the home would be to recognise that the 'right to work' takes on a rather different complexion when there is so much essential work to be done. But it is work that is devalued and unpaid within the masculine definition of 'work' so that men will be reluctant to undertake it as not 'real' work. The problem of mass unemployment would then be described, however, as more specifically a problem with men and how they are to change and adapt their conventional assumptions of masculinity to the new workless future of the west. Rather than indulging in the highly ritualised obsession with 'seeking work' when there is no 'work' available, other than that in the home – given what is objectively a jobless future for so many millions of people and their families – perhaps the definitions of what is appropriate 'work' for men should be suspended and reshaped so that men can participate fully alongside women in the necessary self-defence against unemployment and poverty through domestic labour.

A note of caution is perhaps necessary at this point against the crude ways in which the 'domestic labour debate' has sometimes been approached since the late 1970s, with a dominant tendency to assume that all domestic work always falls to women as their responsibility, to the neglect of important historical and regional variations, as well as a number of 'hidden' aspects of men's contributions to domestic self-provisioning (see Pahl 1984). Nevertheless, the actually existing participation of men is such that it is principally only around pregnancy and childbirth that the division of domestic labour is significantly altered for an extremely short period of time, although even so our knowledge of the precise contribution of fathers to child care and household self-provisioning remains extremely patchy (see McKee 1982). What is clear is that, as things stand, employment status makes very little difference to the division of household labour; so that the vital differences in women's and men's experience of what constitutes 'work' as well as 'unemployment' remain essentially intact.

Of course, one cannot abolish the dominant assumptions of the 'work ethic' and the 'male bread-winner' at a flick of the switch, although it is highly likely that social workers and others who work among the unemployed will increasingly find themselves confronted by the physical and emotional preoccupations which flow from the problems of living in an unemployed household within what will continue to be a work-dominated society, in spite of the stagnancy of mass unemployment. Such a perspective suggests a range of practical welfare strategies, relevant to both the physical and emotional needs of unemployed people (see Pearson 1988b). An overriding consideration should first be to recognise that the received ideas of social work have traditionally acted in such a way as, if anything, to intensify the sexual division of labour. So much of what passes for 'community care', which has been promoted as a central preoccupation within postwar social work, depends upon the unpaid domestic labour of women (see Finch 1984; Finch and Groves 1980, 1982 and 1983; Land 1978; Walker 1982; Abrams 1986; Bulmer 1987). Even so, it was a cause for some astonishment that the Barclay Report on social work managed to spill a great deal of ink on the question of social work opportunities for developing 'informal caring networks' and 'community social work', without any mention of the implied sexual division of caring responsibilities (see Barclay 1982; Pearson 1983b).

The kinds of practical initiatives which might be developed within social work will include a variety of counselling and group work methods, including those adapted from bereavement counselling given that 'loss' is often central to the experience of unemployment, to assist unemployed men and women to fashion and sustain effective and meaningful self-identities, where the prevailing definitions are such as to condemn those without paid employment as worthless (see Pearson 1988b). In devising effective strategies, attention will also need to be given to local needs and circumstances. The impact of unemployment varies enormously in different regions, and even within an area of high unemployment there will be significant local variations. Unemployment and its associated problems do not cast their shadow uniformly across even a single housing estate; rather, there is a tendency for such problems to huddle together in dense pockets of social deprivation which are measured often by only a few streets (see Pearson 1986). Accordingly, although the effects of mass unemployment are likely to have a general significance for social workers whose work has traditionally brought them into contact with the most deprived and often defenceless members of our society, the most effective strategies will be those which are highly localised and attuned to local circumstances; both in terms of local needs and problems and also local resources and traditions of community mobilisation.

As well as the conventional approaches of social work and community work, these strategies directed towards the needs of the unemployed might also include work which draws upon other areas of professional expertise, such as adult literacy programmes; or attention might be given to means by which to assist unemployed people, through schemes of 'domestic science' and 'home economics', to counteract the impact of unemployment on health and diet. The problem of diet has a traditional place in work with the poor since the time of Victorian philanthropists, although it is not suggested that Victorian remedies should be recycled for our present-day consumption. The Victorian philanthropic mentality was often organised around cheerless sermons on how many mouths could be fed by cheap cuts of meat, while stressing the responsibilities of motherhood in rearing a 'virile' imperial race (see Davin 1978). Mrs Helen Bosanquet, doyenne of the Charity Organisation Society, offered some indication of what this hectoring often amounted to:

> Begin with the girls in school, and give them systematic and compulsory instruction in the elementary laws of health and feeding, and care of children, and the wise spending of money. Go on with the young women in evening classes and girls' clubs; and continue with the mothers wherever you can get at them . . . . It has been possible to awaken an intelligent interest in window gardening in the very poorest quarters of our towns, and it ought not to be impossible to awaken a

similar intelligent pride in the care of children . . . . What
we want is a reform which will provide suitable food and
care for the children from the first days of their lives, and
continue it throughout manhood and old age; and there is
no way of securing that except through the mothers and
wives.

(Bosanquet 1904: 73)

It is this kind of thing which has remained in the folk memory
of what Victorian philanthropy amounted to, and to suggest that
social workers might re-invent it would quite rightly provoke
gales of laughter and ridicule of the *Case Con* variety. Even so,
cookery instruction was not always as bad as this, and nor need it
be today. One altered form of earlier philanthropic activity is
described in a remarkable pamphlet from early in the new century, *The Pudding Lady: A New Departure in Social Work,* which was
concerned with the work of the St Pancras School for Mothers in
the Somers Town district of London (Bibby *et al,* 1916). Miss
Florence Petty, who had earned the sobriquet 'The Pudding
Lady' for her endeavours among the poor, had developed a line
of approach which involved working alongside people in their
own homes and using their own kitchen utensils in order to
improve domestic skills and cookery. This was an important
development which worked against the tendency for school-
based cookery classes which employed elaborate forms of kitchen
equipment which were not available in working-class homes, and
which were therefore better suited for training women for
domestic service rather than to their own domestic needs (see
Davin 1978: 27). There was even a hope expressed in the preface
to *The Pudding Lady* that the teaching of domestic skills in schools
and continuation classes should be 'made obligatory for boys as
well as girls' (Bibby *et al,* 1916: xiv). These were the contempo-
raries of the Suffragettes, rather than Mrs Bosanquet, who were
speaking.

I have stressed mention of dietary considerations because
these have not been banished by the 'affluent' society and the
welfare state, even though they often go unrecognised. With the
accelerating tendency towards a 'commodity form' of food – 'fast
food' and 'junk food' in all its forms – access to cheap and
health-promoting forms of food have become, if anything, more
difficult for poor families. This reinforces the need to devise
effective strategies of dietary defence for the poor. So much conventional health education advice and philosophy is also inappropriate to poor families, as Hilary Graham makes clear:

On a day-to-day level, where the struggle to establish a healthier lifestyle begins, the evidence suggests there is little flexibility in the routines of many families. Poverty limits a parent's command over, and thus choice about, the family's lifestyle. A diet high in fresh fruit may be preferred, but cannot be chosen, unless the mother reneges on equally vital health obligations: the rent and fuel bills, for example. Similarly, single parents, constrained by their childcare responsibilities as well as by their income, have little opportunity to choose the more labour-intensive methods of promoting health, like walking and jogging.

(Graham 1984: 187)

The development of local initiatives on health care and health education by women's groups is one possible resource here, although they are very uneven developments which probably do not reach the poorest families and neighbourhoods. Bearing in mind the lesson of the Pudding Lady, it is also necessary to fashion strategies which are relevant to the customary dietary practices and cultural preferences of working-class people. For social workers and health educators to preach among the poor on the virtue of high-fibre diets, advocating pulses to replace animal protein, and other versions of middle-class vegetarianism would be merely to reproduce the worst features of aloof Victorian philanthropy.

If material issues which impinge upon the health and diet of the poor should not be neglected in devising relevant strategies for work with the unemployed, then these strategies must also be directed towards the subtly damaging social psychology of the aimless, disrupted time-routines imposed by unemployment. Because no matter what assistance of a material nature might be offered, it will be difficult for people to make full use of this if their lives and mentalities remain constrained by the demoralising impact of the experience of unemployment.

The destruction of the habitual time-structures which order so much of the everyday life of those who are in employment, and which was fancifully imagined to be the gift of increased 'leisure' opportunities in the coming 'post-industrial' society, is one of the most psychologically damaging consequences of unemployment. As Marie Jahoda described it from Marienthal in the 1930s, the enforced leisure of unemployment proved to be a 'tragic gift':

Anyone who knows how tenaciously the working class has fought for more leisure ever since it began to fight for its rights might think that even amid the misery of unemployment, men would still benefit from having unlimited free time. On examination this leisure proves to be a tragic gift . . . . Now that they are no longer under any pressure, they undertake nothing new and drift gradually out of an ordered existence into one that is undisciplined and empty. Looking back over any period of free time, they are unable to recall anything worth mentioning. For hours on end, the men stand around in the street . . . . They carry on leisurely conversations for which they have unlimited time. Nothing is urgent anymore; they have forgotten how to hurry.

(Jahoda *et al.* 1972: 66)

From New York in the 1960s, Ed Preble and James Casey made a directly similar observation in their study of the street life of heroin addicts in ghetto neighbourhoods, who by the nature of their addiction must sustain a hectic lifestyle which is dominated by the rigid time-routines of hustling, scoring drugs, avoiding the police, and then hustling again. 'The surest way to identify heroin users in slum neighbourhoods', they wrote, 'is to observe the way people walk. The heroin user walks with a fast, purposeful stride, as if he is late for an important appointment – indeed, he is' (Preble and Casey 1969: 2). The way in which heroin misuse enforces a metronome logic upon life which structures the addict's daily routines is one significant mechanism by which heroin misuse and unemployment come to be so tragically connected (see Pearson 1987a and 1987b).

The 'free' time of unemployment will also often be released into various forms of activity within the hidden economy, thereby leading to the possibility of a further denigration of the poor within dominant discourses as 'scroungers' and cheats. Nevertheless, there is nothing at all new in the tendency for poor people to attempt to extend their economic resources, and where they are denied access to the licit economy during times of mass unemployment then the only available economic forms of exchange will be through the 'hidden' economic domain – which is, in fact, hidden only in the sense that it involves income generation which is not visible for taxation purposes, since it is perfectly visible to most people most of the time. Marie Jahoda in her 1930s study of a mining community in the Welsh valleys – a study only very recently made available for publication – found a variety of forms of pilfering, theft and dishonesty organised around the co-operative employment scheme which had been

established in the area, including the re-sale of co-operative produce to neighbours who were not members of the scheme and
therefore ineligible under its rules to benefit from its work (see
Jahoda 1987). The hidden economy will often beckon to the
unemployed, in so many different ways, as a necessary means of
bolstering the domestic economy, placing difficult areas of moral
judgement in the path of social workers who will thereby find
their obligations of confidentiality severely tested in work with
the poor (see Pearson 1975b).

Perhaps one of the major objectives of welfare strategies directed towards the unemployed should be to help people to avoid
the more self-destructive forms of involvement in the hidden
economy. It is difficult to see what other relevant response there
could be, since the hidden economy is not only one important
way in which human resourcefulness is given expression in hard
times, but it is also a means by which the unemployed invent
activity to combat the otherwise disorienting effects of idleness.

It is easily recognised that so much of this psychology of unemployment, with its stress upon idleness and the disruption of
time-structures, is not a universally applicable phenomenon in
that it once more circles around the specific problems of men.
Considerable stress was laid upon this aspect of the sexual differ-
entiation of time in Marie Jahoda's study of Marienthal.
Nevertheless, it is important to recognise the continuing existence and significance of the potential for apathetic resignation
among unemployed people and their families. Jahoda found
large variations in the extent of demoralisation and apathy in her
two 1930s studies, when Marienthal was set against her Welsh valleys study where evidence of total despair was less obvious,
although apathy and resignation were still dominant issues (see
Jahoda 1987). Variations within this aspect of the experience of
unemployment are also to be expected for workers of different
ages. It is something of a surprise, for example, given the stress
placed upon youth unemployment, that young men appear to be
less likely to suffer from its disorienting effects than older workers. It is men in mid-life who become unemployed who suffer
most, whereas for those nearing retirement and already preparing themselves for 'worklessness', together with young people
who have not become sufficiently dependent on the time-routines of work disciplines or self-identities arranged around work
status, the effects appear to be less severe (Jahoda 1982).

Generally speaking, however, the aimless time disciplines of
unemployment eat away at morale and self-identity. To be cast
into the 'free' time of unemployment, and yet be unable to make

constructive use of that time is as Jahoda (1982: 23) describes it a 'heavy psychological burden'. To assist unemployed people in making sense of this purposelessness as something other than an individual failing, but the result of the 'destruction of a culturally imposed time structure' (ibid.: 23) should be a major object of social work intervention. This drifting hopelessness is what characterises the ways by which the unemployed come to terms with their situation, through a recognisable 'cycle of adjustment' (see Zawadski and Lazarsfeld 1935; Bakke 1933 and 1960; Jahoda 1982). After the initial shock of becoming unemployed, feelings of fear and distress are replaced by numbness and apathy. Periods of agitated activity to find employment prove increasingly futile. Interspersed by experiences of anger and loss, the unemployed eventually settle into an unquestioning and fatalistic acquiescence. The extent to which unemployed people become resigned to their position is indicated by a recent research finding that as many as one-fifth of the very poorest people express themselves to be 'satisfied' with their living standards (Mack and Lansley 1985: 166).

In a sense, this is the most effective rejoinder to those earlier traditions of social work 'radicalism' which argued that social workers should not help poor people to accommodate themselves to their situation. With or without social work assistance, the unemployed will soon enough adapt themselves to poverty and its associated lifestyle. The danger is, however, that this adaptation will assume the form of apathetic disregard and impoverished self-esteem. One aim of social work must be to alleviate wherever possible this slide into demoralisation, and to offer forms of defence and protection against what will otherwise prove to be serious injuries to the self and others. Demoralised and incapacitated people are no better equipped to deal with the external world, even if their engagement with the external world has shrunk to the confines of a social security office where they must negotiate and argue the case for their limited rights, than they are to deal with the 'internal worlds' of their families, friends, and lovers.

We know the slogan 'The personal is political', born out of 'affluence' and implying a need to attend to personal lifestyle if the world is to change. Under the stagnant conditions of mass unemployment, a new slogan must be learned: 'The political is personal.'

© 1989 Geoffrey Pearson

References

Abel-Smith, B. and Townsend, P. (1967) *The Poor and the Poorest*, London: Bell.

Abrams, P. (1986) *Neighbours: The Work of Philip Abrams*, Cambridge: (ed.) M. Bulmer. Cambridge University Press.

Allen, S. Waton, A., Purcell, K. and Wood, S. (eds) (1986) *The Experience of Unemployment*, London: Macmillan.

Arts Council (1981) *Spencer in the Shipyard: Paintings and Drawings by Stanley Spencer and Photographs by Cecil Beaton from the Imperial War Museum*, London: Arts Council of Great Britain.

Bakke, E.W. (1933) *The Unemployed Man*, London: Nisbet.

Bakke, E.W. (1960) 'The cycle of adjustment to unemployment' , in N.W. Bell and E.F. Vogel (eds) *A Modern Introduction to the Family*, New York: Free Press.

Barclay, P. (1982) *Social Workers: their Roles and Tasks*, London: Bedford Square Press.

Bentham, J. (1791) *Panopticon, or the Inspection House*, in J. Bowring (ed.) *The Works of Jeremy Bentham*, vol. 3, London: Wm. Tait, 1838 edn.

Beveridge, W. (1942) *Report on the Social Insurance and Allied Services*. Cmnd 6404, HMSO.

Bibby, M.E., Colles, E.G., Petty, F. and Sykes, J.F.J. (1916) *The Pudding Lady: a New Departure in Social Work*, London: National Food Reform Association.

Booth, General W. (1890) *Darkest England and the Way Out*, London: Salvation Army.

Bosanquet, H. (1904) 'Physical degeneration and the poverty line', *Contemporary Review*, Jan.

Box, S. (1987) *Recession, Crime and Punishment*, London: Macmillan.

Bright, J. and Petterson, G. (1984) *The Safe Neighbourhoods Unit*, London: NACRO.

British Medical Association (1987) *Deprivation and Ill-Health*, London BMA.

Brown, G. (1978) 'Depression: a sociological view', in D. Tuckett and J.M. Kaufert (eds) *Basic Readings in Medical Sociology*, London: Tavistock.

Brown, G. and Harris, T. (1978) *Social Origins of Depression*, London: Tavistock.

Bulmer, M. (1987) *The Social Basis of Community Care*, London: Allen & Unwin.

Castells, M. (1983) *The City and the Grassroots*, London: Edward Arnold.

Chein, I. *et al* (1964) *The Road to H: Narcotics, Delinquency and Social Policy*, London: Tavistock.

Community Relations Council (1974) *Unemployment and Homelessness*, HMSO.

Crow, I. and Simon, F. (1987) *Unemployment and Magistrates' Courts*, London: NACRO.

Davin, A. (1978) 'Imperialism and Motherhood', *History Workshop* 5.

Davis, F. (1967) 'Why all of us may be hippies some day', *Transaction* 5, no. 2.

Downes, D. (1983) *Law and Order: Theft of an Issue.* Fabian Tract no. 490. London: Fabian Society.

Echange et Mouvement (1979) *The Refusal of Work,* Paris: Echanges et Mouvement.

Feldman, H. (1968) 'Ideological supports to becoming and remaining a heroin addict', *Journal of Health and Social Behaviour* 9, no. 2s

Finch, J. (1984) 'Community care: developing non-sexist alternatives', *Critical Social Policy* 9.

Finch, J. and Groves, D. (1980) 'Community care and the family: a case for equal opportunities?', *Journal of Social Policy* 9.

Finch, J. and Groves, D. (1982) 'By women, for women: caring for the frail elderly', *Women's Studies International Forum* 5, no.4.

Finch, J. and Groves, D. (eds) (1983) *A Labour of Love: Women, Work and Caring,* London: Routledge and Kegan Paul.

Foucault, M. (1977) *Discipline and Punish,* London: Allen Lane.

Fryer, D. and Ullah, P. (eds) (1987) *Unemployed People: Social and Psychological Perspectives,* Milton Keynes: Open University Press.

Fyvel, T.R. (1963) *The Insecure Offenders,* Harmondsworth: Penguin Books.

Garland, D. (1985) *Punishment and Welfare,* Aldershot: Gower.

Gilroy, P. (1987) *There Ain't No Black in the Union Jack: the Cultural Politics of Race and Nation,* London: Hutchinson.

Gorz, A. (1982) *Farewell to the Working Class,* London: Pluto.

Gorz, A. (1985) *Paths to Paradise: on the Liberation from Work,* London: Pluto.

Gouldner, A. (1971) *The Coming Crisis of Western Sociology,* London: Pluto.

Graham, H. (1984) *Women, Health and the Family,* Brighton: Harvester.

Griffin, C. (1985a) *Typical Girls? Young Women from School to the Job Market,* London: Routledge and Kegan Paul.

Griffin, C. (1985b) 'Turning the tables: feminist analysis of youth unemployment', *Youth and Policy* 14.

Hakim, C. (1982) 'The Social Consequences of High Unemployment', *Journal of Social Policy* 11, no. 4.

Hannington, W. (1973) *Unemployed Struggles: 1919-1936,* EP Publishing.

Heimler, E. (1967) *Mental Illness and Social Work,* Harmondsworth: Penguin Books.

Hill, M. (1853) *Juvenile Delinquency,* London: Smith, Elder & Co.

Home Office (1965) *Probation of Offenders: the Probation Rules,* HMSO.

Hough, M. and Mayhew, P. (1985) *Taking Account of Crime: Key Findings from the Second British Crime Survey.* Home Office Research Study no. 85, HMSO.

Ignatieff, M. (1978) *A Just Measure of Pain,* London: Macmillan.

Jahoda, M. (1982) *Employment and Unemployment: a Social-Psychological Analysis,* Cambridge: Cambridge University Press.

Jahoda, M. (1987) 'Unemployed men at work', in D. Fryer and P. Ullah (eds) *Unemployed People,* Milton Keynes: Open University Press.

Jahoda, M., Lazarsfeld, P. and Zeisel, H. (1972) *Marienthal: the Sociography of an Unemployed Community,* London: Tavistock.

Jay, M. (1973) *The Dialectical Imagination,* London: Heinemann.

Jeffreys, S. (1986) *The Spinster and Her Enemies,* London: Pandora.

Johnson, B.D. *et al* (1985) *Taking Care of Business: the Economics of Crime by Heroin Abusers,* Lexington: Lexington University Press.

Kasl, S.V., Gore, S. and Cobb, S. (1975) 'The experience of losing a job: reported changes in health, symptoms and illness behaviour', *Psychosomatic Medicine* 37.

Land, H. (1978) 'Who cares for the family?' *Journal of Social Policy* 7.

Leeson, C. (1917) *The Child and the War,* London: King.

Liazos, A. (1972) 'The poverty of the sociology of deviance: nuts, sluts and perverts', *Social Problems* 20, no. 1.

McKee, L. (1982) 'Fathers' participation in infant care: a critique', in L. McKee and M. O'Brien (eds), *The Father Figure,* London: Tavistock.

McKee, L. and Bell, C. (1986) 'His unemployment, her problem: the domestic and marital consequences of male unemployment', in S. Allen *et al* (eds) *The Experience of Unemployment,* London: Macmillan.

Mack, J. and Lansley, S. (1985) *Poor Britain,* London: Allen & Unwin.

Marcuse, H. (1968) *One-Dimensional Man,* London: Sphere.

Marcuse, H. (1969) *An Essay on Liberation,* Harmondsworth: Penguin Books.

Mayer, J. and Timms, N. (1970) *The Client Speaks,* London: Routledge & Kegan Paul.

Melucci, A. (1980) 'The new social movements: a theoretical approach', *Social Science Information* 19, no. 2.

Mitchell, J. (1975) *Psychoanalysis and Feminism,* Harmondsworth: Penguin Books.

Pahl, R.E. (1984) *Divisions of Labour,* Oxford: Blackwell.

Parker, H.J., Bakx, K. and Newcombe, R. (1986) *Drug Misuse in Wirral,* Liverpool: University of Liverpool Press.

Pearson, G. (1975a) *The Deviant Imagination,* London: Macmillan.

Pearson, G. (1975b) 'Making social workers: bad promises and good omens', in R. Bailey and M. Brake (eds) *Radical Social Work,* London: Edward Arnold.

Pearson, G. (1978) 'Welfare on the Move, 1945-1975', in The Open University, *Introduction to Welfare: Iron Fist and Velvet Glove,* Unit 4, Block 1, Social Work, Community Work and Society, Course DE 206, Milton Keynes: The Open University Press.

Pearson, G. (1983a) *Hooligan: a History of Respectable Fears,* London: Macmillan.

Pearson, G. (1983b) 'The Barclay Report and community social work: Samuel Smiles re-visited?', *Critical Social Policy* 2, no. 3.

Pearson, G. (1986) 'Developing a local research strategy', in P. Wedge (ed.) *Social Work: Research into Practice,* London: BASW.

Pearson, G. (1987a) *The New Heroin Users,* Oxford: Blackwell.

Pearson, G. (1987b) 'Social deprivation, unemployment and patterns of heroin use', in N. Dorn and N. South (eds) *A Land Fit for Heroin? Drug Policies, Prevention and Practice,* London: Macmillan.

Pearson, G. (1987c) 'Short memories: street violence in the past and in the present', in E. Moonman (ed.) *The Violent Society,* London: Frank Cass.

Pearson, G. (1988a) 'The violent society', in The Open University, *Social Problems and Social Welfare,* Course D211, Open University.

Pearson, G. (1988b) 'Social work and unemployment', in M. Langan and P. Lee (eds) *Radical Social Work Today: Social Work in the Recession,* London: Hutchinson.

Pearson, G., Gilman, M. and McIver, S. (1986) *Young People and Heroin:*

an *Examination of Heroin Use in the North of England,* London: Health Education Council and Gower.

Pearson, G., Yelloly, M. and Treseder, J. (eds) (1988) *Social Work and the Legacy of Freud,* London: Macmillan.

Peck, D. and Plant, M. (1986) 'Unemployment and illegal drug use: concordant evidence from a prospective study and from national trends', *British Medical Journal* 293, 11 Oct.

Pilgrim Trust (1938) *Men without Work,* Cambridge: Cambridge University Press.

Popay, J., Dhooge, Y. and Shipman C. (1986) *Unemployment and Health: What Roles for the Health Services?* Research Report No. 3 London: Health Education Council.

Preble, E. and Casey, J.J. (1969) 'Taking care of business: the heroin user's life on the streets', *International Journal of Addictions* 4 no. 1.

Riley, D. (1979) 'War in the nursery', *Feminist Review* 2.

Riley, D. (1981) 'The free mothers: pronatalism and working women in industry at the end of the last war in Britain', *History Workshop* 11.

Riley, D. (1983) *War in the Nursery: Theories of the Child and Mother,* London: Virago.

Rose, H. (1974) 'Up against the welfare state: the claimants unions', in R. Miliband and J. Saville (eds) *Social Register 1973,* London: Merlin.

Rusche, G. and Kirchheimer, O. (1939) *Punishment and Social Structure ,* New York: Columbia University Press.

Scheff, T.J. (1968) 'Negotiating reality: notes on power in the assessment of responsibility', *Social Problems* 16, no. 1.

Stedman Jones, G. (1971) *Outcast London,* Oxford: Oxford University Press.

Stevenson, J. and Cook, C. (1979) *The Slump,* London: Quartet.

Touraine, A. (1981) *The Voice and the Eye: an Analysis of Social Movements,* Cambridge: Cambridge University Press.

Touraine, A. (1983) *Anti-Nuclear Protest: the Opposition to Nuclear Energy in France,* Cambridge: Cambridge University Press.

Townsend, P. (1987) *Poverty and Labour in London,* London: Low Pay Unit.

Walker, A. (ed.) (1982) *Community Care: the Family, the State and Social Policy,* Oxford: Blackwell.

Warr, P.B. (1984) 'Job loss, unemployment and psychological well-being', in V. Allen and E. Van de Vliert (eds) *Role Transitions,* London: Plenum Press.

Whitehead, M. (1987) *The Health Divide,* London: Health Education Council.

Wilson, E. (1977) *Women and the Welfare State,* London: Tavistock.

Zawadski, B. and Lazarsfeld, P.F. (1935) 'The psychological consequences of unemployment', *Journal of Social Psychology* 6.

2

Finding the right response: Social work, AIDS, and HIV infection

Geraldine Peacock

Little more than two years ago, if you mentioned AIDS in a social services department you would have been referred to the District Occupational Therapist. In a short space of time a simple word has undergone a transformation of meaning and now signifies anxiety, ignorance, death and sex. For social services departments the onslaught of AIDS (Acquired Immunodeficiency Syndrome) presents an enormous challenge, not least because of the climate of fear it has generated. AIDS is a fatal disease; it has no known cure. Since the onset of monitoring the course of the disease in this country, we know that at least 700 people have died, that 8000 people are infected with the HIV virus, and that the numbers of infected people are doubling every ten months (Dec. 1987 figures). It has been described as the 'gay plague', 'the black death', 'the judgement of God', and used to vilify and morally exclude blacks, gay men, drug users, and promiscuous lifestyles. Chief constables have ranted, archbishops preached, doctors diagnosed and government ministers investigated. AIDS has provided a vehicle for groups, whose vested interests lie in the maintenance of the 'status quo', to vindicate all they see as immoral or unnatural in society. It has also given rise to a group of people, often young, who are in dire need of help. What can social services departments do to provide support, understanding, and practical help for these people?

In helping people with AIDS and HIV infection social workers have to cope with public hysteria, government decisions, client needs and fears, and their own belief systems. This is nothing new. Social workers often work with people who pose threats to society, who are stigmatised or outcast. But AIDS and HIV infection put social work departments on the horns of many dilemmas simultaneously. In the public mind and, indeed, the government one, AIDS is seen as a medical problem. Despite enormous psychological and social implications the public focus is on finding a cure and preventing the spread of the disease. However, there are many gaps in medical knowledge which, with the help of the media representation, have fuelled speculation about routes of transmission through irresponsible, unnatural or promiscuous lifestyles. Such speculation is the breeding ground for fantasy and scapegoating that leaves the public, of which social workers are a part, half-informed, wondering, and vulnerable.

In this chapter I want to suggest that the public presentation of the AIDS phenomenon gave rise to received ideas which inhibited social work action. I further suggest that the language of public discourse about AIDS and HIV infection often influences and confuses possible working responses. Communication about AIDS and HIV infection has left social workers responding to imagined fears and false realities. Eighteen months into the 'public' recognition of AIDS and HIV infection, there is still evidence that many social services departments are struggling to identify an appropriate role to play in the crisis and that the government has failed to acknowledge the importance of a social services response. Social workers, because of their marginal power position in society and low public image, are not in a strong position to counteract scaremongering or to lobby for appropriate action. Despite this, I would suggest that social work does have a vital role to play in the co-ordination and provision of caring services for people with AIDS and HIV infection. Adequate funding and effective training could help social workers provide a relevant and enlightened service. In pursuing these ideas the first half of this chapter concentrates on the public presentation of the AIDS phenomenon and the second on a social work response.

Myths, medicine, and morality

Public images of AIDS

Social Workers are used to confronting taboo topics; it is part of a day's work. AIDS however provides an overload of taboos: sexuality, death, disease, drug addiction, racism and promiscuity for a start! When the government advertising campaign invaded our letter boxes, newspapers, and TV screens in late 1986 and early 1987, public tension about AIDS was already high. People were worried about whom they could safely sit next to, the dangers of wet toilet seats, kissing strangers and sharing cups. Misinformation was rife; James Anderton, Chief Constable of Greater Manchester, famously pronounced that everywhere he went he saw 'increasing evidence of people sinking in a human cesspit of their own making . . . . We must ask why homosexuals freely engage in sodomy and other obnoxious practices knowing the dangers involved?' (*Guardian,* 12 Dec. 1986) The Archbishop of York, Dr John Hapgood, had declared the world to be on 'the brink of the biggest and most destructive epidemic in recorded history.' (*Guardian,* 29 Dec. 1986) Rock Hudson had died a very public death, and Tony Newton had declared 'AIDS to be the most serious health challenge any government has ever faced.' (*New Society* 14 Nov.1986: 10)

From America there had been tales of Lyndon La Roche's Proposition 64, in which he maintained that 'homosexuals and drug users are creating a human reservoir of infection in the population . . . . I'm afraid we'll get into a fourteenth century Black Death type of scenario and the people would go berserk' (*New Statesman* 7 Nov. 1986, pp.7,8,9). Proposition 64 recommended the isolation of people with AIDS in desert 'institutions', whilst elsewhere there were suggestions of branding and castration. There had been tales of the spread of AIDS at a horrendous rate amongst the heterosexual population of Uganda, and in Britain, heavy press exposure of the scandalous plight of 'innocent victims' infected through blood transfusions.

Theories about cause and transmission abounded. They included suggestions of germ warfare against black people, Africans eating the uncooked brains of the green monkey in which a similar virus had been detected and voodoo practices amongst Haitians. Transmission was mainly attributed to forms of 'deviant' practice, particularly sexual practice. Homosexuality topped the 'blame' list with an emphasis on promiscuity and anal sex. Following in its wake came needle sharing amongst drug addicts, promiscuous heterosexual activity, and the transfusion of unchecked blood. 'High risk groups' were identified: homosexuals, drug takers, Africans, Haitians and Americans.

Uncertainty was high, ignorance great, and fear enormous. A potentially explosive situation existed. Panic reactions had already occurred. In America, as Dennis Altman records, 'people . . . avoided restaurants that employed gay waiters . . . bus drivers . . . feared AIDS could be transmitted through paper transfers' (Altman 1986: 2). In Australia people worried about catching AIDS from swimming pools and withdrew their children from schools where there were HIV-positive children. In Britain, home helps in Camden refused to go into the homes of people with AIDS, and a man, whose neighbours learnt he had AIDS when the police arrived in 'space suits' to arrest him, had his home burnt down. Another man was deemed intentionally homeless by a housing department which viewed AIDS as a self-inflicted condition. Unions looked at issues of employment and confidentiality, funeral directors refused to bury 'contaminated' bodies, prison officials isolated prisoners who were HIV-positive, and insurance companies refused cover for infected people. There was a climate of 'holocausts', 'moral retribution', and 'doom'.

From the start, the dominant representation of AIDS in the media was as 'the gay plague'. As Jeffrey Weeks informs us:

> The first major newspaper breaking of the story was in the *New York Times*, 3rd July, 1981, which headlined its story 'Rare cancer seen in 41 homosexuals'. From this it was a short step to blaming the abnormal sexual practices of gay men for the spread of the disease – particularly their promiscuity.
>
> (Weeks 1985: 46)

Frank Mort points out that

> the disease has produced gay men as its victims and their sexuality as the problem . . . . Doctors concluded that given the abnormally high promiscuity of gay men, some form of sexually transmitted virus or exposure to a common lifestyle played a critical role in establishing immunodeficiency.
>
> (Mort 1987: 2)

This led to the stigmatisation of the gay community, homophobia reached epidemic proportions and drew on Christian morality for its *raison d'etre*. AIDS was a punishment from God for unnatural and promiscuous sex.

As more information about AIDS and HIV infection became available, other groups faced scapegoating: prostitutes, drug users, Africans, promiscuous heterosexuals; as Mort observes, 'more and more sexual undesirables have been twinned with the socially undesirable' (Mort 1987: 2). The permissiveness and libertarianism of the sixties was blamed. 'Might it not also, with some justification,' wrote Digby Anderson in *The Times* (15 Sept. 1986), 'prise the sixties prophets of sexual freedom out of their retirement and call them to account for encouraging others to promiscuity?' AIDS provided a perfect link for marrying social, political, moral and religious indignation.

Facts and figures

Figures and projections were a media favourite: numbers of deaths, numbers of infected people, projections of numbers into the twenty-first century, the proportions of infected people who died – these quickly became public preoccupations. Daily 'scoreboards' were available in the tabloids all differing from one another! Fitzpatrick and Milligan point out:

> fears about the rapid spread of AIDS have been intensified by the widespread practice of publicising *cumulative totals* of those with the syndrome, rather than simply noting *new cases*. This creates steeply rising curves and general alarm. Studies of the spread of infectious diseases other than AIDS generally rely on figures for new cases.
>
> (Fitzpatrick and Milligan 1987: 10)

They go on to point out that, compared with other causes of death such as heart disease, cancer and road accidents, AIDS is a marginal health hazard. The public at large, however, including people who worked with people with AIDS and HIV infection, was afraid. Figures meant facts and the figures they saw were frightening. In an age where medicine had found an answer for so many things, here was a new and terrible challenge: a disease for which the 'experts' could find no cure nor any easy way of prolonging the life of infected people. Death from AIDS was uncomfortable and demise, once the full blown syndrome was diagnosed, was certain. There were no absolute points of reference, no real authorities, little you could do and, as Altman wrote, 'in the hysteria around AIDS one sees the rational fears of disease and contagion mixed in with irrational fears of sexuality and "otherness".' (Altman 1986: 59) The only 'innocent victims' were haemophiliacs, people who had received infected blood through transfusion, and infected children born to sero-positive mothers. Even then stories were sensationalised. A *New York Post* article (26 Aug. 1987) reported Mrs Cavaliere, whose husband died of AIDS after receiving infected blood during a bypass operation, as saying:

> In 1981 someone donated or sold blood which was contaminated with the AIDS virus and my husband was killed. The high risk category for this dread disease seems to be homosexuals, intravenous drug users, and promiscuous sexually active people . . . extensive publicity should be made to beg these people to refrain from donating their blood.

The picture painted was of social outcasts inflicting the just deserts of their deviant ways on their innocent fellow citizens. The figures indicated that this was happening at a rapidly increasing rate.

A medical matter?

The media presented AIDS and HIV infection as health problems. Solutions lay in medical hands; salvation was possible only if doctors could determine the aetiology of AIDS and find a cure. To the public at large this did not seem to be happening fast. What the press portrayed was the confusion of the medical world, which fostered public anxiety and oppression. Because every possible 'theory' about AIDS was presented publicly social reactions occurred. The fact that some unproven medical theories suggested AIDS originated in Africa was enough to make the Blood Transfusion Service initially identify black people as a 'high risk' donation group. Other running debates in the press about infection through saliva and breast milk, the possible high risks to care staff through infected blood and needles, and the risks of spreading infection through dental care, fuelled ignorance and fear. Reports about different 'miracle' cures promoted false hope and disillusionment.

Ironically, medical research was both helped and hindered by media attention. On the one hand, the press seemed to believe that the more horrendous and scaremongering their reports, the more impetus would be given to raising funds for medical research. On the other hand, the homophobic fears promoted by press campaigns were a powerful barrier to initiating research; Altman writes:

> several researchers have told me that they were 'discouraged' by colleagues from becoming too involved in work on a 'homosexual disease', and Dr Brandt has referred to 'some difficulty in attracting researchers because AIDS has become a gay rights issue'.
>
> Altman (1986: 49)

The public watched and waited for the medical world to 'do' something. Encouraged by the press and government reaction a kind of medico-blindness occurred. The answer lay *only* in medicine: AIDS was a killer disease, which required treatment in hospitals, and separation from everyday life. Public funds were made available to finance hospitals to provide care, and for doctors to undertake research; the government's concentration was upon health services, health education, prevention and cure. The overt medicalisation of AIDS also meant that no money was given to local authorities to establish community systems of support; hospitals were the focus of activity, with voluntary organisations being left to pick up the issues of counselling, group support and self-help.

Both news and advertising campaigns focused on AIDS. AIDS is *not* the virus concerned but a full-blown syndrome caused by opportunistic infection resulting from the breakdown of an individual's immune system, due to the presence of the human immunodeficiency virus (HIV). Not everyone who is HIV-positive (sero-positive) develops AIDS; present knowledge would appear to show that between 10 and 15 per cent of sero-positive people progress through related conditions to develop full-blown AIDS in three years; others may develop conditions such as lymphadenopathy, acute retroviral illness, or AIDS-related complex (ARC), all of which present their own problems and dilemmas. Such an exclusive focus on AIDS misrepresented the problem. Attentions were directed to the fatality of the disease and the medical needs of terminally ill people rather than the difficulties of living with the knowledge that you are HIV positive and the uncertainties this involves, or the more positive aspects of the disease, such as the development of active community and support groups.

Health problems are tangible. Even if there is no present cure the problem has been defined. But such a definition clouds the senses of governments and obscures the important but perhaps less obvious needs of people with AIDS and HIV infection, for emotional, psychological and social support.

The campaign

The first stage of the government health education campaign did little to alleviate public anxiety and much to foster fear. The approach was geared to opening everyones eyes to 'the facts' – a difficult task when there were so few. 'Don't Die of Ignorance' screamed the posters. 'AIDS is not prejudiced' warned the newspaper advertisements; 'it can kill anyone.' The envelope through our doors announced, 'This is being sent to every household in the country to inform everyone about AIDS, in order to help stop the spread of this serious disease. It deals with matters of health and sex that may be disturbing.'

£20 million were spent on a health promotion campaign using posters, leaflets, TV and cinema advertising. On the cinema and TV screens pneumatic drills vibrated and icebergs loomed whilst funereal music played and doom-laden voices told us that 'there is now a deadly virus'.

The coy language of the early leaflets became more explicit with the second stage of the campaign, which included much TV coverage. Condoms and anal sex became nightly topics for debate. Schools launched AIDS education campaigns and games of tag in the junior playground changed from 'touched you – you're it' to 'touched you – you've got AIDS'.

The results of this onslaught of publicity were mixed but as Fitzpatrick and Milligan explain:

> in one way it constituted an officially sponsored AIDS scare
> .... One of us, working as a GP was appalled at the distress caused to people who had not the slightest risk of contracting AIDS. Elderly men worried about some sexual misdemeanour 30 years ago, anxious parents terrified about the dangers to their children in school changing rooms and public swimming baths, women working alongside gay men – all came rushing for advice and reassurance.
>
> (Fitzpatrick and Milligan 1987: 1)

They maintain that the anxiety caused was out of all proportion, and conclude that 'for millions of pensioners who learnt that importance of shunning promiscuity and using condoms, hypothermia was a much more serious threat to life' (Fitzpatrick and Milligan 1987: 33).

The publicity created a new group of people, 'Fraids', who suffered from the fear that they had AIDS or could be at risk. As Andrea Breach found in her job as a social worker in a haemotology unit:

> particularly after the government campaign on AIDS . . . . the disease has made many people frightened and concerned about their own health. Unfortunately, the television campaign raised anxieties but did not always give information about where people could discuss their own personal worries face to face.
>
> (Breach 1987: 10)

These worries applied as much to social workers as to any other member of the public.

The government campaign added to both knowledge and confusion. Surveys to monitor its efficacy found that people knew more about how AIDS was transmitted and what it was, but that many had not actively changed their sexual practices. Interviews with young people on *Weekend World* demonstrated an 'it could not happen to us' attitude. It left people confused about the real risks. The campaign also lacked back-up. Voluntary agencies such as the Terrence Higgins Trust found their 'help lines' jammed with calls and social services departments, along with GPs and health centres, found themselves flooded with enquiries which they were not equipped to handle. On the positive side, many taboos were broken: condom advertising was allowed on television, sexual behaviour was discussed more openly, and the gay community gained public admiration for the way it rapidly organised itself into an effective pressure group. However, the government campaign left society reeling, particularly its care support systems.

Panic, the real plague

Society responds acutely to 'moral panic'. People seize upon a threat to society, typecast its main actors and highlight their differences. This encourages belief that the perceived threat exists and provokes public concern. The fabric of society is examined, moral positions are assumed and sanctions adopted. Stigmatisation, restrictions and curtailment produce a new and stronger equilibrium leaving people reassured in the strength of society and the protection it offers them. Many authors (Weeks, Mort, Fitzpatrick and Milligan, and Altman) have already documented how the AIDS scare had many ingredients of 'moral panic' (first outlined by Cohen 1972.) From the early *Sunday Times* headlines in August 1983, which proclaimed 'AIDS scare now become a phobia', to the 'Gay Plague' headlines of 1986 – the AIDS panic flared, fanned by media representation and government campaigns. As social work agencies struggled to produce a response, public hysteria grew. In the country's eagerness to combat something portrayed as a threat to social order and family life, fear and panic often led to irrational action and a deafness to the stated needs of people with AIDS and HIV infection.

Moral panics make people feel better. To identify and rally against a problem creates a common bond and a target against which to channel discontents. AIDS offers a combination of problems : health, sex and deviance. Weeks writes:

> disease sanctions govern and encode many of our responses to sex. It is this which makes the moral panic around AIDS . . . so important. It conditions a number of social stresses and throws unprecedented light on them. What is so striking about the whole moral panic around AIDS is that its victims are often blamed for illness.
>
> (Weeks 1985: 45)

The highlighting of certain 'out groups' in this way reinforces the social fabric. This is a form of social control which has long been practised, but unfortunately AIDS presents a more complex problem – the more we know about it, the more people can be classified as 'victims' until your 'out group' contains potentially everyone. The more this realisation dawns the greater the moralising and the greater the panic.

Some authors (Mort, Marshall, and Weeks) have argued that such a moral panic serves the interests of the medical profession, for whom it provides a source of power. Disease cannot be viewed in medical isolation; politics, ideology and social expectations all prevail. Mort clearly chronicles how, in early panics about disease, doctors were largely involved in medico-moral discourse:

> the substance of our history is the continuing power of medical discourse to define the sexual, setting the parameters of what can and cannot be said . . . but medico/moral discourse is not a conspiracy . . . . It is a distinctive regime of power/knowledge relations, rooted in institutions which circulate authoritative representations of sex.
>
> (Mort 1987: 217)

Medical power is also a source of political and moral power. As the country looked to medics to provide guidelines and answers for AIDS, medical statements became translated into moral judgements giving rise to witch hunts and influencing policy. As Marshall warns,

> unless we are all alerted to the manner in which scientific knowledge becomes politicised and, in turn, is used to political ends the medical profession may well find itself at the epicentre of a political debate with far reaching effects upon minority civil rights.
>
> (Marshall 1987: 33)

Moral panic around disease gives overstated power to medicine to provide all the answers – the danger is that it ignores social consequences.

Fitzpatrick and Milligan suggest other reasons for a moral panic. With the impending general election, government activity around AIDS provided an effective smokescreen to other social crises. It provided a new foe, a new national crisis against which the government could be seen to be fighting actively. The timing of the AIDS crisis was opportune and, some would suggest, in the light of the election result and the comparative lack of follow up to the government campaign, served its purpose.

Whatever the reasons and dilemmas, moral panic prevailed, blinding people from logic, freezing them into inaction. In the wake of the enormous publicity about AIDS, prejudice loomed large. Petitions were signed against hospices being set up for people dying from AIDS, various occupational groups started wearing protective clothing and refusing to handle people with AIDS, homosexuals and black people were oppressed. Tom Mangold writing in the *Listener* (2 July 1987) observed:

> as the tide of AIDS moves deceptively into recession, it leaves in its deadly wake a plague mentality that threatens civil liberties no less than the AIDS virus itself threatens the bodies it has invaded . . . . AIDS hysteria, compounded by public ignorance, prejudice, self serving politicians and blinkered guardians of law and order will affect not only those likely to be infected with the virus, in its erosion of civil liberties it will touch us all.
>
> (Mangold 1987: 5,6)

Speaking of AIDS

One of the most obvious, but often unrecognised, vehicles of anxiety mobilised in the process of public debate about AIDS, is the language used to describe the disease and the lives of people associated with it. Peter Randall, a co-founder of Body Positive (a self-help group for people who are sero-positive) describes it as a 'punishing language, it is aggressive and violent, it lacks care and it lacks understanding and that increases the isolation for individuals' (quoted in Maclachlan 10 Sept. 1987: 15–18).

The terms in which the AIDS phenomenon is described, and written about convey 'received wisdoms'. The press consistently failed to discriminate between AIDS and HIV infection, they have used AIDS as the generic term to convey a doom-laden image of the disease to the public. The most horrendous aspects of the disease have been emphasised in scaremongering terms. It is hard for the public, including social workers, to be understanding when they are consistently bludgeoned with reports about 'plagues' and 'deadly viruses'. For the press, AIDS is both terrifying and titillating – above all it is news; it sells newspapers, and the more outrageous the stories, the more profitable it becomes to report them. Even the more reputable press succumbed to 'doom merchanting'. Andrew Vietch writing in the *Guardian* warned that 'the worst possibility is a holocaust, a third of the British population dead by the turn of the century, America and Western Europe in a state of political and economic collapse, Africa left to the lions' (21 Nov. 1986). In *The Times* Digby Anderson, Director of the Social Affairs Unit, thundered, 'if something is not done within six years, according to a recent *British Medical Journal* Editorial, deaths per month will be the equivalent of the crash of a fully loaded Jumbo jet' (15 Sept. 1986). If they were not forecasting chaos, articles focused on 'risk'. The risk to health care workers from contaminated blood, risks to patients from being treated by doctors who have AIDS, risk to everyone from the time-bomb effect of HIV. Reports used alarmist language and created a climate of misinformation. People felt deceived when information changed daily and unsure of what they were facing. Press language overall conveyed the idea that we were all involved in a fatal battle against the great, deadly unknown. AIDS became 'the bogeyman'.

A second strand to considering the use of language in portraying received ideas about AIDS, is that it often signifies a moral stance. It has been suggested (Randall 1987, Watney 1987) that apart from being emotive and irrational, the public terms of reference and debate about AIDS and HIV infection have also been oppressive. The common parlance refers to 'AIDS sufferers', and 'AIDS victims', denoting a powerlessness and degree of blame in people who are infected. 'Victims' of what? – either their own irresponsible actions or others' selfish acts. 'Sufferers' – people who are struggling with a self-imposed burden or who are prey to the outcomes of others' perversions. Randall identifies that the language of the government campaign 'Don't Aid AIDS' and 'Don't Die of Ignorance' implies, in the first case, ostracism of people who already have AIDS and, in the latter, implications of stupidity. Such terms deny dignity and hope to people with AIDS and HIV infection : they are undermining and demoralising; they imply 'affliction, weakness and helplessness'. They do not accurately reflect the feelings of people living with the disease or motivate carers to work positively.

These may seem simple, obvious points, but they are important to the public perception of AIDS. The ways in which we think about and describe the disease affect both the attitudes of people infected, the care givers who provide help, and the social climate in which both have to function. Language creates and embodies received ideas. Because it is the mechanism through which they are transformed into action, it is therefore an important source of power and a determinant of 'reality'. Watney suggests that

> the language used to describe every aspect of the epidemic, together with the public shaming of people with HIV infection or AIDS, and their friends, loved ones and families, evidences levels of barbarism in contemporary Britain which we would all be foolish and naive to ignore.
>
> (Watney 1987: 11)

So what has all this got to do with social work?

I have spent several pages considering public images of AIDS and HIV infection. The role of social services departments and their employees has been greatly affected by such public images, and in the second part of this chapter I want to examine why this might be the case, what social work *can* offer, and how it is attempting to overcome initial hurdles.

Firstly, the portrayal of AIDS and HIV infection as primarily a 'medical problem' detracted from the contribution that social work had to make. This has occurred at both practical and ideological levels. The focus of financial support and government attention has been on medical research, treatment and health education. Publicity and reporting has concentrated on the causes, prognosis, and outcome of the disease. With the overall lack of public knowledge this has often fuelled anxiety. On the other hand, it has also indicated that the pattern of the disease does not always necessitate hospital treatment which is expensive, but can respond better to community-based forms of care. So far no funds have been made available to social services departments to meet this identified need. Although £20 million has been poured into medical research and training health care staff, no specific funds have been made available for training social workers and home care staff or providing special community services. At present, a person with AIDS in Britain spends an average of 86 days in hospital during the course of treatment, the comparable period in San Francisco is 16 days. In Britain there is little choice, care for people with AIDS is in hospitals (which receive the most resources) thus determining their pattern of death. As Christopher Spence, Director of the London Lighthouse says:

> People have two fears, the first is the fear of death. . . but the second is the fear of a bad death. Eventually the issue is not whether we die – or even when we die – but how we die. I found it very difficult to reassure the people I was seeing because their fears of a painful isolated and alienated death were well founded.
>
> (quoted in Smith 10 Sept 1987: 12-13)

The public focus on medical solutions, minimised the expectations and undermined the confidence of social services departments that they could and should offer appropriate help.

Early government statements and guidelines have fostered the medical mystique and have given no encouragement to social work to provide more than small-scale back up support. The establishment of the National AIDS Trust, initiated by Norman Fowler in May 1987, also reinforced this. Set up to co-ordinate voluntary efforts it consists of representatives from medicine, health and voluntary bodies but no one from the social services. However, at the time of writing (Dec. 1987) the latest report of the House of Commons Social Services Committee 'Problems Associated with AIDS' identifies for the first time the need for sufficient resources to be allocated to help health and social services to cope together. The committee was disturbed by 'evidence of under-resourcing' and, in advocating a co-ordinated programme of community care, commented that joint funding was inevitable and should be encouraged and facilitated at the national, as well as the local, level. The report, whilst praising the Government's initial approach, noted that resources were being channelled away from superficially less pressing areas of concern and called for serious consideration and funding of sociological resources to augment existing and future medical research. It also reiterated the call of the Association of Directors of Social Services for a national co-ordinating body to be set up to bring together statutory and voluntary sectors and unions in work around AIDS and HIV infection.

The medicalisation of AIDS did a disservice to the co-ordination of care. People with AIDS and HIV infection need a continuum of care: this means people from all sectors planning, providing and delivering services together. This does not mean resourcing one sector and not others; it does not mean expecting sectors to meet challenges without resources or looking to the voluntary agencies to fill gaps in provision.

The public image of AIDS and HIV infection has created fear and doubt in social workers and their managers. Social workers, just like other members of the general public, are influenced by reported beliefs. In the absence of enlightened information they too believe what they read. But for social workers, more than many other members of the general public, the fears have to be confronted. They do meet people with AIDS and HIV infection who need their care and help.

Initially, no specific information regarding AIDS, other than health and safety guidelines, was made available to employees of social services departments and no specific resources were made available to train staff; social workers like everyone else had to rely on what they could pick up because they were not identified as having a specific role to play. Therefore, social workers faced working with people with AIDS and HIV infection, with many publicly gained apprehensions, such as basic fears about the transmission of the disease and the dangers of infection; fears about having to confront and deal with homosexuality as an overt factor; fears about working with people who are young, dying or deteriorating mentally; and fears about whether traditional skills would stand them in good stead. AIDS and HIV infection also brought to the forefront of social workers' attention many taboo areas that are not specifically tackled on social work training courses: sexuality, racial discrimination, terminal care and drug taking are often 'special options' rather than core elements of a curriculum.

Additionally, as Reg Vernon points out, 'Social work has concentrated particularly strongly on the conventional heterosexual family, somewhat to the detriment of other units, and there is certainly very little about homosexual lifestyles in social work literature.' (Vernon 1987: 161) The public image of AIDS has left social workers struggling with their own beliefs and responses, and those engendered through training.

The media depiction of people with AIDS and HIV infection as victims and sufferers, people who need pity but who, through their sexual and deviant habits, have played an active part in their own demise, also left social workers wondering. How would they cope with the knowledge that one of their clients had AIDS: what problems of confidentiality would this impose? Would they be able to avoid making value judgements or assumptions about that person's way of life? Social workers felt uneasy about their own knowledge base, both in terms of factual information about the transmission and prognosis of the disease and also about their ability to deal with the beliefs and lifestyles of potential clients. Could the social worker simultaneously cope with his/her own fears and anxieties, those of clients, their friends and family, in addition to the public at large? Would their employing agencies provide support? Public campaigns left social workers fearful, and government action made them feel the problem had little to do with them.

In London, and especially in inner boroughs like Hammersmith and Fulham, and Kensington and Chelsea where the problem was keenly felt, there was enlightened and pioneering action. The first AIDS Policy Development Officer, Terry Cotton, appointed to Hammersmith and Fulham Social Services Department, said 'Fear and ignorance which AIDS arouses has to be squarely faced . . . too many people in Britain still see AIDS as primarily a health problem.' Andrew Henderson, ex-Director of Social Services in Kensington and Chelsea further commented, 'There is every indication that not enough attention is being paid to the social implications of AIDS and the build up of an adequate network of support services without which the NHS facilities are soon going to be in danger of being overwhelmed.' (Both cited in Peter Morris 4 Feb. 1986: 3)

Received ideas and language used to present the AIDS and HIV problem publicly, created doubts and fears for social services departments. I would argue that these forestalled the immediate development of relevant community services. The image of AIDS as a problem to be tackled and contained by medical services and/or voluntary groups providing self-help, left the vital role of social work marginalised. Therefore its initial response was patchy, piecemeal and ill-informed.

How is this changing? What can social work offer?

As the number of people with AIDS and HIV infection increases and more is known about the disease, received wisdom begins to change. Regardless of media speculation, certain working ideas have become established amongst the population of care givers, not least of which is the theme of co-operation. Despite the initial uncertainty and fear on behalf of social workers, there is now a growing conviction about the vital role they have to play. Much of this has been learnt through experience and through training. Despite limited resources, social services departments around the country, and most noticeably in London and Edinburgh where the problem is immediate, have provided a range of responses, often working closely with medical and voluntary organisations. In the wake of public panic, ways forward have emerged with social services/social work departments, who have had to deal with AIDS related problems, learning on their feet and providing a new body of ideas and 'wisdom' for their colleagues.

Part of the initial difficulty in knowing how to work with people with AIDS and HIV infection stems from the fact that the majority of social workers have never been in contact with anyone who is infected. Pioneering work in London, especially in the Boroughs of Hammersmith and Fulham, Kensington and Chelsea, and through the Terrence Higgins Trust, PACE, Body Positive and the London Boroughs' Training Committee (to name but a few) highlights the felt needs of people with AIDS and HIV infection – above all the need and the right to live and die at home. People with AIDS and HIV infection come from a range of backgrounds, and can have become infected by a number of routes. Whatever the route, the effects are the same – stigmatisation, loneliness, fear. Pauline Howard, a social worker at the Middlesex Hospital, described people with AIDS as feeling 'out of control of their lives [they] are aware of the loss of body image, suffer from low self-esteem and guilt'. Dr Tony Pinching from St Mary's Hospital, Paddington, urged social workers to dispel these myths about AIDS 'we've got to make sure people get their facts right and ensure patients with AIDS are received into the community in a proper fashion. Social workers are in a key position to do this' (*Social Work Today*, 30 June 1986 p.6). The response from the voluntary sector has been pioneering. As Marek Kohn writes in the *New Statesman*:

> One of the less remarked but more remarkable phenomena surrounding the AIDS epidemic in this country is the Terrence Higgins Trust. With striking adroitness, it turned to its advantage the reluctance of the state to address the crisis: the product of a marginalised social movement, it occupied the vacuum and built an alliance that has permitted it to channel some of the power of the medical profession into the service of its own goals. An important aspect

of this strategy has been the willingness of many individuals around the Trust to control their justifiable anger and build a dialogue – with Conservative politicians; with parts of the media.

(11 Dec. 1988: 28)

The Terrence Higgins Trust is perhaps the best known voluntary group involved in this work, but many others, including PACE, Body Positive and Front Liners, have made their mark. Gathering strength from a common oppressed position, and unity from ostracism, they have broken through barriers, raised money and hope, and pioneered new systems of care. The social services have dithered in comparison. However, when the problem hits, responses have been good. In Lothian and Tayside, for example, where significant numbers of drugs takers are HIV positive or have AIDS, imaginative moves have been made to develop policies for the fostering and adoption of babies born to sero-positive mothers, to develop needle exchanges for addicts and counselling services.

It is difficult for social services to work constructively towards policies and programmes of care for people with AIDS and HIV infection without public backing. The image of social workers, created by the media, as ineffectual and bumbling (particularly in child protection work) does not help establish their own and public belief in the vital skills they have to offer to emerging problems around AIDS and HIV infection. Although a great deal of time has been given to looking at the medical causes and implications of the disease, little consideration has been given to examining how people are actually going to *live* with it. By this I do not just mean people with AIDS and HIV infection, although undoubtedly their needs are enormous, but their parents, friends, children, partners, and the carers who will provide them with support.

The social work contribution: co-ordinated caring

During late 1986 and 1987 many working groups were established to look at the role of social services in relation to AIDS and HIV infection. The DHSS, the ADSS, the LADSS and the AMA have spearheaded some of these initiatives. There have been national conferences and debates. From this a growing recognition of a right response from social work has emerged. Such a response has crucially involved the co-ordination of activities aimed at providing help and care for people with AIDS and HIV infection. Social services departments are seen as being well placed to form a vital link between medical and voluntary organisations in order to make care in the community a genuine choice. This requires foresight. At present more people are dying of hypothermia, smoking, and cancer than AIDS related conditions, but AIDS and HIV infection are like time bombs: if effective planning is not achieved now, five more years will witness chaos.

Social work staff are already well equipped to work with people with AIDS and HIV infection. Counselling skills, working with interpersonal relationships, dealing with loss, advocacy skills, links with health, education, housing and voluntary agencies are all part of the social work task: the basic values of social work emphasise the need for self-determination and respect for the client – both fundamental needs of people with AIDS and HIV infection. What social workers lack is confidence. They need to be reassured and convinced that their skills and what they have to offer are needed. This can be achieved by information sharing and dispelling myths. Social workers need to realise that people with AIDS and HIV infection are not different from many other client groups. What *is* different about their situation is that they are surrounded by fear and anxiety linked to societal taboos, particularly about death and sexuality. It is the effect of these that needs confronting, with good information and examples of innovative practice.

Each person's experience of AIDS and HIV infection is different: there is no set pattern. No one is yet sure of the proportion of people who are HIV- positive and go on to develop full blown AIDS. The incubation time is lengthening, and the need for periods in and out of hospital differ, so help needs to be flexible and responsive. Most importantly care givers need to listen to what people with AIDS and HIV infection want. Jonathon Grimshaw, Director of Lambeth AIDS Action, who is HIV- positive himself, says:

> 'it seems to be the role of social services to ensure that windows of opportunity for self determination are kept open, SSD's should listen to the people with HIV and not the publicity which surrounds them'. In a plea to social workers he continued, 'We are being deprived of the physical, emotional and material resources we need in order to maintain our quality of life, our physical and moral well being and our sense of identity. We will need the best that you can give.'
>
> (*Community Care* 24 Sept. 1987: 6)

Sensitivity to the needs of people with AIDS and HIV infection is sometimes difficult to obtain but can be achieved through effective training provision. Training is perhaps the key to most successful social work initiatives. It is not just a supportive activity but crucial to the effective planning and provision of services. Training can be used to provide factual information and dispel myths, particularly when it involves people who have AIDS or who are HIV-positive as trainers. Through training, departments can assuage fears, build confidence and foster interdisciplinary collaboration.

If AIDS and HIV infection are to be coped with sympathetically and effectively, people from senior management downwards need to understand and respond appropriately. This means making money and the means available to equip people to cope – not just care staff but people with AIDS and HIV infection, their friends, families, and support systems. Training is needed, in many areas, from information giving, to the development of in-depth counselling skills, to policy development, and planning for services and their delivery. This involves the government making resources available to enable social work and care staff to learn to cope – so far no money has been earmarked for this purpose. Departments are expected to provide from existing budgets.

AIDS and HIV infection present many complexities apart from health needs. Associated problems occur: stress, social isolation, withdrawal of family support, housing problems due to failing health, special medical needs or eviction due to prejudice, the loss of income due to failure to work, financial insecurity for families due to the inability to be insured, feelings of anger, hopelessness and frustration, and a need to prepare for death. The implications of these problems for social services departments are manifold. The complexity and intensity of needs will necessitate training and education for all staff (not just social workers), the increase of domiciliary and day care provision, including specialist care for young people with dementia, rehabilitation facilities and strategies, services for children who are HIV-positive and their families, the development of links with voluntary, health and other local authority organisations and government departments, the development of policies on health and safety issues, confidentiality, and adoption and fostering.

All this suggests that social workers and their departments have a multi-faceted role to play in organising provision, advising, counselling and supporting people with AIDS and HIV infection to ensure they play an active role in managing their own destinies. Peter Jones writes:

All of us working in the medical and social services, and with the responsibility of providing care for people with this sad and lonely disease, should follow the lead set by the voluntary societies, and exemplified in their 'buddy' systems, which aim to ensure that those in need are befriended by suitably trained people. The sharing of involvement in the management of AIDS is crucial both to those infected and their carers.

(*Social Work Today* 9 Feb. 1987: 11)

Conclusion

In this article I have attempted to show how a social work response to AIDS and HIV infection was delayed and undermined by media coverage and government action. The marginal position of social workers in our society fuelled doubts, raised by 'received ideas', that social workers had a vital role to play. Social work has been slow to recover from that position, but in recognising, often through direct experience and training, the 'unreality' of many of the 'public truths', it has begun to forge a creative way forward, identifying action and lobbying for resources to implement it.

There is still a long way to go. Social workers have an important role to play in changing public attitudes and ideas about AIDS by working effectively with health authorities and voluntary agencies to promote the dispersal of accurate information and ideas.

AIDS and HIV infection offer social work the chance for positive action. In demonstrating how it can transcend the morass of 'received wisdom' and inaccurate language to offer effective help to the perceived needs of people with the disease, social work has the opportunity to effect a sea change in the received ideas about social work in general.

© 1989 Geraldine Peacock

Postscript

This chapter was written in December 1987. The whole field of work with HIV infection has grown rapidly since this time; numbers have changed, language altered, and services developed. Publishing schedules make it impossible to update, so readers must take into account this chapter's 'historical' context!

References

Altman, D. (1986) *AIDS and the New Puritanism,* London: Pluto Press.

Breach, A. (1986) 'Do social workers have a special role to play in helping AIDS patients?', *Social Work Today* 26 Oct. : 10-11.

Cohen, H. (1983) 'AIDS scare now becomes a phobia', *Sunday Times* 14 Aug.: 4.

Cohen, S. (1972). *Folk Devils and Moral Panics,* London: McGibbon & Kee.

Fitzpatrick, M. and Milligan, D. (1987) *The Truth about the AIDS Panic,* London: Junius Publications, BCMJPL Ltd 1987.

Grimshaw, J. (1987) 'AIDS raises opportunities for change', *Community Care,* 24 Sept.:6.

Jones, P. (1987) 'AIDS, planning for our future', *Social Work Today* 9 Feb.: 10-11.

Kohn, M. (1987) 'Ways of seeing pornography', *The New Statesman,* 11 Dec.: 28.

Maclachlan, R. (1987) 'Beyond hope and hopelessness', *Community Care,* 9 Dec.: 15-18.

Mangold, T. (1987) 'The plague mentality makes victims of us all', *Listener,* 2 July: 5-6.

Marshall, S. (1987) 'The politics of prejudice', *Nursing Times,* 4 March: 31-33.

Morris, Peter (1986) 'Getting to grips with the AIDS epidemic', *Community Care,* 4 Dec.: 3.

Mort, F. (1987) *Dangerous Sexualities: Medico-Moral Politics in England since 1830,* London: Routledge and Kegan Paul.

Randall, P. (1987) 'AIDS – the language of oppression' *Body Positive Newsletter* 34, 6 Oct.:2,3,4,21.

Smith, P. (1987) 'Lighting their home', *Community Care,* 10 Sept.:12-13.

Vernon, R. (1987) 'Responding to AIDS : practice and policy', in Horobin, G. (ed) *Sex, Gender and Care Work, Research Highlights in Social Work* 15, St. Martins Press/Jessica Kingsley Publishers.

Watney, S. (1987) 'AIDS babble', *Body Positive Newsletter* 38, 1 Dec.:9-11.

Weeks, J. (1985) *Sexuality and its Discontents: Meanings, Myths and Modern Sexualities,* London: Routledge and Kegan Paul.

3

'Mad, bad, and dangerous to know': Social work with drug users

Patricia Kearney

> Making allowances for constitutional differences, I should say that in less than a hundred and twenty days no habit could be formed strong enough to call for any extraordinary self-conquest in renouncing it, or even suddenly renouncing it.
>
> (De Quincey)

> One hit and you're dead
>
> (Pete Townshend)

Over one hundred years separate these two very different statements, although both could have been made yesterday. Drugs and drug users provide a rich source of myth, fascination and misinformation. As Marek Kohn has recently argued, heroin 'acts as a sign under which some of the deepest concerns of a people can gather. It creates channels for the transmission and discharge of anxieties more massive than the actual issue of heroin would merit' (Kohn, 1987: xi). Social Services departments are currently invited to consider themselves as part of the help offered to drug users. If social workers are to be clear about how they can best respond, they need to separate myth from reality and to note where their own professional anxieties find a reflection in 'the drug problem'. In this chapter I shall look at some of those myths and at how they feed social workers' own presumptions about work with drug users. Traditionally in this country, such work has been done by specialist agencies, and generic workers now must consider the relevance of their own existing skills and whether they are expected to acquire new ones.

Since 1965 it has been possible to chart a qualified picture of drug misuse with the introduction, then, of the Home Office notification system. Although a partial picture, for reasons I shall give below, it shows that rates of use, methods of use, and characteristics of users are varied and changeable. Despite this information, popular opinion about drug use remains fairly constant. Public views influence both drug workers and users, and this influence needs to be recognised as the first stage of any examination of social work with drug problems. In the last twenty years or so there have been rapid changes: the non-medical use of drugs has always been affected by legal, political and economic factors, as have official responses to such use. In the last few years another massive influence has been added, that of HIV infection and the AIDS syndrome. The social and moral context of professional behaviour is arguably nowhere more acute than in drugs work, and it is an area in which service planning is currently akin to star-gazing: who knows what the practice issues will be in five years' time?

Social Service departments, like other welfare services, are faced with the task of organising priorities under increasing fiscal and ideological stringencies. At the same time, they are faced with a new area of work, that of problem drug use. This extra pressure is dealt with in the same way as other demands upon the service: by definition and allocation of work that afford both agency and worker some sense of control over what they are dealing with.

Thus clients and their needs are defined in terms of what social workers think they can offer, rather than services developed in response to need defined in other ways, including by the client. Morever, the stereotypes that surround drugs make positive definitions hard to make. If social workers are to be clear about what they can do, they need to be aware of such ideas, otherwise drugs work will be perceived as an uncomfortable and unprofitable challenge.

The history of drug use

The use of mood-altering substances in western society is well described (Gossop 1982), and we clearly have long-established ways of improving how we feel. What changes is the choice of substance and public attitudes to it. If a substance gains a reputation as pleasure giving, it may then attract public hostility and possibly formal restriction. The popularity of a substance can be increased by such attention and it may even lose much of its attraction, irrespective of its actual pharmacological effect when another newly fashionable substance emerges. Use is affected by class and by culture: when a new substance is introduced to our society its use is often controlled by its cost. As long as it is restricted to a rich minority it is deemed to be used safely and responsibly or, at least, in a relatively restricted way. As its reputation grows or as a familiar substance is discovered to be pleasurably mood-altering, it obeys the law of supply and demand. Becoming cheaper, and its use widespread, it is deemed dangerous. Nicotine, tea, coffee and gin have all followed this pattern, irrespective of their actual pharmacological effect. Prohibitive laws, which add to the attraction, may be the next step, whether by high taxation, as upon tea two centuries ago, or by outlawing, as with alcohol in the Prohibition era: 'Is pot helping to change the world? . . . Yes, as long as it remains illegal' (Neville 1971: 114).

Official responses to the drug problem

In 1926, the Rolleston Committee set down the principles underlying official attitudes to drug users in this country, and laid the foundation for what has been seen by other countries as the liberal and humane 'British system'. That is, people addicted to drugs are to be regarded as patients entitled to medical treatment rather than as criminals requiring punishment. At the time of the Rolleston Committee, Britain had a small number of people with drug problems, who were usually dependent upon morphine or cocaine. They fell into two groups: the 'therapeutic' addicts who had developed their habit through injudicious prescribing in the course of medical or surgical treatment; and those who, by virtue of their occupation, had access to such drugs. These were, most usually, doctors, nurses, and dentists. It was considered that both groups could continue as stable, valuable members of society provided that they had a legal supply of their drugs. For the next thirty years, official figures remained relatively constant at between 400 and 500 such addicts per year, who continued to live free of legal and medical problems. This stable situation was controlled by the 1920 Dangerous Drugs Act, by which morphine and cocaine could be obtained only by a doctor's prescription.

In the late 1950s this picture changed markedly, with a rise in official statistics from 454 users in 1959 to 753 in 1964. Barbiturates, cannabis, LSD, and amphetamine began to figure as drugs of abuse. Drug users were no longer therapeutic addicts or from those groups professionally at risk; they were younger, and were using drugs recreationally with friends. Drugs were something to be enjoyed and shared, and obtaining them began to involve theft, deception, and unscrupulous prescribing.

In the light of these changes, the Brain Committee was re-convened in 1965 (HMSO 1965). It had first met in 1960 when it reported that changes in drug use did not at that time require a change in policy (HMSO 1961).

The Brain Committee's new recommendations were embodied in the 1967 Dangerous Drugs Act by which heroin and cocaine were limited to prescription by Home Office licensed doctors, if for the purpose of treating addiction. (All doctors could and can still prescribe these drugs for other conditions.) In effect, licences were mainly held by those doctors working in the new treatment centres, Drug Dependency Units (DDUs), which addicts were now obliged to attend if they wanted legal drugs. The committee also established the notification system to keep track of the extent of the drug problem. This requires any doctor seeing a patient concerning, or whom he suspects of, addiction, to notify the Home Office. This system remains the basis of current official statistics.

The 1971 Misuse of Drugs Act brought together all previous drug legislation and organised drugs of misuse, 'controlled' drugs, into categories A, B or C, with penalties for possession and supply depending upon the category of substance, class 'A' drugs carrying the severest penalties. In theory, a drug can change class, be removed from, or added to a classification. In practice, drugs have yet to be demoted or removed, and it requires a lengthy process to add them. This was done when barbiturates were included in the provision of the Act on 1 January 1985, and when the majority of minor tranquillisers were included, on 1 January 1986. The Act attempts to regulate irresponsible and ignorant prescribing, although drug misuse extends beyond the prescription pad: solvents are not included nor are naturally occurring hallucinogenic mushrooms, unless in a prepared form. The hierarchy of classification does not distinguish drugs by their relatively harmful pharmacological effect: for example, cannabis mainly carries heavier penalties than Valium yet it is the latter that has dangerous side effects in withdrawal.

The prevalence of drug use

The Home Office notification system shows that the number of addicts has increased annually from 1949 in 1976 to 5869 in 1985

(HMSO 1986). This is an incomplete picture since it identifies only those people who come forward for treatment. Conviction rates and local drug indicator surveys suggest that this is the minority of opiate users and that, for many people, heroin is not their first or only drug of use. It is likely that the notification system identifies a trend but substantially underestimates it.

Since the mid-1970s British users have had access to heroin from South-east Asia, which can be smoked as well as injected. This has made heroin a much more attractive drug, especially to those already smoking cannabis. Coupled with increased and cheap availability, this accounts in part for the dramatic rise in heroin use over the past decade.

Some definitions

In recognition of this increase in drug use, the Advisory Council on the Misuse of Drugs, established under the 1971 Misuse of Drugs Act, distinguished different levels and patterns of drug taking in an attempt to identify at which points use would give cause for concern. The term 'addiction' was increasingly less useful as a general description, since not all substances are truly addictive. That is, they do not result in a physical withdrawal syndrome on sudden cessation. Heroin, if taken sufficiently regularly, does have a withdrawal syndrome, but solvents and cocaine do not. Non-addictive drugs do, however, produce problems of psychological dependence, and giving them up can leave people with cravings, anxieties, and distressed feelings that last much longer than the few weeks of most withdrawals. The addictive drugs also produce problems of dependence once the initial withdrawal is over. The committee noted that there is a spectrum of using behaviour, ranging from the experimental, through the casual and controlled, to the dependent and chaotic.

Of course, there is overlap between these categories, and their characteristics are not exclusive. Experimental drug use, for example, among young glue sniffers, may not be well controlled because the implications of sniffing and risking intoxication in a dangerous place, such as a railway embankment, is not appreciated. Casual use of drugs – that is, irregular or infrequent use – might be either recreational and controlled by context or may indicate chaotic or binge use, similar to that shown by some problem drinkers. These definitions begin to broaden professionals' understanding of the problems of drug use. They are based on the pattern of use, rather than on specific substances and acknowledge the possibility both of non-problematic and potentially problematic drug use. The view moves outside the relatively narrow focus of the specialist services, since these are less likely to come across people using drugs intermittently or in a relatively controlled way. Residential and generic social workers are arguably much better placed to identify potential problem use and less obviously drug-related difficulties. The committee's definition of a problem drug user is of someone who 'experiences social, psychological, physical or legal problems related to intoxication and/or excessive consumption and/or dependence as a consequence of his own use of drugs or other chemical substances' (HMSO 1982: 34).

If taking drugs lands you in court or results in your parents throwing you out, or your partner threatening to leave you, then you have a drug-related problem, even though you may not be addicted to heroin. This focus begins to make sense to generic social workers since they are familiar with problem-solving ways of working even if they are not familiar with drugs. They may well meet problem drug taking at one remove: for instance, when their clients come to them via the courts, or fall into rent arrears or start to have child-care difficulties. They may begin to relate such difficulties to drug use at a stage when their client may well not want to perceive them as such.

Stereotypes

Despite such approaches, the myths about drug-taking are still strong. An example of the difficulty of clear thinking is given by the evolution of the drugs laws, where the humane ideals of the Rolleston Committee have become the contradictions and ambivalences of current practice.

Are drug users sick or bad, victims or predators, free spirits or slaves? How professionals perceive drug users will determine our behaviour towards them; do we offer care or control, and how do we distinguish between the two? This issue is familiar to social workers in other contexts when they have to decide what their own role is within the legislative framework; for example, when working with adolescents or depressed shop-lifters or abusing parents.

The resolved attitudes that lie behind such practice debates are seen quite clearly in the mass media's presentation of drugs issues. The frame of reference implicit in much media presentation is one which presumes a shared sense, with the audience, of the normal and the deviant. This framework offers a sort of resolution and both reflects and informs public opinion.

This position is considered by Jock Young, who identifies a classification of society presented by the media as follows:

(a) sick (who can't help it)
(b) innocent (who are corrupted)
(c) wicked (who are corrupt)
and a number of (d) the normal

(Young 1973: 332)

In this way, the media dispenses with uncertainty by attributing otherwise contradictory characteristics to distinct sets of people. This classification, put into drug terms, creates 'pushers' whose aim is to make 'sick addicts' out of passive victims. By extension, the drugs themselves take on the supposed power and qualities of the corruptors and become themselves evil yet irresistible. These images bear little comparison to reality where the borders between personal use, scoring for friends and 'doing a bit of business' often to finance one's own habit, are blurred. The familiar media image of strangers at the school gate has been tracked down by Marek Kohn to a single, alleged incident reported in a 1983 *Daily Telegraph* article (Kohn 1987: 122-3). For most users of illicit drugs, compliant friends are their most usual introduction. Social workers will recognise the parallels with public views on child sexual abuse: that the danger lies with strangers, not with relatives or family friends.

Because this framework dispenses with awkward questions it is a strong one. It can be strong enough to withstand contradictory evidence and resists informed opinion from professionals and users that some forms of use might be unproblematic or even non-deviant. This is seen in attitudes to alcohol, where there is still great resistance to recognising drink-related problems in anyone not 'down and out'.

Such attacks upon the status quo are dealt with by the myth of inevitability: 'Namely that those individuals who violate the natural law ineluctably suffer in the long term' (Young 1973: 333). Thus, individual drug use is seen as an unavoidable progression from soft to hard drugs, from initial pleasure to ultimate degradation and death. The myth is a persuasive and dangerous one for workers and users alike, since it destroys hope. Preventive work, even at an early stage, seems pointless; users fear they have no control over their drugs but are controlled by them, and workers think they can offer nothing to help to break the chain. Media coverage and popular ideas attribute specific characteristics to individual drugs and to those who choose them. The 'junkie' stereotype ignores the fact that many users of street drugs have jobs and families and do not conform to the picture of white, male, single and drifting. It does not allow for those problem drug users whose source of supply is their GP. In recent years, public disapproval of drugs has focused on heroin, so that 'Heroin is a special drug because it is perceived as a special drug. It occupies a position as the demon drug of demon drugs' (Woodcock 1985). Heroin mirrors the position held by LSD in the late 1960s when the media response was that good trips make bad news. William Braden (1973) shows how coverage of LSD changed over a decade from lauding a new 'wonder drug' in the treatment of mental illness to condemning it and its users as degenerate. LSD was eventually regularly described as a cause of brain damage and cancer despite the lack of research findings to validate such statements.

Stereotypes of drug taking do more than offer easy copy: they are a powerful influence upon professionals. When social workers find that their clients don't fit their preconceptions, then the simplest response is to deny the problem, not the media presentation. Similarly, users decide to ignore the advice and information given to them since it does not tally with their own experience.

An example of this was the first stage of the government's anti-heroin campaign. Young people using heroin, or with using friends, found little in common with the wasted figure on the posters. They either ignored the message or elevated the model to pin-up status: a truly Romantic hero. Social workers, perceiving the hype, may respond by deciding that there isn't an issue to deal with after all.

Response to drug use is currently paralleled by responses to child sexual abuse, and for similar reasons: it is awesome to think of these things happening on a large scale and even worse to be expected to provide some sort of solution.

Our personal attitudes to pleasurable drug use are complicated. Hedonism threatens the status quo since it questions the rules of effort and reward by which we attempt to live. The hedonist is 'mad, bad, and dangerous to know', and the means by which he obtains his pleasures are, by association, similarly dangerous. Society's discomfort can be translated into moral indignation. This allows condemnation whilst exercising a vicarious interest. The process is, of course, not confined to drug-taking:

'We know of no spectacle so ridiculous as the British public in one of its periodical fits of morality . . . . Once in every six or seven years our virtue becomes outrageous . . . . We must make a stand against vice' (Macaulay 1880: 143).

The rise in illicit drug use in the late 1970s offered an ideal opportunity for the outbreak of a moral panic. In the early 1980s heroin became the focus of much media attention with the *Daily Express* and the *Daily Mirror* running anti-heroin campaigns or, as the latter paper called it, 'chasing the dragon'. These campaigns did have an impact, not least upon the parents I saw at the time who financed their adult children's habit, since both thought that withdrawal was literally fatal. Newspapers and television were often the main source of information for social workers too. Unless they worked in a drugs-related setting they may have had very little to balance the supply of misinformation they were exposed to.

The established drug services are also affected, as it seems that their responses both to changes in the drug scene and their own lack of homogeneity in how to view drug users involve disagreement and uncertainty. They recognise that many drug users do not want or cannot imagine a life without drugs. Many drugs specialists would argue that it is impossible to 'cure' addiction but that this is something users will decide for themselves: they will 'grow out of it'. One of the issues for the DDUs currently is whether long-term prescribing helps or hinders the user's chance of eventually becoming free of dependence upon drugs. Prescribers and the agencies they work in have to consider whether their function is purely medical or socially protective. 'The dichotomy [is] not between using drugs and getting off them, but between clean drugs from a clinic and dirty drugs from the gangsters' (Marks 1987).

Alternatively, do they see themselves as offering drug users the opportunity to make choices – that is, made with a clear brain, in an environment where feelings such as ambivalence, fear, and regret can be safely expressed, and where the consequences of drug use can be faced and acknowledged. It is worth looking at the issues facing specialist services since it seems that the more they expand their remit, the closer they come to a definition that already fits the activities undertaken by generic and residential social workers and probation officers.

The invitation to social work

It is in this atmosphere of media hype, professional 'expert' disagreement and a changing drug scene that Social Services Departments have been invited to consider their role in working with drug users.

The formal and positive invitation is expressed by the Advisory Council on the Misuse of Drugs (HMSO 1982). It recommends that problem drug use should no longer be the safe concern of the existing specialist services but that the generic agencies, including general practitioners and Social Services Departments, have a useful part to play. By definition, the council considers problem drug use to have a social context and so must look to community-based and primary care agencies for part of the solution.

The rate of increase in drug taking means a consequent normalising of drug use. For this reason, social workers in generic agencies are increasingly likely to come across clients who use drugs. This may or may not be problematic for the individual client but certainly will be for social workers and social work agencies that are unclear of their role in the drugs field.

Another reason why Social Services Departments are likely to become professionally involved with drug use is because they can be seen to fill gaps in the existing service which are created both by changing patterns of drug use and the already sparse nature of specialist drugs services.

Both the NHS, where drug dependency services are not available in every health authority catchment area, and the non-statutory services, who, to date, have provided a larger part of the counselling and rehabilitation help available, are under increasing financial pressure. It takes time and money to identify and respond to changes in drug use. For example, the small number of residential rehabilitation houses that exist can, as yet, offer very few facilities to drug-using mothers who wish to keep their children with them. Social Services Departments on the other hand, may well look like holding more appropriate resources, such as family centres, under fives services, I.T. projects, than either the DDUs or the non-statutory drug agencies.

The reluctance to respond

It is unfortunate that the drug problem is regarded with such apprehension by many social workers and social work managers – not least because of the role they can play in it.

(McCarthy 1986)

This apprehension takes several forms. One is that social workers are as affected by negative images as everyone else and they have little acknowledged professional experience of drug takers to balance against this. Whilst social workers have experience of working with other supposedly discrete and stigmatised groups, such as the mentally ill or abusing parents, they have the justification and the confidence given by statutory obligation and responsibility. Social workers have no such link with drug users, who are therefore easily defined as the authors of their own predicament and, as such, require or perhaps deserve no social work involvement. It is not surprising that the group of social workers traditionally involved with drug users outside of the specialist services are probation officers. Drug use is, for the probation service, an acknowledgeable issue, especially if its clients' initial contact is via the courts because of a drugs offence: problem drug use is both identifiable and definable for client and worker. Probation officers work with the reality of legal consequences, which is a framework they can use positively as motivation for their clients to begin to acknowledge their problems and the possibility of change.

Another cause of reluctance is the current pressure upon Social Services departments to prioritise their activities within a setting of financial stringency. Social workers are expected to justify their activities on criteria with which they may profoundly disagree. It is a difficult and demoralised climate in which to make positive assertions about new areas of work. However, welfare organisations experience perennial difficulties in ordering their activities. These processes are worth examining for the insight they give to the problems that social work agencies have when considering what help they might offer to drug users.

Smith and Harris's study of Social Services departments was undertaken at the time of the Kilbrandon and Seebohm reports, and has immediacy and relevance when applied to current issues about the relationship between drugs work and how social workers perceive their own activities. Smith and Harris consider how social work departments 'Fail to assign a significant role to the organisational members' own subjective ideas about the phenomena in question' (Smith and Harris 1972: 27). They describe the process of decision making within area teams, how cases are allocated, to whom, and for what purpose. They identify the importance of 'need ideologies': 'the general system of ideas in terms of which social work professionals make sure of their everyday practice and of the administrative structure within which this occurs' (ibid.: 28). The study sees these based primarily upon an individualistic ideology with the individual client as the basic 'unit of need'. By implication, this requires a set of specialist skills which come to be regarded as embodied in specific individual 'specialist' workers. This process can be seen in drugs work, where contact with users is siphoned off to particular settings, such as DDUs and away from generic social work teams.

The causes of need are similarly ideologically defined by workers and take the form of, for example, material need or individual psychopathology, or even a moralistic definition by which clients can be considered for attention. In this context, the function of such causal ideologies is 'to provide social workers with a rationale for considerably reducing their workload' (ibid.: 40) since a distinction between 'real' clients and the undeserving others allows a lessening of demand upon social workers and their agency's energies and resources.

The concept of 'units of need' can be seen at work in the specialist drug agencies. DDUs are part of the NHS adult psychiatric services, and so a medical service style predominates; that is, with the focus upon the individual patient. The principle of medical confidentiality operates alongside this, which further disposes the service to deal with discrete individuals. This is carried through to record- and statistics-keeping and makes styles of work with a family or community focus difficult to define and operate. It is hard to identify patients as members of a particular family or as members of a particular community, whether by age, address, or culture.

Generic agencies are arguably better suited to developing services that allow a range of client definitions: they may operate a patch system, or have community workers on the team or organise a sub-office in a specific locality such as a housing estate.

Individualistic ideologies can result in teams producing 'specialists'. In the context of avoiding problematic work, this means a designated social worker to whom all referrals of a certain type are allocated. This protects the rest of the team from a particular brand of clients and their problems. It also perpetuates stereotypical responses in workers, partly because they gain little experience to counteract them, and partly because only those clients clearly exhibiting such problems are so identified. This means that any less obvious presentation of problem drug use is missed.

In generic teams, the drugs 'specialist' fulfils the role of protecting the team as a whole from discomfort, change, and the potential for new ways of working. This can even result in the worker carrying the same stigma as the clients: it is always that worker's clients who are late or abusive.

Training in drugs work will perpetuate the tendency if it is used to create 'experts' in this way. Drug training needs to be a pan-agency responsibility so that experience and subsequent expertise is not confined to individual unsupported workers with no sense of an appropriate agency structure behind them.

Social workers need to examine how their existing skills can help them to include work with drug users within their generic repertoire. Such work should be incorporated within existing agency procedures rather than lead to the creation of new ones. An example of this is child abuse procedure, where parental drug use should be seen as one of the factors to be considered when assessing parenting ability. It should not mean the setting up of separate criteria, which would suppose that such children do not have the same needs and rights as others. Making sense of the transferability of existing skills does a great deal towards giving generic workers a sense of confidence in dealing with drugs. It offers them a positive alternative to stereotypical images that are both unrealistic and uncomfortably defensive. I suggest that the skills social workers use in the rest of their practice are highly applicable to work with drug users – in particular, those of assessment and problem-solving approaches.

An initial assessment

This would aim to clarify the following:

Are drugs a problem in their own right?
Are there other problems?
What does the client see as the problem?

To answer the first point, the worker should establish:

what drug(s) are used;
how often;
how long;
the method of use;
whether the user has had any withdrawal symptoms;
have there been any associated medical problems e.g,
accidental overdose?

If the client is using addictive drugs almost daily and for at least a couple of weeks, then it is likely that he or she has developed a physical addiction and will have withdrawal symptoms on stop-

ping. A medically supervised detoxification plan may be something the client wishes to consider undertaking.

If the client is injecting drugs, even if they are non-addictive
(such as amphetamine), he is running a high risk of damaging
veins and skin tissue and of hepatitis and HIV infection.

It may be that none of this applies but that the client's drug
use causes related problems. These may be legal, financial, or
social, with the client finding it difficult to maintain school, work,
or family responsibilities.

It may be that the client uses drugs because they provide a
solution to problems, and it may be that the client has problems
independent of drug use. For example, a client of mine found
that heroin helped to keep him calm when he was at work. His
work of choice was burglary, since that way he didn't have to mix
with job colleagues.

Going through this process with the client allows the worker to
engage with the client in establishing a consensus about the difficulties that exist and the best forms of help. Some of this will
come from others, such as lawyers, family, or GP. The social
worker's role may consist in part of initiating and co-ordinating a
system of service.

A full assessment

If drugs do seem to be having a major impact on the client's life,
then a full drug assessment should be made. This includes a
detailed look at use, including a diary-type account of several
days' drug taking, noting such things as mood, effect, and precip-
itating event. It also begins to look more closely at the client's
life story.

At this stage, client and worker are considering moving into
longer-term work, where goals may include safer drug use or no
drugs at all. The generic worker needs to consider who is best to
undertake this assessment with the client. It is important that it
is someone who will continue to work with the client. It is of little benefit to the client to open up and face painful exploration
of the past and the future only to be handed on to another agency or series of workers. Social workers must negotiate on each
individual case as to whether this should be held by them, with
extra help, say, from a GP, or jointly with another agency, or
whether referring the client on means closing the case.

A full drug assessment is where causal explanations of drug use
can be incorporated into the work. They do not necessarily pro-

vide explanations of the past or solutions for the future but they can generate useful questions and distinctions; for example, why someone begins to use drugs and why they then continue to do so. Drugs can start to be seen as solutions to problems as well as the cause of them. A distinction can be made between history and the possibility of change so that it becomes possible to focus on achievable goals and to gain some hope for the future.

Can social workers deal with drugs?

Stereotypical ideas about drugs feed society's ambivalence about drug taking: they influence social workers as members of society and affect their professional practice. However, social workers are no strangers to difficult clients, complex issues, and the need to keep a clear head amongst public prejudices and reactions. Working with drug users is not perhaps so different from the rest of social work. The practice issues that discourage social workers from involvement with drug users are precisely the ones that they can make use of: I shall discuss below three such issues, those of motivation, failure, and loss:

> Perhaps, the most important thing to realise at the very beginning about help is that most people do not want to be helped in any significant way. The great majority of those who even ask for help are at the same time very much afraid of it. They may, in fact, actively wish to render it fruitless at the same time as they ask for it.
>
> (Keith-Lucas 1972: 20)

Alan Keith-Lucas' description of the helping process is illuminating in its applicability to working with a client group that tends to be perceived as homogeneous, ambivalent, distrusting, and bizarre. He describes the initial stages of the process as when the individual cannot see that they have any problem at all. Drug users may define 'problems' in terms of addiction, with no examination of the consequences that drug use may be having on themselves or their families. They may put boundaries on problematic drug use, such as whether or not they inject their drugs. These boundaries shift as they are overstepped – it is usually only in retrospect that clients can see supposedly stable periods as having been highly problematical.

Individuals who admit to difficulty may project it outside themselves and cope with it by adapting and creating conditions within which the problem is manageable. For drug users this is often the point at which they most clearly regard themselves as powerless *vis-à-vis* their drugs. They too are as influenced by stereotypes as the rest of us. 'Once a junkie always a junkie' is a belief held by many users when at their most desperate and hopeless. Narcotics Anonymous (NA), the self-help drugs organisation, turns this around to a positive expression. Those drug users who find a solution to their drug problems in the NA approach consider themselves as always at risk, and therefore follow total abstinence from all mood-altering substances, including alcohol. They make a protective and self-enhancing device and principle out of an attitude that otherwise traps users in a sense of hopelessness that enables them to avoid painful changes.

Users' myths also have a basis in reality: parents are extremely reluctant to admit to drug problems for fear that their children will be taken away. Social workers must give clear information about powers and procedures as well as putting this in the context of their own department's application of policy on child care and its attitude to drug-using parents.

Social workers, particularly those working within a statutory framework, are familiar with reluctant or unforthcoming clients. When suspicion and stereotypical expectations exist on both sides, the importance of a rapport and the difficulties of achieving it seem yet another barrier for social workers. The user's sense of impotence is often transmitted to the worker at an unacknowledged level. Social workers can feel as useless as their drug-using clients. In this atmosphere, the false solution flourishes, when the client says, 'All I need is . . . .' Although there are undeniably potent arguments for offering clean needles, detoxification, decent housing, and welfare advice, demands for the legalisation of heroin or a new life in the country are not within the social worker's power or even pertinent to the client's immediate needs. Demanding and greedy clients, who avoid help by such behaviour, are a phenomenon known to social workers already.

The inherent paradox of false solutions de-skills all workers and can make social workers fulfil their clients' worst expectations of them. Thus, clients can blame the helpers if, having taken the major step of asking for help, their problems don't quickly resolve themselves. Detoxification and rehabilitation programmes have to be seen as useless if clients are to bear the sense of failure they have at not completing them. Workers can be put down either because they are 'experts' and supposed to succeed for the user, or because they 'know nothing about taking drugs' since they are based in a generic agency. This process, if unrecognised, de-skills all workers, by touching upon an Achilles' heel, and enables the clients to protect against both self-hatred and their need to take responsibility for making changes in their lives.

The redefinition of these situations as expected – and indeed, necessary – stages in the helping process allows social workers to look beyond the immediacy and the fascination of drugs and to help their clients to do so. They can prepare clients for some of the unlooked-for consequences of asking for help. These include motivation, failure and loss.

Clients are often hindered by what they see as insufficient motivation in themselves to change. They consider their ambivalence and their awareness that drugs solve some problems as major barriers. They think that nothing short of a 'light on the road to Damascus' can get them off drugs. Social workers need to show them that ambivalence is a normal part of decision making. They can point out that 'motivation' is not a moral attribute, but whatever gets the client to ask for help; e.g. their dealer has just been busted and they can't get hold of any drugs.

Since statistics suggest that the majority of users give up without recourse to professional help, it is arguable that those who do come to the attention of workers have particular difficulties. Preparing clients for the possibility of relapse is important work. Being able to point to change and improvement is extremely encouraging to the client. For example, a return to drug use may be to a less chaotic style than before, or to smoking instead of injecting. At the least, the user will have had an experience of drug-free time. They can build on that at the next attempt and start to see that they can have control over their drugs. They will also begin to find out their vulnerable areas and the strategies that are most helpful to them. They can begin to consider what they can realistically achieve or actually want. For example, they may decide that they do want to continue using but find ways of doing so less problematically.

There will always be losses in giving up drugs, and very often positive gains are not immediately forthcoming. If drug taking has helped a client to ease or ignore other difficulties, these will have to be faced. There are real benefits to be lost when drugs are given up: users may make their living by dealing. As importantly, they may thereby hold a prestigious role in a drug-using community. A client of mine left a large squat as part of his attempt to give up heroin. In the squat he had been respected as someone who knew about welfare benefits, sick children, and the law, as well as where to score. He lost this when he moved and was regarded with suspicion by his new, respectable neighbours. Users who are parents and job-holders may be terrified that the loss of drugs may mean the loss of dignity and self-respect. In some ways the process of giving up drugs, or of less problematic use, mirrors the stages of mourning. Social workers have already learnt to apply bereavement work in other contexts, such as limb loss or adoption, and could use some of these skills with drug users.

What social workers, and their managers, can do

Firstly, social workers are already seeing drug-using clients, whether or not such use is openly acknowledged. This ranges across the spectrum of use, from experimenting teenagers in care to elderly people sedated in residential homes. This 'hidden' use may or may not be problematical for the client and, at the least, social workers can provide information about the effects of drugs and the kind of help available locally. Workers based in residential and primary health settings have a particularly important role regarding prevention and education.

Secondly, it is clear that most drug users do not make use of drug-orientated services. It may be that Social Services, particularly when there is already contact with a social worker, can offer a more acceptable form of help. For example, those dependent on tranquillisers through the medium of a legitimate prescription may well find a social worker attached to a general practice, working in collaboration with the GP, far more comfortable to approach than a drugs agency.

Thirdly, Social Services offices may be more readily accessible than specialist drug services. They are truly local and, as said above, offer resources that are not automatically thought of as helpful to drug users. Agency emphasis allows workers to consider the social context of individual drug use more readily than, say, hospital-based services.

At a wider level, agency function is as important as individual workers' skills: Social Service departments have their own specialisms such as child-care practice. Workers in specialist drug settings parallel the difficulties that generic workers have about drugs when drugs agencies do consider child-care issues. It is hard to acknowledge that this may be a legitimate concern because they do not know what to do. A Social Services department that can consider parental drug use within a child-care context will be of major help to drug agencies and to the development of services to drug-using families. Users tend to be regarded in the same way as their drugs: they are seen to be special because they are perceived as special. Service provision carries the risk of labelling clients, and users often keep away from drug agencies precisely because they do not regard themselves as 'that sort of drug taker' or because they fear that to attend would be to give up hope. Social Services departments could offer a less stigmatising service to certain groups of problem drug users.

If social workers have an idea about what they can offer to drug users, it follows that they can define what is beyond their remit. This begins to make the prospect of working with drug users a manageable one. Social Services departments do not need to be overwhelmed by the prospect of having to offer the whole range of help that this non-homogeneous group might require. They can offer a specific part of it and be aware of what other agencies have to offer and how they can work together. A multi-agency approach to drugs work seems to be the only one that can manage a problem that is protean and multi-factorial. The fall in heroin use noted by the Scottish police during 1986 is attributed by them to developments in multi-agency work (Morrison 1987).

Social Services departments have a series of tasks to perform to enable them to work with drug users. Workers and their managers need basic information about problem drug use. They need to know about the existence and function of other agencies with regard to drugs. They need the confidence to acknowledge drug use as a legitimate use of resources and define boundaries on their work that help make explicit the nature and extent of other agencies' remits.

Social Services departments have a managerial responsibility for devising guidelines for such inter-agency work and for the assimilation of confident drug assessment within the generic task. This will free individual workers from trying to cope with cases whilst battling out agency policy at the same time. Otherwise, social workers will be left working with and reflecting a client group that has nothing much in common other than a sense of failure, isolation, and hopelessness.

© 1989 Patricia Kierney

References

Braden, William (1973) 'LSD, and the press', reprinted in Cohen and Young: *The Manufacture of News: Social Problems, Deviance and the Mass Media*, London: Constable,

Cohen and Young (1973) *The Manufacture of News: Social Problems, Deviance and the Mass Media*, London: Constable.

Gossop, Michael *(1982) Living with Drugs*, London: Temple Smith.

HMSO (1961) *Drug Addiction: Report of the Interdepartmental Committee*, Ministry of Health and the Department of Health for Scotland.

HMSO (1965) *Drug Addiction: Second Report of the Interdepartmental Committee*, Ministry of Health and the Department of Health for Scotland.

HMSO (1982) *Treatment and Rehabilitation: Report of the Advisory Council on the Misuse of Drugs*.

HMSO (1986) *Drug Addicts known to the Home Office, 1985*, Statistical Bulletin 40/86.

Keith-Lucas, Alan (1972). *Giving and Taking Help*, Chapel Hill, NC: University of North Carolina.

Kohn, Marek (1987) *Narcomania – On Heroin*, London: Faber & Faber.

McCarthy, Mike (1986) 'Cycle of desperation', in *Social Work Today* 17 Nov.

Macaulay, William (1880) *Moore's Life of Lord Byron; Collected Essays*, London: Longmans.

Marks, John (1987) 'State rationed drugs', *Druglink, Institute for Studies of Drug Dependency* 2, No. 4, July, Aug.

Morrison, Alexander (1987) Annual Report of the Chief Inspector for Constabulary in Scotland.

Neville, Richard (1971) *Play Power*, London: Paladin, Granada,

De Quincey, Thomas (1822) *Confessions of an English Opium Eater*, London.

Smith, G. and Harris, R. (1972) 'Ideologies of need and the organisation of social work departments', *British Journal of Social Work*, vol. 2, no. 1.

Townshend, Peter (1984) Address given to Young Conservatives at Conservative Party Conference, Brighton, 10 Oct.

Woodcock, Jasper (1984) 'Working with drug users, a video package for professionals', produced for the Health Departments of Great Britain and the NHS Training Unit, Dec.

Young, Jock (1973) 'The myth of drug takers in the mass media', reprinted in Cohen and Young (1973) *The Manufacture of News: Social Problems, Deviance and the Mass Media*, London: Constable.

4

Users fight back:
Collectives in social work

Stewart Collins and Mike Stein

The background

The Barclay Report, published in 1982, suggested 'that personal social services must develop a close working partnership with citizens focusing more closely on the community and its strength' (Barclay 1982: 198). The report went on to state: 'We believe there is no one way in which partnerships between those involved in using and providing social care should be developed. Each statutory and voluntary agency must consider the geographical area, the nature of the people and the communities it serves' (ibid.: 198).

Sharing of caring is a repeated theme in the report. 'The community approach we are advocating seeks to share more fully with citizens the satisfactions and burdens of providing social care' (ibid.: 199). At the same time 'citizens' are seen as partners who merit opportunity for direct participation in agency decision making, thus 'allowing informal carers and communities direct influence on how resources are used' (ibid.: 214). Social workers are perceived as being involved in multiple accountability to elected members, clients, informal carers, and others with whom they act in partnership: 'They [social workers] will also have a duty to give an account of their actions and decisions not only to individual clients and client groups but also to informal carers with whom they are in partnership' (ibid.: 215).

The idea of citizen participation was also commented on in the Seebohm Report (1968), with its conception of a community-based, family-oriented service, while during the late 1960s and up to the mid-1970s, the setting up of Community Development Projects led to explorations within deprived communities to discover more about the needs of local people and attempt to help them meet their needs. A parallel development to the re-examination of the needs of local communities was seen in the revival of the Settlement Movement in the late 1960s, with one of its traditional aims being to reduce the distance between local people and settlement staff/management committees, in order to enable the settlements to be seen as 'owned' by the local community.

More recently, experiments with 'patch' and neighbourhood social work have included a strand of user participation, with Social Services workers being seen as accountable to direct, indirect, and potential users of social services in their locality. Decentralisation has been one of the key themes linked in with 'patch' and community social work thinking. This has emphasised the 'greater accessibility and acceptability of staff to the community and clients, to get services (and decisions about services) nearer street level' (Henderson and Miller 1982: 12). This message has emerged from both professionals and politicians: 'The former express their concern to design services that will respond visibly and flexibly to people's needs; the latter articulate the theme more in terms of the civic and political rights/obligations of consumers and local people and of the need to involve them more in the democratic process' (ibid.: 12).

These two themes have been emphasised more recently by Hoggett and Hambleton. They have stressed the distinction between service *responsiveness* to users and collective approaches which emphasise *democracy*. In particular, they contrast *representative democracy* and its emphasis on the activities of the major political parties with *direct democracy* and its stress on participation and non-party forms of self-organisation. Participatory democracy is seen to hinge on the collective activities of those who express either the needs of geographical communities or 'communities of interest', which express the needs of particular user groups such as the disabled, handicapped, or elderly (Hoggett and Hambleton 1987: 54). Hoggett and Hambleton go on to say, 'People *do* participate, *do* organise, *do* take on responsibilities so long as . . . organisations directly relate to their interests and so long as they feel they are exercising real control' (ibid.: 69).

This brief sketch does suggest that user participation has been on the welfare agenda in recent years. Nevertheless, 'participation' still remains an elusive and highly problematic concept, as well as an undeveloped practice. Why should this be so? Part of the conceptual confusion is that participation can mean anything from manipulation to user control including, as Arnstein has highlighted, non-participation, and varying degrees of tokenism or degrees of user power (Arnstein 1969). Very few of the advocates of greater participation in the personal social services make a clear statement of the level of participation or the extent of redistribution of power they consider appropriate, or their underlying rationale. And, in similar vein, some of the other problematic issues are swept under the carpet: the relationship between professionalism and participation, social control and democracy, consumerism and elected representation. These issues will simply not go away by just ignoring them. Is not our failure to develop credible participatory structures within the personal social services partly a reflection of the poverty of our exploration of these issues?

Local welfare advisory committees

The Barclay Report proposed local welfare advisory committees, 'to provide a forum in which representatives of clients, employers and social workers could discuss agency policies with respect to the rights of clients, including such issues as confidentiality, access to information and criteria for resource allocation' (Barclay 1982: 192). Again, such a proposal is not new. The Seebohm Committee had recommended advisory bodies and the co-option of users on to Social Services committees and sub-committees in an attempt to remedy any imbalance towards Social Services departmental bureaucracy and professionalism, at the expense of taking power away from users and communities.

The Barclay Report suggested that the local welfare advisory committee would 'test out new ideas and policies and comment on the structure and operation of social services agencies' (ibid.: 193). It was intended that each agency in consultation with the local advisory committee, would 'adopt procedures for dealing with complaints or appeals' (ibid.: 193). The report went on to distinguish between various kinds of complaints. It suggested that some formal vehicle was necessary to enable clients to maximise their rights, in line with expectations that publicly funded agencies with extensive powers over individuals should provide such safeguards. Such provision might 'impose a healthy discipline on social work practice' (ibid.: 196). This would encourage workers and their agencies to think more clearly about what kind of service they were offering; its purpose and the part to be played by the user in such a service.

Barclay's proposals were clearly pitched at the level of giving information and receiving complaints. But even these modest proposals have resulted in very little action and most Social Services departments still do not have a comprehensive complaints procedure.

Restraints on the user

Within organisations as complex as Social Services Departments which are legally responsible for a range of care and control functions, there may well be arguments for different levels of participation, depending upon the prime task. For example, for those living in residential care (the elderly, young people, mentally disordered, physically handicapped), delegated power and participation must feature on the agenda. At the most basic level all users should be given information.

Users of social work agencies are often unable to seek practical information and counselling help from other sources. They may have little choice but to accept a user role; they may be either reluctant users of the agency or they may be receiving a service against their wishes. It is reasonable to expect that users should be fully informed of the grounds upon which decisions may have been made within an agency. On occasions social workers have been accused of inadequately explaining reasons for decisions; of not being open about restrictions on resources; of failing to make clear to users their rights; of failing to explain their own powers. Social workers have been criticised for 'hidden agendas' which emerge at a relatively late stage in some relationships, such as child-care cases when a child is at risk. If rights have not been adequately explained, if the grounds for decision making have not been made clear, then the user has a right to complain, to consult with other members of the social worker's organisation. This is not easy. Complaints or requests for information have been often 'turned back' to the social worker concerned, and a second opinion from a line manager or director is difficult to obtain in many departments. It is hard for most users to complain in the first place, operating from a disadvantaged position and usually with no collective to whom they might refer to support their grievance. Furthermore, specific decisions regarding an individual may be a reflection of agency policy at a higher level, and the user has no real means available to influence such policy. A collective response is required which could be channelled through an appropriate body to impose more effective pressure upon decision makers.

Studies of user opinion have revealed that the role of local welfare committees advocated in the Barclay Report has remained a minimal one. By 1985 only seven committees had been established, and objections were raised by the Association of County Councils and the Association of Metropolitan Authorities as well as the Association of Directors of Social Services. One suggestion was that such committees impinged upon the role of elected members, bringing confusion to the democratic process and the more 'normal' machinery of local government. Such thinking, of course, may have overestimated the ability of local councillors to ensure an appropriate amount of citizen involvement. Councillors are already often over-burdened with numerous responsibilities, decreased powers, and the concentration of overall council power into only a few hands. It has been clearly pointed out that 'It is also difficult to find a way of involving them [local councillors] in structures for grassroots participation without them either dominating these or creating conflicts and inconsistencies between them' (Beresford and Croft 1986: 249). Furthermore, in Deakin and Willmott's study of two London boroughs, it was concluded that 'representing the consumer voice did not seem to be a high priority for councillors at least over social service matters' (Deakin and Willmott 1979: 15).

Therefore, the rhetoric of, and exhortations for, user involvement has not been matched by grassroots movements which might invest clients with real power. Deakin and Willmott's study of participation also emphasised that there was very little involvement by users and local people, with constraints being evident on all sides. In particular, there was a 'lack of direct access to the decision making process' when considering planning and provision of services (ibid.: 16). Although there was an avowed commitment to participation, with much reflective thinking and public pronouncement in support of this, 'we encountered some scepticism about implementation, at least at policy and planning levels' (ibid.: 16). It was intended to set up a committee on participation in one of the two boroughs examined in their study, but this intention was abandoned.

Several other studies on participation have produced similarly negative results. For example, Tyne, in exploring the position of families where a member had a mental handicap, suggested that Social Services Departments were not willing to allow parents to participate in processes of policy making or to use the expert experience and information of the parents themselves in expanding or modifying existing services (Tyne 1978). Similar difficulties were experienced in the inadequacies of formal machinery set up to encourage participation for people with disabilities (Low, Rose, and Cranshaw 1979; Oliver 1985). Beresford and Croft have gone so far as to say: 'Many groups found their dealings with formal systems of representation like consultative committees and advisory bodies to be deeply frustrating and indeed they could often be diversionary' (Beresford and Croft 1986: 208). In fact, in many situations consultation has occurred but often at the expense of genuine power sharing and without any real intentions to transfer power to users.

The promise of patch and decentralisation

Recent developments in patch-based social work held the promise of a movement away from bureaucratic and centralised services to a greater emphasis on partnership with users and the anticipation of more genuine power sharing.

'In this philosophy the user is not only a client, but also a partner in the planning and provision of services' (Hadley and McGrath 1984: 15). The minority Barclay Report had also argued that patch-based services would 'lead to greater participation from the community . . . as partners in formulating policies on social service departments and also in criticising and evaluating existing services' (Barclay 1982: 229). Yet again such rhetoric has not matched reality. As Beresford and Croft have trenchantly emphasised in their survey of user opinion in Brighton, East Sussex, 'very few knew of the patch reorganisation so their ideas about local social services would often be unaffected by any of the claims made for it or the administrative charges that it entailed' (Beresford and Croft 1986: 199). Indeed, after reorganisation respondents in this survey still identified developments *away* from the participatory management of social services, commenting on the increased size of the local authority, the transfer of headquarters away from the patch surveyed, and an increasingly directive and controlling role by central government.

It is not only in East Sussex that impressive claims have been made for the increased opportunities for client participation within a patch-based approach. Such claims have been seen as one of the five major principles of patch identified in 'Going Local' – the principle of 'the right of local communities to share in decision making' (Hadley and McGrath 1980: 10). Dinnington and Normanton are seen as two major examples of patch working. The Dinnington Project was committed to community involvement and a joint management committee which would involve members of the local community. The focus, unfortunately, was placed upon the deployment of statutory workers, and the community representatives were seen to take a nominal role. In Normanton it was not clear that increased involvement for users followed the setting up of the patch initiative. The Social Care Assembly for Normanton did enable groups and individuals to bring forward matters for debate and provided an opportunity to develop community involvement fully. It did not, however, have access to the Social Services Department or give local users any say in it. The evidence available then, about patch-based operations, so far reveals that 'Its aspirations to increase the say and involvement of service users . . . remains the one most difficult to achieve' and 'patch seems no more likely to take us further toward increased citizen participation than the Seebohm Report's earlier rhetoric did' (Beresford and Croft 1986: 218 and 219).

Negative comments could be made also about moves towards decentralisation and the failure of plans intended to provide advisory or consultative powers for users. Such plans have avoided fundamental changes in structures. It has been claimed that in arrangements 'for decentralisation in twelve local authorities surveyed in 1985 in no case had there been any devolution of executive powers or control' (ibid.: 219). Therefore, close centralised managerial power has been maintained, with top–bottom control predominating. We have already mentioned one intentional, or unintentional, example of tokenism in user representation in Dinnington. Similarly, in East Sussex, according to the Director, 'specific consultation exercises with particular client groups' were set up. These occurred in the establishment of meetings to obtain the views of children in care and residents in homes, but in other instances did not take place. For example, a consultation paper examining a possible general redistribution of residential resources in child care to community provision did not include the views of parents or children. Additionally, although a working party report on services for the mentally handicapped and their families did recommend parental involvement in planning and running alternative family placements and that all day care services and assessment conferences should include trainees or parents, the working party itself did not include representation from groups of parents or the mentally handicapped themselves.

Abuse of the community?

It is hard to avoid the conclusion that while the intentions of patch and decentralisation for greater user involvement are commendable, in practice, reality does not match the intentions. Structures for enabling users to have greater say remain tokenistic. It is debatable whether genuine democratisation has occurred in any significant way, with managers maintaining both power and control. On the other hand, there is evidence to suggest that participation by users and consumers in Social Services can have other meanings – meanings linked to the provision of voluntary or low-paid work. As the Barclay Report has stated: 'An important feature of the community is the capacity of networks of people within it to mobilize individual and collective responses to adversity. . . . The community approach we are advocating seeks to share more fully with citizens the satisfactions and burdens of providing social care' (Barclay 1982: 199).

Beresford and Croft have commented upon this in a critical and questioning manner: 'Thus people's "weaknesses" are when the Department has to intervene; their "strengths" code for things it is thought they can do for the Department or to relieve the Department of further demands' (Beresford and Croft 1986: 283). Clearly, women will be, and are, a primary target in view of the assistance they might give in providing 'social care'. Volunteers may be seen as an additional resource and as another potential weapon in the social care armoury. However, is this what people want? In Beresford and Croft's survey in East Sussex, users did not see themselves as volunteers, as part of the support system for patch. They were more concerned with access to mainstream services and with resolution of material issues to meet social and employment needs.

These are not new phenomena. The experience of one of the authors in the Probation Service some years ago highlighted the mismatch of user need with agency provision. A team specifically designed to work with homeless offenders took great pride in the casework service it provided to men recently discharged from prison. By 'casework' was meant a counselling service, opportunities for discussion, talk about problems. This approach was spelled out explicitly in an agency policy document. Yet at the same time research by a team of academics revealed that members of the user group concerned, upon release from prison, were primarily interested in accommodation, jobs and money (Corden 1983)! Therefore, there was an almost complete mismatch between user need and agency provision. Fortunately, the service to homeless offenders has now been modified to take account of the research work. The point of this example is to illustrate the discrepancy between the collective wants of a particular client group in contrast to the actual service provided.

The findings of the Beresford and Croft study come as no surprise to experienced social workers, when they state that

> while Social Services, including patch, are framed primarily in terms of care and support, most people do not seem to conceive the meeting of their needs in these terms . . . . 'Care', 'independence' and 'prevention' all seem to have acquired specialist meanings in Social Services and patch . . . different from those amongst the people we spoke to.
>
> (Beresford and Croft 1986: 196)

'Care' in social services has become a blanket term for the actions of Social Services.

> So we have day care, care services, care workers and reception into care. This usage does more than add a label. It also changes the sense, giving it idiosyncratic meanings far removed from people's day to day definitions. There are connotations of storage, control, passivity and keeping people occupied. So instead of the positive values that are placed on careful work or caring relationships, it is these passive meanings – looking after, minding, a caretaker role – that are more often attached to welfare.
>
> (ibid.: 266)

It is very easy, therefore, for users to become dependent objects of care, and with the meanings above attached to 'care', can the social services respond appropriately to people's needs?

Clients in collectives

Some groups of users now focus upon greater independence and assertiveness in their thinking and action, in collective action. Such thinking argues for a redefinition of terms such as 'care'. 'Support' is no longer seen as being 'dependent', 'cared for', or 'looked after' and the call is for equal participation – explicitly exemplified in the ideas of the Derbyshire Coalition of Disabled People: 'Our aim [is] full participation or equality for all disabled people . . . disabled people are the only people who can translate this aim into reality' (Davies 1985: 46).

Such a statement stands in contrast to ideas of 'care' and 'dependence' way beyond passive, placatory reliance on others.

Clearly, there are some users who wish to make a collective stand for their rights and for independent living. It should not be thought that all users will be as active and forthright as the Derbyshire Coalition of Disabled People. Some are obviously dependent upon statutory agencies for both services and support, and they may be afraid to criticise the department offering such help as a result.

Equally, Social Services clients form a large, diverse group of people with different wants, interests, needs, and concerns. We have, we hope, convincingly illustrated the limitations that exist in the present provision for users to change democratically and collectively the structure of the Social Services from within. There are examples of users imposing collective pressure and action from outside Social Services Departments. The range of such collective groups is diverse, ranging from active, national campaigning groups such as PROP, to local self-help discussion groups comprising only a few members. Equally, the part played by statutory social workers in these collectives may be minimal, such as in claimants unions, or they may have been more active, in an advisory or enabling role as with the National Association of Young People in Care (NAYPIC). Users themselves are often involved with social services in difficult and demanding circumstances. The contact may have arisen, as we have said earlier, through Supervision Orders and compulsory admissions to care of varying kinds. These have directly involved the controlling elements in social work, where much power rests with the social worker and very little power with the user, who may be resentful and annoyed. Thus, it is not surprising that many people do not feel any strong sense of affiliation to Social Services and may find the service to be stigmatising and unpalatable. Therefore, it is also not surprising that they should want to organise primarily, outside social service provision, sometimes rightly motivated by frustration, dissatisfaction, and anger. However, there is another side to the coin. Learned helplessness, acquired apathy, and developed inertia are all problems with which most users have struggled during years of strife, put-downs, let-downs, and being placed on the bottom rung of society's ladder. What then, are the chances for users to organise themselves when traditionally they have been placed in a dependent, deferential role, often characterised by fatalism, low esteem, and blind resentment? Typical comments from users who might be asked to consider working together are on the lines of: 'It's useless'; 'What can we do to change things?'; 'We're on our own'; 'No one wants to know us'.

Some problems of collectives

It is important to note that most users are placed on the fringes of society, often outside the main bonds of so-called productive activity. They are, of course, as we have stated already, a diverse group and include the elderly, people with disabilities of various kinds, the unemployed and offenders. Even *within* specific interest groups there can be a wide range of attitude, opinions, and wishes. For example, Cook quotes one study of groups of physically handicapped people which found that 'in England the younger, more articulate spokesmen of the physically handicapped, especially amongst those who have not been disabled from birth, strongly oppose efforts to improve institutional care and concentrated instead on improving community services' (Kramer 1981). Similarly, a study of a self-help group of parents of mentally handicapped children revealed 'that young parents of mentally handicapped children could feel little sense of kinship with the elderly parents and would not join the groups' (Cook 1987: 15).

Some writers have expressed pessimism about the possibilities of users combining together in collectives in view of their powerlessness. There have been criticisms of existing collectives such as Claimants Unions. They have been described as having been a 'virtual failure' and of being 'unable to make any impact on Social Security services, and even to sustain themselves as an effective critical movement' (ibid.: 12). Similar criticisms have been made of NAYPIC, where so-called 'problems of organisation, transient membership and long lines of communication have limited the impact which might otherwise have been made' (Smith 1987: 84). As Smith goes on to observe, 'The relative powerlessness of clients, both absolutely in society as a whole and relative to the organisations from whom they request help, must be a starting point to the debate' (ibid.: 82). Judy Wilson, a supporter of user collectives, has also urged caution when considering the problems which users may face having set up a group, in that 'lack of experience of organising, over-ambition as to what they can achieve, lack of resources, hostility or inertia among professionals, lack of visibility and domination by a few key members' may all present problems (Wilson 1987: 117). Even Mike Simpkin, an advocate of socialist and collective enterprise, expresses uncertainty when he states, 'It is not always possible for users to act for themselves without a great deal of support', feeling that 'clients as a whole are neither organised nor possessed of much political weight' (Simpkin 1983: 180 and 192).

The marginality of client groups

It is the recent writing of Peter Leonard which has most clearly delineated the marginality of user groups and emphasised the very different experiences which accompany such marginality (Leonard 1984). It follows that users are often usually amongst the poorest of the working class. They are placed *outside* their own class *by* their own class. Within working-class culture there is often much antagonism towards those who occupy roles as social work users, tendencies to see them as non-respectables, as 'scroungers', 'idlers', 'nutters', 'wasters', and 'no-hopers' who 'get what they deserve'. In fact, many users stand outside traditional working-class power bases such as established trades unions on account of their youth, their excessive age, and either physical or mental handicaps. These groups are criticised for their dependency, their lack of contribution to society. In particular, so-called 'problem families' and offenders are likely to suffer most of all as they present more obvious active difficulties to a local community. They are seen as an aggressive threat; as groups who 'lower the tone of the neighbourhood' and 'give the area a bad name'. 'Respectable' working-class organisations do not want these people, while users in turn may have the utmost difficulty in forming their own collectives. Coates and Silburn noted that 'problem families' in St Anne's, Nottingham, 'certainly found formal association of any kind more difficult than other people and they tend to live at some distance morally speaking from their neighbours . . . . Reviled by many residents as the cause of all St Anne's difficulties, labelled by the authorities as multi-problem families, not only do they not accept any common identity, but will frequently express the most caustic opinions of one another' (Coates and Silburn 1970: 154).

Meanings and ideologies

Chris Jones highlights the isolation and individualism of many social work users who attempt to survive in hostile and uncaring environments, and comments that, 'for many clients the sheer struggle to survive compels them to adopt the most individualistic and introverted strategies which are completely at odds with the traditions of collective action which have developed within the organised working class both in their communities and in their workplaces' (Jones 1983: 57). Yet, in addition to the isolation and individualism forced upon so many users is the fact that many of the labels and definitions imposed upon social work users who are offenders, disabled, elderly, or unemployed have come from within *dominant* ideologies; that is, definitions and meanings have been ascribed by those who have not offended – by the able, non-elderly, and employed – and these tend to concentrate on psychopathology. Sometimes so-called 'experts' from the fields of medicine and social work tend to devalue the definitions and meanings provided by users themselves. Consider this example from a Director of Social Services: 'Social Service consumers are, of course, handicapped by their relative inarticulateness, and views will often have to be gained at second hand through the experience of practitioners' (Smith 1987: 84).

It is, then, a very easy step to negate the anger, resentment and annoyance felt by users; to move away from the poverty, stress and material deprivation which they may experience; to deny the need for better resources; to fail to accept definitions by users of their own needs and to provide only minimal advice and support. Thus, dominant ideologies, definitions and meanings triumph; marginalised user groups are then placed under enormous pressure to incorporate such definitions into their *own* thinking, to subordinate their own definitions, terminology, and meanings. For unemployed users, continued unemployment leads them to be exposed more and more to disapproval and negative comment, to be exposed more and more to psychological pressure eroding a sense of identity, well-being, and health. Those users who are disabled are likely to be exposed to lack of attention, misunderstanding, and expectations of passivity – to the extent that, in some instances, 'the person' is seen as a recipient and a bystander, not as an initiator, an instigator, and an actor.

Some benefits of collectives

We have established then, the impact of marginalisation and the pressures of dominant ideologies upon users. This has profound implications for self-respect, feelings of worth and dignity, and it is here that collectivity can offer some strength, giving support to individual dignity as well as providing a forum for the sharing of common experience. In other words, collective action by users can provide a vehicle, a means for psychological growth:

> If we conceive a revolutionary activity as a process often taking place over long periods of time involving individuals in collective action, we can see that such activity helps the

individual to be rid of the psychological 'muck' (guilt, lack
of self-confidence, low self-esteem) which subordinacy to
the social order often entails.

(Leonard 1984: 206)

Leonard goes on to suggest that such activity can lead to changes
in the conception of self and the development of new capacities.
These include a sharing of experiences, thoughts, and feelings, a
moving away from a sense of isolation and rejection towards
developing the skills necessary to help others share their experiences, thoughts, and feelings. Anger, resentment, and negative
feelings are thus more likely to be expressed outwards – towards
social structures – rather than being turned inwards, in expres-
sions of apathy, defeatism, and depression. It enables the individual to become more aware of the social relations of which they
are a part. Therefore, a capacity for questioning the existing
social order develops, a revelation of possible alternative courses
of actions is made available, and an awareness of potential for
change is established which is opposed to the existing dominant
ideology.

It has been suggested that possibilities for collective action may
be expressed in two major ways: either through practice which is
consciousness-oriented or through practice which is action-oriented. Firstly, action-oriented practice is said to place

> great emphasis on the achievement of material changes
> through collective action. Focus centres upon the common
> material interests and concerns of those involved and the
> practical means by which material improvements can be
> obtained. Within this form of practice substantial changes
> in consciousness are a possible outcome but not a primary
> objective of the practice.

(Leonard 1984: 209)

Examples of action-oriented practice would include trade-union
activity with its major focus upon obtaining material advances for
its membership. More particularly, claimants unions exemplify
this approach.

On the other hand, consciousness-oriented practice puts more
of an emphasis on changes in consciousness before action can
take place. Developing understanding of oneself as part of a
wider society rather than any immediate material gain is seen as
particularly important. Women's consciousness-raising groups
are a particularly good example of this kind of practice, and

97

Mitchell describes this as a 'process of transforming the hidden, individual fears of people into a shared awareness of the meaning of them as social problems, the release of anger, anxiety, the struggle of proclaiming the painful and transforming it into the political' (Mitchell 1975: 61)

Clearly, these models are presented in simplified terms, and in practice will overlap to some extent. Nevertheless, they do provide an opportunity for exploring both the ideological and material conditions within which collective action is likely to occur.

Collectives in practice

Lest it be thought that we are in danger of excessive theorisation, of losing touch with the realities of practice, it is perhaps important at this stage to consider some practice examples of user collectives operating in the day-to-day world outside statutory Social Services and Probation Departments. These collectives may reveal varying degrees of participation by social workers. Equally, collective groups may operate on a national level or on a purely parochial level – or in some combination of these forms.

Large-scale, well-known action-oriented collectives include claimants unions (dating from 1969), The National Association of Young People in Care, Preservation of the Rights of Prisoners, and Survivors Speak Out. Other examples might include the relatives of clients who have combined together for mutual support and campaigning – for example, the National Schizophrenia Fellowship and the Alzheimers' Disease Society.

On a self-help, consciousness-raising level, one might include AA as the prime example of a client collective operating on a mutual-support basis without a campaigning element, but still functioning on a local and nationwide basis. If one goes on to list the range of self-help groups available, then this task can become quite daunting in view of their profusion and diversity. Some may have had lengthy lives with a nationwide network and many members such as AA. Others may exist in only one locality and have very few members. Some may have an active and campaigning thread to their work; others may not. It is not easy, therefore, to generalise about the activities of self-help groups. One specific example, however, may be useful at this point. Nigel Stone describes an example of self-help amongst prisoners; an example which seems particularly noteworthy in view of ex-prisoners' general reluctance to acknowledge their own status and identity. He describes the North London Baggshott Group as a 'pioneering self-supporting housing and work co-operative . . . set up by ex-prisoners for ex-prisoners, in democratic manner without funding or patronage and independent of helping agencies', which 'seeks to offer members ideas for regaining control of their lives without crime, by using personal and collective resources and opportunities' (Stone 1985: 63).

'Regaining control of their lives . . . by using personal and collective resources and opportunities' is an important concept. The idea of developing control, of offering mutual support, is an important one for self-help groups. The joining together of those who have mutual concerns, leads to identification of shared concerns and ultimately to constructive work on those concerns. Often such groups are in a positive position in that 'they can speak about [their problems] from first hand experience and they have little to lose by speaking out' (Wilson 1987: 120). Allied to this, the inadequacies of services provided by professional social workers may be highlighted – or, more particularly, the patronising attitudes of some professional social workers. However, it is perhaps the development of coping skills and confidence as a result of successes that is the most significant part of such collectives, and 'with this comes a confidence in . . . an ability to share care with professionals and be more assertive about the need for partnership and involvement' (ibid.: 122).

The National Association of Young People in Care (NAYPIC)

A current example of a user collective which has displayed both action-oriented elements and consciousness-raising elements is the National Association of Young People in Care (NAYPIC). Developments within NAYPIC have reflected some of the key themes discussed throughout this chapter, such as 'participation', 'partnership', 'campaigning', and 'collective action'. The struggles involved, the beginnings, and the development of this collective over several years can be found in an earlier account (Stein 1983). It is, nevertheless, interesting to consider the different stages and layers of development of NAYPIC, tracing the move from its 1973 origins in a small group of young people in care in Leeds, to a national organisation which also comprises numerous local groups. Initially, the group was set up by two social workers with young people who were about to leave care and looked at some of the problems involved – not only about leaving care but about being in care. Part of this effort was concentrated in challenging existing policies and campaigning for defined rights such as being able *themselves* to pay for dinners at school instead of the Social Services Departments arranging this, and to pay for clothes in local shops with money instead of using the departmental clothes order book.

Young people found that the group helped them to gain confidence – a highly significant benefit of such collective endeavours – and to develop self-awareness and increase self-esteem. Linked to this, feelings of guilt and stigma were reduced. In the group, members were able to discuss and work out their thoughts and feelings about growing up in care, to consider different types of care, and to meet and make friends with other young people in care. Also, adult members of the group and other social workers became more aware of, and more sensitive to, the meaning of care for the young people, and successful attempts were made to influence policy as outlined above.

The Leeds AdLib Group, although a small-scale project in client participation, was, as far as young people in care were concerned, a pioneering movement. It represented a break with behaviourist or psychoanalytically based approaches by giving credibility to the intention and rationality of its members.

> Prior to the setting up of AdLib in 1973, there was little evidence of young people in care coming together with or without adults to talk about or collectively express their views and opinions about care . . . . Between 1973 and 1975 it was the only group of its type and there was still very little publicity given to what children and young people were saying as clients or consumers.
>
> (Stein 1983: 91)

From local beginnings, a national movement emerged in 1975, following a national one-day conference organised by the National Children's Bureau. Again, a vociferous response had emerged from the young people, and anger was expressed about their experiences. There are signposts here 'that progressive social workers should be working alongside clients . . . in order to identify those pressures which undermine essential human characteristics, perhaps rekindling a rage against those pressures' (Jones 1983: 69).

In the case of the Who Cares? project, a working group of young people was established, their taped discussions were used in *Who Cares? Young People in Care Speak Out* (Page and Clark 1977). Several issues were raised, including the process of reception into care, the stigma of care, discipline in care, six-monthly reviews, and the end of care. A Charter of Rights was also included in the book, and four new regional Who Cares? groups were established in various parts of the country. A dominant theme expressed in these groups was the lack of power experienced by young people in care. This manifested itself in restricted opportunities for participation – at reviews, in the use of money, and in decision making in children's homes. Magazines and videos were produced by the groups and two national conferences took place in 1978. The termination of funding by the National Children's Bureau that year left the Who Cares? representatives without a formal organisation for meetings and contact and a sense of frustration in the young people that there had been constant talk about issues but little opportunity for campaigning about policy. The young people wanted an organisation which could take action on issues as well as talk about them.

In 1979 the National Association of Young People in Care was formed following a meeting of representatives from ten 'in care' groups. A management committee of young people was established, which included representatives from all the local groups and three co-opted adults. The aims of the Association were defined:

(a) To improve conditions for children and young people in care.
(b) To make information and advice available to young people in care.
(c) To promote the views and opinions of young people in care.
(d) To help start, support and develop local groups.

(Stein 1983: 95)

Adults were not to form more than one-third of the management committee. By 1981 the role of NAYPIC as a national campaigning body was established; the collective was comprised predominantly of those who were in care or had been in care. Thus, the organisation came from users (or ex-users). It focused upon issues drawn out by users, and these issues were acted upon by the same people. Two of the early national campaigns were launched around the abolition of clothing order books and the right of young people in care to attend their own reviews.

NAYPIC's momentum during its early days came mainly from the enthusiasm and commitment of its young people. July 1983 marked a new phase in its development when it received funding from the DHSS for three full-time workers (who had all been in care themselves). This has enabled both wider and more systematic work to be carried out than had formerly been possible. Between 1983 and 1988 this has included four major areas of work.

First of all, NAYPIC has influenced national child-care policy. In 1983 NAYPIC submitted substantial written evidence 'Sharing Care' (1983), to the House of Commons Committee on Social Services, Children in Care. Their evidence was quoted by the committee in a number of contexts, including support for attendance at reviews by young people and access to files. The committee in its report commented, 'NAYPIC's growth has given children a voice of their own' (1984). Then in 1987 NAYPIC prepared evidence to the Wagner working group 'A review of residential care'. It made its own position on participation clear to that group:

> In general NAYPIC supports policies and practices that involve young people and that encourages them to take greater control over their lives. It is recognised that we [young people] need help and assistance from skilled workers in doing this and that we will make mistakes – like young people not in care! NAYPIC is against policies and practices that deny young people opportunities to participate and make them feel different from other young people. We do recognise that learning about life is a gradual process and at times a difficult experience which involves responsibilities to others as well as ourselves. But we do need the opportunities to learn, to make mistakes, to find out about ourselves and others – otherwise we will not be prepared for making our own way in the world.
>
> (NAYPIC 1987: 5)

The main issues raised by NAYPIC in their evidence included:

(a) Criticisms of the large number of authorities which still operate bulk buying for food, clothes and toiletries,

(b) The case for a charter of rights for young people in care, and

(c) The need for more flexible care.

The evidence continues:

> Residential care could have a far more *positive image* as a key part of community based child care provision. Children's

homes could become more widely used as neighbourhood resources, e.g. when young people need 'time out' of a family for a short period . . . the main official attitude should not be to keep young people out of care at all costs. This very negative view contributes to the stigma of care as a 'bad' last resort . . . . Children's homes could develop far more positive links with neighbourhoods and offer a system of *shared care* to families at times of difficulty.

(NAYPIC 1987: 7)

NAYPIC also argued for complaints procedures to be linked to greater opportunities for participation.

Secondly, NAYPIC has carried out a number of user surveys, including *Reviews and Young People in Care* (Stein and Ellis 1983), *Access to Files* (Denton 1984), *Leaving Care* (Stein and Maynard 1985), *Guidebooks and Young People in Care* (Stein and Ellis 1988). These and other issues have been followed up by local and national conferences.

Thirdly, NAYPIC's full-time workers have been involved in working with Social Services Departments on a number of key issues; for example, setting up complaints procedures and establishing working groups on leaving care. In addition, they have contributed regularly to training courses and in-service programmes.

Finally, NAYPIC has provided support for the development of local groups. Perhaps the most significant initiative in this area has been the creation in 1985 of 'Black and in Care' as a forum for discussion of the problems faced by black young people in a predominantly 'white' care system.

NAYPIC has operated at a large number of levels. It has moved from its roots as a social worker-initiated discussion group for young people, through to a group striving for self-help and greater participation in local policy and decision making, to become a democratic collective organised by users and ex-users which has self-help elements and campaigns at both local and national level. This is a major achievement. Rhetoric has become reality; slogans have come alive, and empty words have become concrete actions. NAYPIC, therefore, symbolises and represents a significant step forward in the development of user collectives.

Clearly, these developments have not occurred without a struggle to overcome obstacles, without effort, and without pain. Many new members of in-care groups may lack confidence and have poor self-esteem. They may find it difficult to talk about their ideas and views. They may lack a sense of power and control over their own lives, let alone the lives of others. Societal stigma and labelling has to be fought against; the kids 'from the home' can be seen as outsiders, as misfits, even as 'wrong-doers', as those who haven't got 'mums and dads'. The process of entering care can leave scars. Inevitably there have been significant upheavals in friendships, family, and local ties which may further undermine a sense of identity and purpose. A sense of powerlessness can easily develop, and being moved between a number of different settings in care is likely to exacerbate that process. Therefore, local group membership can change suddenly as a result of such movement and adversely affect the cohesion of local groups. Also, feelings shared in common with many other user groups may have been experienced which are hard to leave behind – feelings of guilt and fatalism – all of which may need to be overcome. Young people in care who have been designated 'clients' with connotations of difficulties, problems, dependence, and limited power have to struggle with problems associated with this label. At the same time they are designated 'adolescents' with devaluing connotations of rebelliousness, aggressiveness, waywardness, disorganisation, problems of identity, and purposelessness in the eyes of many members of the general public. NAYPIC members, then, face a double struggle, being labelled 'clients' and being 'adolescents'. This dilemma for the organisation has been captured by Stein (1983):

> How can an organisation of young people who are also in care (and thus carry the label of 'client') achieve respect and credibility? In reality young people possess little political, economic or social power and this reflects a strong consensus about the limited role young people should play in our society. But NAYPIC is not just an organisation of young people; it is an organisation of young people in care.

Accompanying the implications of 'client' and 'adolescent' labels which can be attached to members of NAYPIC groups is the problematic relationship with adults who might be attached to, or interested in, the organisation. NAYPIC has spelt out this relationship quite clearly:

> Adults who get involved should remember the 'in care' groups are 'for young people in care – run by young people in care'. They are there to help young people do things for *themselves* not to do it for them, despite the fact that it might be easier, quicker, etc. For example, chairing a meeting,

writing letters, taking minutes, can all be done by young
people in the groups, even if minutes can sometimes be a bit
chaotic or spelling in the minutes gets rather erratic . . . .
Adults should be careful to check out that the young people
want them to be involved or stay at the meeting – not
assume that it's okay to be there just because their motives
are good.

(Stein 1983: 9)

The role of adults in the in-care movement has changed considerably over time. In the early Who Cares? days they were the key
organisers, in reality exercising considerable influence. Following
the creation of NAYPIC, their involvement gradually decreased,
becoming minimal with the appointment of the full-time ex-care
workers. After a while the workers, particularly when newly
appointed, and other new members felt unsupported and unable
to deal with all the demands upon their time. Therefore, at present the relationship between young people and adults is again
under discussion, and what is being suggested is an advisory and
supportive role that enhances the ability of the members to carry
out NAYPIC's aims effectively. This is without doubt a very skilful
and subtle adult role – enabling, assisting, advising – without
undermining or taking over.

Indeed, the NAYPIC Action Pack goes on to suggest that adults
might be invited to special open meetings of 'in-care' groups or,
alternatively, set up their own groups to work with 'in-care' representatives and other interested parties. However, even given the
supporting role of social workers, NAYPIC is clearly different from
some groups which campaign on behalf of users, represent them,
and speak on their behalf, such as the Child Poverty Action
Group, the Voice of the Child in Care and the Family Rights
Group; NAYPIC is comprised of, organised by, and campaigns for,
young people in care. It places the problems of young people in
care firmly into a collective, agency, and societal context; away
from a major focus upon the individuals themselves, thus developing an 'understanding of oneself in the context of the social
order', and helps the young person become 'substantially more
aware of the ensemble of social relations of which she/he is con-
stituted . . . . Such changes in the individual are especially directed against those "common sense" meanings and understandings
which render subordinacy as natural . . . and see no alternative to
the existing social order' (Leonard 1984: 210 and 212). A collective like NAYPIC therefore places what seem to be individual
problems into a social context with social definitions.

It would be a misunderstanding to see NAYPIC *solely* as an organisation struggling for increased participation by young people in formal situations such as reviews and case conferences. It is not difficult to construct situations that allow token participation (for example, young people invited to the last few minutes of a review). For NAYPIC, any changes in the direction of 'open' policy and practice must be combined with modes of participation and approaches that provide genuine opportunities for young people to gain increased power over their lives. Local group meetings, for example, provide a much more realistic opportunity for young people to share concerns, experience genuine power, and then put that power into practice. Therefore the psychological benefits for NAYPIC members should not be underestimated. Leonard's comments about the black and anti-racist movements are surely as equally applicable to NAYPIC:

> The fact that it is possible . . . to make headway through collective action, in overcoming some of the psychological obstacles produced by subordinacy – deference, fatalism, self-destructive anger . . . provides a basis for forms of collective action which attempt not only to achieve material results but also to change the consciousness of those involved in the action. Thus the development of concrete capacities and changes in the conception of self may be seen as complementary and overlapping psychological benefits of collective action.
>
> (Leonard 1984: 205, 212)

Significantly, NAYPIC has gone further than psychological boosting in that new skills have been acquired by its members; skills in organising meetings, chairing meetings, taking notes, writing letters, producing magazines and negotiating with significant others. In addition, NAYPIC has created its own *democratic structure*, with committees at national and local level and with membership being democratically elected. Therefore, collective action has provided an opportunity for young people in care to develop what Leonard has called 'capacities necessary to effective struggle' (Leonard 1984: 118) – capacities such as organising and negotiating. Mike Simpkin has also acknowledged the positive aspects of this approach, stating, 'users will be able to set up much more effective structures than some of the present well intentioned, but feeble, attempts at democracy' but 'without organised networks, they will continue as passive recipients (or non-recipients) of services' (Simpkin 1983: 180 and 181).

NAYPIC's struggles and the struggles of other user collectives do raise some questions about their relationships with statutory social workers. The latter inevitably have different perspectives on users' situations, influenced by professional training, professional language, varied workloads and location in agencies with specific priorities and restraints on resources. Indeed, the language of 'the professionals' and 'users' has been said by some to be 'in worlds apart' (Robinson 1978). Very few social workers have had the experience of being in care. They can make an attempt at understanding. They can offer empathy, but they cannot have the same strength of feeling, the same experience of the user which, on occasions, gives rise to so much heartfelt anger and depression. Channelled into effective, structured, collective action, anger and depression can be shared, worked on and used as a platform for change at several levels. Such change can provide greater degrees of satisfaction and fulfilment, both for the collective and for the individual who is part of that collective. The successful development of NAYPIC illustrates that change is possible, and other user collectives may well follow this example in the future.

© 1989 Stewart Collins and Mike Stein

References

Arnstein, S. (1969) 'A ladder of citizen participation', *Journal of the American Institute and Planners*.

Barclay Report (1982) *Social Workers: Their Roles and Tasks*, London: Bedford Square Press.

Beresford, P. and Croft, S. (1986) *Whose Welfare?* Brighton Polytechnic: Lewis Cohen Urban Studies Centre.

Coates, K. and Silburn, R. (1970) *Poverty: the Forgotten Englishmen*, Harmondsworth: Penguin.

Cook, T. (1987) 'Participation' in D. Clode, C. Parker, and S. Etherington *Towards the Sensitive Bureaucracy*, Aldershot: Gower.

Corden, J. (1983) 'Persistent petty offenders: problems and patterns of multiple deprivation', *Howard Journal* xxii.

Davies, K. (1985) 'The politics of independent living: keeping the movement radical', *The Bulletin* (on social policy), 16 (Winter).

Deakin, R. and Willmott, P. (1979) *Participation in Social Services: an Exploratory Study*, London: Personal Social Services Council.

Denton, A. (1984) *For Whose Eyes Only: Files and Young People in Care* , NAYPIC.

Hadley, R. and McGrath, M. (1980) *Going Local*, London: Bedford Square Press.

Collectives in social work

Hadley, R. and McGrath, M. (1984) *When Social Services are Local: the Normanton Experience*, London: George Allen & Unwin.

Henderson, P. and Miller, C. (1982) 'The content of community social work'. Unpublished paper, London: National Institute of Social Work.

Hoggett, P. and Hambleton, R. (1987) *Decentralisation and Democracy*, Bristol: University of Bristol.

Jones, C. (1983) *State Social Work and the Working Class*, London: Macmillan.

Kramer, R.M. (1981) *Voluntary Agencies and the Welfare State*, London: University of California Press.

Leonard, P. (1984) *Personality and Ideology*, London: Macmillan.

Low, C., Rose, G. and Cranshaw, B. (1979) *Participation in Services for the Handicapped: Two Contrasting Models*, London: Personal Social Services Council.

Mitchell, J. (1975) *Psychoanalysis and Feminism*, Harmondsworth: Penguin.

NAYPIC (1980) *Running an In Care Group*, NAYPIC.

NAYPIC (1983) *Sharing Care*, NAYPIC.

NAYPIC (1987) *Evidence to the Wagner Working Group 'A Review of Residential Care'*, NAYPIC.

Oliver, M. (1985) *Social Work with Disabled People*, London: Macmillan.

Page, R. and Clark, G. (eds) (1977) *Who Cares?* National Children's Bureau.

Robinson, T. (1978) *In Worlds Apart*, London: Bedford Square Press.

Simpkin, M (1983) *Trapped Within Welfare*, London: Macmillan.

Smith, J. (1987) 'Social Services' in D. Clode, C. Parker, and S. Etherington, *Towards the Sensitive Bureaucracy*, Aldershot: Gower.

Stein, M. (1983) 'Protest in care', in B. Jordan and N. Parton. *The Political Dimensions of Social Work*, Oxford: Blackwell.

Stein, M. and Ellis, S. (1983) *Gizza Say, Reviews and Young People in Care*, NAYPIC.

Stein, M. and Ellis, S. (1988) *Guidebooks and Young People in Care*, NAYPIC.

Stein, M. and Maynard, C. (1985) *I've Never Been so Lonely*, NAYPIC.

Stone, N. (1985) 'Prison based work', in H. Walker and B. Beaumont, *Working with Offenders*, London: Macmillan.

Tyne, A. (1973) *Participation by Families of Mentally Handicapped People in Policy-making and Planning*, London: Personal Social Services Council.

Wilson, J. (1987) 'Self help and consumerism', in D. Clode, C. Parker, and S. Etherington, *Towards the Sensitive Bureaucracy*, Aldershot: Gower.

5

The sound of silence:
Who cares about the quality of
social work with older people?

Mary Marshall

A neglected field of social work

Most people who read this book will skip this chapter. Social work with old people is not the heart and soul of social work. It is a peripheral activity practised well by a small and silent band of converts. It is more commonly practised badly by unwilling, unsupported, and often untrained staff. The quality of most social work with older people would profoundly shock the public if it was subject to the same scrutiny as some child abuse cases – or would it? Is this hidden world neglected because nobody is interested – not the public, nor the media, nor the politicians? Laying the blame is not the purpose of this chapter; it merely attempts to examine critically the state of social work with old people on the basis that attitudes are the fundamental explanation for the longstanding neglect of this field of work.

Social work with elderly people is such an underdeveloped field of social work that it is littered with unchallenged, usually negative, received ideas. These ideas are often not put into words but are carried into social work from society generally. They are to a large extent an expression of an ageist society. There is plenty of evidence that we live in an ageist society where the term 'old' is an insult, where we tolerate well over half the pensioner population living in poverty, where cuts to the incomes of older people relative to the rest of us are of little interest, where it is common to hear that old people are a 'burden', and where one member of Parliament recently joked in the House of Commons that old people should be shot by the IRA. The notion that old people are a burden is used to justify increasingly shabby treatment of poorer old people by the government. Yet there is no general outrage about this.

'Care in the community'

The main plank of government welfare policy for vulnerable older people is 'care in the community'. This has an increasingly hollow ring to it as all other government policies combine to make this daily more difficult. The new Social Security Act, for example, although it can pay grants for helping people to come out or remain out of institutional care, actually reduces incomes for large numbers of poor people, thus undermining frail older people and their carers. Changes to housing benefit have the same effect for those just above basic social security levels. Limitations on funds available to all local authority departments is another policy which undermines 'care in the community'. Warm and dry housing is equally important a factor in 'care in the community' as the provision of domiciliary support services and skilled social workers. A financially restricted National Health Service cannot provide the expansion in community health services which is so urgently needed. The growth of the private residential and nursing-home sector has for several years sat uneasily beside a policy of 'care in the community'. Increasingly, people are questioning the government's commitment to *care* in the community. Older people usually want to remain in their own homes and so applaud this policy, but, given rapidly increasing numbers of very frail older people, we have to ask whether what is really going on is in fact *neglect* in the community. The rhetoric will inevitably be exposed for what it is before very long.

Some critiques and received ideas

Social work with old people is perceived as so peripheral to mainstream social work theory and practice that concepts such as Marxism and feminism have barely touched it. Where they have touched the predicament of older people, they have shed some useful light. Chris Phillipson (1982) is a sociologist educationalist and not a social worker but he has produced one of the few Marxist-style critiques of the treatment of old people. He has explained that the low status of older people is due to the need for a reserve of low paid labour available. Thus, for example, pensions are low so that old people would be delighted to join the labour force should the need arise. Barbara Macdonald (1984) is a feminist now in her seventies who writes most usefully about the way the women's movement relates to older women.

She sees the women's movement as being white, middle class, and young. In its relations with older women it is stereotyped and rejecting.

One of the rare attempts to link feminism and social work practice with older people is Raymond Jack's article in *Insight* (1987) where he looked at gender issues in old people's homes. He maintains that a predominantly female staff caring for predominantly female older people compounds the low status that both characteristics elicit. It is important to recognise from the outset that most older people are women. There are twice as many women as men in the age group between retirement and eighty and nearly three times as many thereafter. Issues of feminism could therefore be most usefully supplied to this group but very seldom are; such is the general lack of interest in older people.

So what sort of received ideas affect social work with old people? The first is seldom put into words but it is something like: 'old people are worthless'. Few people would accept such a harsh statement yet the evidence of this view abounds in social work: the ever-increasingly used 'investment' argument being a good example. Social workers justifying the far better trained staff, better resources, and infinitely greater amount of attention given to children or adolescents will say that this is right because we are investing in our future. They imply that it is not a good investment to put the best resources into work with old people. At a basic level this ignores the fact that many old people are part of families, and that failing to assist them puts a strain on the entire family. At a higher level one must ask about the morality of such a view. Why should assistance for distressed, unhappy, and suffering people be determined by their age?

Lack of training and planning

Worthlessness is seldom a concept put into words, but how else are we to judge the fact that managers in social work or Social Services departments are seldom required to have any skills or experience with old people in spite of the fact that the majority of people seeking or referred for help from these departments are old people? How else do we judge the dire lack of training in this field?

Training is the key to improving standards since it is about improving knowledge, skills, and attitudes. We have a petrol-pump model of social work training in Britain: one fill-up for the whole journey. This makes basic professional training the crucial time for a major input about social work with older people. There are almost no teachers on social work courses in Scotland with experience of working with old people. People in charge of courses argue that, even when they advertise for this speciality, appropriate people do not come forward. This may be true, and if it is then it must be addressed as a very serious issue which may need special measures like job-sharing or special recruitment. It is surely essential in 1988 that, when more carers care for older people than care for children, when there are more people over retirement age than there are children in school, and when the number of people aged over eighty is going up by 80 per cent between 1981 and 2011, we have properly trained social workers.

The most exasperating aspect of this gloomy scenario is that it is actually possible to plan for older people. We know what future numbers are and what the likely characteristics and there-fore needs of older people are. We could plan now for the next century. This is quite unlike services for children where we can-not predict the birthrate, or for mentally ill people where we can-not predict new drugs and treatments. We should have had a crash course fifteen years ago to train social workers to work with older people so that we would now have social workers to man-age services and social workers to teach. Interestingly, now that there are more senior posts for social work managers in this field, the transfer from child care is not as unsatisfactory as might have been expected. At least people moving into management posts with child-care experience have got standards. They know what good practice looks like, and they do not usually seem to fall into the trap of treating very old and frail people like children.

Another area where worthlessness is demonstrated is in the low priority given to helping elderly people in most social work and Social Services departments. The thinking behind generi-cism is that elderly people experience the same quality of social work as other clients and that to some extent this results in a recognition of the extent to which their problems are the same as any other age group. This has not been the result of the generic model. Instead, informal systems grow up where crises are dealt with, but older people seldom become long-term social work clients. Alternatively, they go on a pile merely to be 'assessed for services'. In many of these systems older people never see a qualified social worker. They are allocated to social work assistants, or a judgement is made on the referral and it goes straight to the occupational therapist or the home help organiser. Where specialism exists there does seem to be a much greater interest and enjoyment in working with old people. However, the general picture is that even with the rapid developments in specialisation, staff working with old people are usually less well trained, expected to have bigger caseloads, and their work is given lower priority than that with children. A few departments have made work with elderly people a priority, but it is often more a pious intention than a real commitment of resources. This is all understandable given the weight of public opinion and government policy, but it is really not acceptable for social workers who know the relative proportions of referrals. One can only assume that the majority of social workers do not themselves perceive a need for social work for elderly people.

Most social workers are guilty of seeing social work with old people as being about the provision of social services rather than social work. Tim Booth, in an article in *Community Care* (1987), remarked on the 'common observation that elderly people receive social services while social work is reserved for the young'. This view is upheld in most social work department policy papers which are preoccupied with service delivery. Often this is reflected in departmental classification lists for elderly clients, where they are classified under services: 'Part III/Part IV application' or 'need a home help'. Similarly, much social work with old people is perceived as an assessment process – but a very particular kind of social work assessment process which is assessment only of eligibility for particular services. If the client is found to be ineligible for services, the matter is dropped. There even used to be departments where assessments for residential care were filed for a waiting list that could be anything up to two years, and yet no other social work input was envisaged in between.

The criticism of social workers perceiving the needs of elderly people as social service rather than social work needs is not meant to be a criticism of those social services or, indeed, a view of social work that precludes service delivery. The point is that even if the need of the old person is for a range of social work skills, he or she is likely to be seen merely as an applicant for a practical service. It is important in this discussion not to downgrade the service provided by home helps, occupational therapists, and care assistants in the care they give to old people. These inadequately paid, often poorly supported, usually overworked staff provide essential and much appreciated assistance to old people – but this is a book about social work. Social workers should offer a range of skills from the direct, interpersonal skills of counselling, advice, support, organising packages of services, and advocacy for individuals, families, and groups right through to the indirect skills of working on behalf of old people both within social work and Social Services departments and with other agencies. This is accepted with child care, and it is to standards set in this high-status field that we should look for the best.

Problems facing elderly people

It is perhaps worth for a moment reflecting on the kinds of problems older people face in order to give more substance to the view that they need social work, as much as if not more than the rest of us. To a large extent the problems of old people are no different. They have stresses and strains within families, marital problems, problems of poverty and poor housing. Many live alone without relatives nearby. Some may need twenty-four-hour care because they have special needs. The sad difference for old people requiring extra help compared with other client groups is the lack of choice: family placements and family group homes being very underdeveloped, for example, whereas the institutional sector is very substantial. It is interesting to compare the interest of both the public and social workers in child abuse with the interest in abuse of frail old people. The problem of physical and sexual abuse of vulnerable and relatively defenceless people is the same, yet the degree of concern expressed is totally different. It is easy to say that social workers' lack of concern for abused older people simply and accurately reflects the public mind, but it is not really an adequate excuse.

Although many of the problems facing older people are the same as those facing any group, it seems to me that there are three special characteristics of social work with old people: the importance of the health component, the experiences of loss, and the need for strong advocacy. Health is not always an issue but, especially with the older age groups, it usually is. This does not mean that illness is inevitable in old age – indeed, it is useful to take the opposite view and insist that illness can and must be treated in old people. There is another unformulated received idea lurking here, which is that everyone gets frailer and sicker as they grow older. This is not inevitable, in fact. Some people stay fit until they drop, others have a bad patch but stay the same for many years, some people even get better. However, many do become more frail. Many people enter old age in poor health with some long-standing disability. Social workers need to face this idea in two ways. We need to see every individual separately in terms of their pathway through old age, always questioning whether the elderly person needs to be as dependent as he or she appears. We need to know enough about illness when it does occur in order to understand its consequences. Advocacy becomes a very important skill in the health field. We have to insist that our clients get the health care they need. We are up against 'therapeutic pessimism' of truly vast proportions amongst GPs and many acute medical specialists.

This interconnection with health professionals is one of the essential qualities of social work with elderly people. It is what makes this work so special and different from, say, most work with children. Social work with older people seldom has a role on its own. As well as skills in working with older people, we need to have skills in working with doctors, nurses, occupational therapists, physiotherapists, pharmacists, and psychologists. At its best this is immensely exciting, because it is possible to see so many ways of looking at an elderly person and her or his circumstances, and to see how a properly integrated care package can really change things. Working with other professionals can, of course, also be frustrating, infuriating, and depressing. We need to see it as a range of skills: skills in understanding language and behaviour of other professions, skills in communication and group dynamics, skills in working through other people who may relate better to the old person and skills in negotiation, influence, and advocacy. This may not suit the social worker who likes to be independent and all-powerful; but for the genuine, creative collaborator it is without doubt the best way to work. The sad thing is that social workers with this expertise seldom get the respect they deserve.

Another aspect of working in a situation where health is a factor is that social work is often concerned with carers and with the relationship between carers and cared for. Sadly, social workers often find it easier to empathise with carers, whose plight is often so tragic. It is much more difficult to empathise with the person cared for unless you have some personal experience of dependence. A seldom-articulated idea in this work is that the social worker's job is to achieve a compromise between the needs of the carer and the cared for: here the social worker is an arbitrator. This is unlikely to be genuinely workable most of the time. It denies the genuine conflict of interests between carer and cared for. It plays down the intensity of the relationship and the extent to which the balance is uneven. It denies the history and the passion that lies behind these relationships. It is strange that we recognise this conflict of interests in marriage. This is demonstrated by our approach to marital work, and the whole new field of conciliation is a further recognition of the complexity of the marriage relationship even in its break-up. Yet this complexity goes unrecognised in a relationship every bit as intense, potentially violent, potentially exploitative, and, of course, potentially emotionally rewarding as that between carer and cared for. If we gave this relationship its due weight we would at the very least be considering two social workers, one for each person, in situations where conflicts of interest are very difficult and real negotiation to a mutually agreed end is needed. To some extent this can happen between professionals in team meetings, but it needs to be more open and to be recognised as a process.

This points up another problem in the field of social work with older people, which is the extent to which the skills needed are seldom given the recognition and attention they need, not just by the practitioners and managers but by the theorists. There is very little solid and respectable writing in this field beyond basic textbooks like those by Rowlings (1981) and Marshall (1983). There is very little especially about the application of high-status skills such as family therapy or psychotherapy, welfare rights work or community work. Emphasising the potential of highly skilled social work may be the way to get this field of work into the central curricula of social work courses, or into the imaginations of students.

A second special factor which makes social work skills so essential in working with older people is the importance of loss. Old people can experience a great many losses: tangible ones like people and homes, and intangible ones like status and role. For social workers who enjoy and are skilled at the interpersonal skills of this work it is intensely rewarding. Good, solid skills of crisis intervention, bereavement counselling, empathy, and so on really work. 'A little goes a long way' is one of the precepts that should be a received idea in this field. This work is with adults, most of whom will have coped with stresses and strains of an order quite foreign to most of us – such as the Depression and two world wars. They often need only a small amount of the right help at the right time. Good crisis intervention work is thus invaluable. It is impossible to specify what kinds of situations are most common and most applicable to crisis intervention because of the range of problems faced by old people. Maslow's (1954) hierarchy of need is worth remembering. Some old people will actually be facing a crisis of cold or lack of food, others a crisis of companionship and relationships, yet others a crisis of self-esteem.

There is no point in prejudging the nature of the problems. We need to remember a basic precept of crisis intervention, which is that we deal with the crisis as perceived by the client.

The third factor which makes social work so important in this field is the need for advocacy: the need to stand alongside the old person against the forces of ageism, and insist that they deserve and must have at least as much as other people. A simmering anger characterises the best social workers in this field.

Ageism

We have to ask ourselves *why* social work with old people is so underdeveloped. It is helpful to look further at some of the ageist assumptions common throughout society. These assumptions have two major and related origins: one is the age structure of our society, and another is our social structure. The age structure of the population in Britain today is unique. Never before in history have so many people survived into old age. This is the result of both more babies surviving infancy at the turn of the century due to public health measures and better health services thereafter. This is at present a phenomenon of developed countries, but many more prosperous Third World countries will experience it in twenty to thirty years' time.

In a society with small numbers of old people, they can be revered. With 17.3 per cent of the population over retirement age this is unlikely to happen. Changes in social structure affecting attitudes to old age include the change from rural to urban which affects, among other things, the work available for older people. In traditional rural communities it is possible to see how no labour is wasted. The potential of older people to contribute is fully realised, and they are never idle. Chris Phillipson (1982) has analysed more recent social changes and their impact on older people, linking attitudes very much to the availability of work. He maintains that shortages of labour after the Second World War contributed to very positive attitudes to older people as they were drawn into the labour force. They have subsequently been squeezed out, and attitudes have become much more negative in order to justify this treatment.

In the same way that attitudes to older people are related to their work, they are also related to their incomes. The increasing income of young people has led to considerable attention to their needs and demands. Older people are predominantly poor and are ignored, therefore, by the media and the market.

However, the minority of wealthier pensioners are beginning to generate much interest, and there are now several magazines, a holiday company, and special private housing companies all targeted specifically at older people. Another factor behind the slightly increasing public interest in the fitter and wealthier pensioner is the shortage of children and young people. Libraries and educational facilities, for example, are directing their attention increasingly to this group.

Negative assumptions and positive practice

Having digressed to look at some characteristics of social work with older people and some possible causes of ageist attitudes, I want now to return to examining some of these attitudes and their implications for social work. 'Old people cannot learn' is one such widely accepted negative assumption. There is no evidence for this: old people learn differently and can have problems in recall, but they most certainly can learn. Even severely demented people can sometimes learn about a new place or to recognise new people. If social workers believe the myth that old people cannot learn, then many social work skills are inapplicable. What is the point, for example, of good crisis intervention if the client is not able to cope better next time? What is the point of good community development if the skills and confidence that come from being better organised in groups are not retained? Perhaps this accounts for the lack of community work with older people. With some shining exceptions of well-supported pensioners' groups like the Strathclyde Elderly Forum, social workers have failed to recognise the potential of well-organised pensioners' groups. There has been remarkably little work done with frailer older people, such as those using day centres or those living in residential care.

Linked to this ill-informed, but widely held, idea about limitations to learning is the view that one cannot form new relationships of any quality in old age. This is demonstrably untrue, given that most older people have to do this in order to cope with losses of previous relationships. A splendid example is Lady Slane in Vita Sackville-West's novel *All Passion Spent* (1931), who chose a new set of friends when released by her husband's death.

Social workers are no different from most young and middle-aged adults, in that they seldom see the extent to which old people are making new and important relationships because they are seldom long enough in the company of sociable older people.

The people they meet are often those who are very depressed or very isolated for some reason. An evening spent experiencing the richness and intensity of relationships in an Age Concern club would be a good experience for anybody, and especially for professionals working with old people. One of the most serious consequences of this idea that older people do not learn to make new relationships is the negative nature of social work assessments. These are invariably about what the person 'cannot do' or what they 'need'. They are almost never about their potential or what they can contribute to other people or groups of people. This links to something that is not so much a received idea but more of a result of sloppy thinking, which is the assumption of homogeneity amongst older people. It is true that they tend to be poorer, more often on their own, worse housed than the rest of us, but this is no excuse for assuming that they have anything more in' common. To an extraordinary extent, assessments ignore factors like social class, education, beliefs, attitudes – and sometimes even information about family, work history, responsibilities, and positions held.

This assumption of homogeneity takes on even more appalling connotations in the frequent lumping together of elderly and handicapped people as one client group. And worse still is the persistence of language like 'the elderly' and 'the handicapped'. Those of us who remember IYDP – the International Year of Disabled People – will remember how often disabled people had to insist that the word 'people' did not get left off. Usage of the term 'the elderly' is a way of distancing ourselves from them: they become dehumanised.

Social workers, like the rest of society, can have a very passive image of older people. At a training session recently a group of social workers were asked to shut their eyes and imagine themselves aged eighty-three. Almost without exception they saw themselves as cold, alone, and in pain with arthritis. This passive, lifeless image is a strong one in the public mind. It is demonstrated by the media's obsessive interest in attacks on frail older people. Older people are much less likely than people in their early twenties to be viciously attacked, yet they get a great deal more media attention. This is understandable, of course, because it is outrageous when apparently defenceless people are attacked. The result is, however, a widely prevalent image of passive helplessness in older people. Social workers imbued with this image will always feel overwhelmed by their work with older people for whom they feel enormous responsibility. They will not see the potential, the contribution, and the rewards of interaction with frail older people.

Low expectations of old age are the consequences of these negative stereotypes. Perhaps the most tragic assumption is that old people lose their emotions as they grow older. In my view, inasmuch as touch remains a sense as strong in extreme frailty as it ever was, emotions run as strong in spite of often restricted lifestyles and lack of opportunities to show emotion. Many old people are constantly angry such as the old lady befriended by Jane Somers in Doris Lessing's excellent novel (1984). Many relationships are extremely intense – perhaps more so because there can be fewer of them. Many older people have or would like to have passionate affairs. It is a common experience of social workers that the two things older people want to discuss with social workers are sex and death. Social workers with old people often shy away from the intensity of feeling expressed by their older clients, whereas what they ought to be doing is searching out opportunities for this to be shared.

The viewpoint that older people experience less emotion than younger people has perhaps its most poignant consequences in institutional settings such as long-stay hospitals and residential care. Where is the potential for emotional expression, let alone satisfaction, in most institutional settings? What is done to encourage expression of love, of anger, or fear? What is done to promote friendship, or sharing, or love? Many social workers in this field understandably hate admitting older people to institutional settings. They hate it because they do not get time to do the preparatory work with the client first. They hate it because they know it to be not good enough. They hate it because it is so difficult for relatives (and social workers) to go on caring for an old person in an institution. They hate it because they know it is not usually what the old person wants, but twenty-four hour care comes attached to buildings, and to get it you cannot remain in your own home. Sadly, however, for every social worker who hates admissions, there is at least one manager and another social worker who give it little thought, who assume that older people feel less and will therefore survive the experience.

Life in most institutions makes a misery out of this last phase of life. Standards are tolerated which would be inconceivable with any other group of physically dependent people. The proliferation of the private sector demonstrates the lack of interest of society in what happens to frail older people – not because the private sector is necessarily bad. The private sector can often be a lot better than the public. But it can be a lot worse, and it has to be truly unspeakable before anything can be done about it.

This brings me to my final point, which is the received wisdom about those with dementia. It is assumed that those with severe dementia are without feelings at all. This is demonstrably not true if you watch someone who has the time and skill communicating concern and affection to an agitated, demented old lady and compare this with someone who has neither. Communication may have to be allegorical or it may need to be by touch, but it happens, and the emotions of fear, isolation, or anger that underlie the agitation are eased. Quite intolerable standards exist for demented people in some of our institutions where they are locked in or doped. They are also tolerated in families with utterly exhausted carers driven far beyond their ability to share any feelings at all besides desperation and despair. This is not the fault of social workers, but they are in a good position to share their knowledge and assist in work to get more resources and better standards for dementing people. Of course, social workers have first to embrace the idea that dementia is a social as well as a medical diagnosis. The new BASW *Guidelines for Social Workers Working with People with Dementia and their Carers* (Marshall 1988) should make a major contribution to more positive thinking about social work in this complex field.

A challenge

It would be a mistake to end this chapter on such a note of gloom. It would be better to look at another received idea, which is that social work with older people is unrewarding, boring, and dull. The assumption (wholly unproven) is that interviews take longer and get nowhere, that older people moan a lot, and that there is no sparkle and humour and excitement. This is simply not true. It is clear that some social workers transfer negative attitudes from their own life experience where they found their grandparents garrulous and boring. The real truth is that social work with old people is very enjoyable. It provides a real challenge, an opportunity to meet a diverse group of people with complex but fascinating problems, and a chance to see life through the eyes of people with personal biographies so much longer and more interesting that the rest of us.

© 1989 Mary Marshall

References

Booth, T. (1987) 'Camden shows the way', *Community Care*, 2 Feb.

Jack, R. (1987) 'Women in care', *Insight*, 2, no. 12, 20 March.

Lessing, D. (1984) *Diary of Jane Somers*, London: Michael Joseph (Harmondsworth: Penguin Books 1985).

Macdonald, B. and Rich, C. (1984) *Look Me in the Eye: Old Women, Ageing and Ageism*, London: Women's Press,

Marshall, M. (1983) *Social Work with Old People*, British Association of Social Workers,

Marshall, M. (ed.) (1988) *Guidelines for Social Workers Working with People with Dementia and their Carers*, British Association of Social Workers.

Maslow, A. H. (1954) *Motivation and Personality*, New York: Harper & Row.

Phillipson, C. (1982) *Capitalism and the Construction of Old Age*, London: Macmillan,

Rowlings, C. (1981) *Social Work with Elderly People*, London: Allen & Unwin.

Sackville-West, V. (1931) *All Passion Spent*, London: Hogarth (London: Virago, 1986).

6

Social work with black people: What's the difference?

Roger Ballard

Immigration

More than two million people of non-European descent now live in Britain, and their presence has radically transformed the social and cultural characteristics of most major cities. As even the most casual observer can now hardly fail to be aware, not only is our society now significantly multi-racial, but quite overtly poly-ethnic. Even so, it is only very recently that serious consideration has begun to be given to the implications of this transformation for the social and welfare services. And although – largely as a result of the black uprisings of the early eighties – there is now a widespread, if tardy, recognition that something *must* be done to improve existing practices, there is still extreme confusion about what that something should be. Since the reasons for this situation are very deep-seated, it is worth exploring why.

One large obstacle to constructive thought and action has been the limited scope of the models of social inequality used by most social workers, as well as their tutors on CQSW courses. Since almost all – taking their cue from the broad consensus amongst sociologists and social policy makers – have invariably regarded social class and poverty as the primary sources of all social disadvantage, racial inequality, if discussed at all, has been perceived as something which happened elsewhere – in South Africa, the United States, and prewar Germany, for example. Britain, the comfortable assumption ran, was not like that. Racism was thus marginalised into an essentially non-British phenomenon. But in recent years this perspective has become increasingly unrealistic: so salient are the racial fault-lines in the British social order that it is hard to avoid making at least some mention of them. Even so, there is still a marked reluctance, even in radical circles, to treat race – no less than gender – as an

Social work with black people

integral, but distinctive, dimension in the structure of social inequality. Given the strength of Marxist orthodoxy, discussions of racial inequality all too often appear as a peripheral afterthought to the real business: the analysis of social class.

But even though analyses of race and racism are now beginning, however uneasily, to creep inwards from the margins of the agenda, culture and ethnicity have so far fared far worse. Their significance is hardly discussed at all. Why should this be so? The reasons are even more deeply embedded in received opinion. While the new non-European minorities have certainly been particularly active in using their cultural resources to maintain a sense of ethnic distinctiveness – as is evident from the scale and vitality of the ethnic colonies which have now become such a conspicuous feature of inner-city life – it is not the case, whatever hostile white natives may believe and suggest, that the new minorities have *introduced* diversity into a previously homogeneous society. Far from it. Not only did earlier migrant groups – of whom the Jews and the Irish were only the largest – follow similar, if less overtly distinctive, strategies of ethnic aggregation and community formation; there are, and always have been, substantial cultural differences amongst the wholly indigenous population. Yet as members of dominant groups so often do, the English middle classes routinely forget that theirs is but one of the United Kingdom's four provincial components, each with its own cultural tradition; and that although their own lifestyles may provide the dominant norm, working-class lifestyles not only differ, but are also regionally and occupationally diverse.

These variations – which are best understood as the strategic adaptations made by people of differing historical backgrounds, and standing at different positions in the social order, to accommodate themselves as positively as possible to that position, be it of poverty or privilege – are of immense, but largely neglected, significance. Had sociologists and social policy makers taken a more positive interest in them, and especially in the resourcefulness and creativity of those who follow non-standard and otherwise 'deviant' lifestyles, they would at least have had an intellectual framework within which to comprehend similar, although generally much more elaborate, tendencies amongst the new minorities. But that was not the case. Such is the strength of the determinist tradition in British sociology – although exceptions such as Willis (1977), Corrigan (1979), and Seabrook (1957) can certainly be found – remarkably little attention is ever paid to the positive aspects of non-standard lifestyles. Instead, there is a strong tendency to regard them as nothing more than an epiphenomenal, and so implicitly pathological, consequence of poverty and deprivation.

Given such received perspectives, it is a little easier to see why racial and ethnic issues should have remained neglected for so long. Quite apart from the general reluctance of white people to acknowledge that theirs is a position of racial privilege, let alone to examine how they gained and how they now sustain that position, their established conceptual parameters left little or no space for a recognition of the prospect that racial contradictions might become as severe in Britain as they evidently were elsewhere. They similarly obscured the possibility that the new minorities might – especially because of the richness and the vitality of their imported cultural capital – prove particularly adept at using those resources to resist, and wherever possible to challenge, the racial exclusionism they so regularly encountered. But in the absence of an appropriate intellectual framework, these possibilities were – to most white theorists and policy makers – literally unthinkable.

Thus, even when Britain's black[1] population began to grow rapidly – largely because rural Ireland was no longer able to satisfy the demand for additional unskilled industrial manpower precipitated by the postwar boom – sociologists and social policy makers paid remarkably little attention to the changes that were consequently being precipitated in the structure and character of the British social order. Indeed, many made great efforts to *avoid* discussing such issues, and to deny that significant changes were taking place at all. Not, of course, that race and ethnicity were not a subject for public debate; far from it, as from the late fifties onwards these issues have always loomed large in British politics. Hence, for example, the introduction of a whole series of Immigration Acts – whose purpose was quite overtly to keep black people out of Britain – by Labour and Conservative administrations. And the reason for their passage was clear: there was widespread popular support for these obviously racist measures. And much to the embarrassment of those wishing to maintain a liberal stance, some of the most overtly racist attitudes were to be found amongst white working-class people. It was they who were initially most fearful of black competition for jobs, and most alarmed by the rapid growth of Asian and Afro-Caribbean ethnic colonies.

Yet most white commentators (all too many of whom had little or no first-hand experience of inner-city life) sought to down-play the significance of these contradictions. And so great was their concern to dismiss popular feelings as alarmist, irrational, and ill-informed, they closed their eyes most effectively to the extent and the permanence of the changes that were taking place. Thus for many years the intensity of racial conflict, especially in inner-city areas, was underplayed; the extent and the consequences of racism, especially in its more covert forms, was grossly underestimated; the size, and the likely future growth of Britain's black population was consistently, and very seriously, under-estimated,[2] as was the extent to which the newcomers might wish (or be driven) to band together on their own terms, the better to protect their own interests and concerns. Anyone who had paid any attention to the history of immigration in the last century would have recognised that Asian and Afro-Caribbean settlers were no less determined, and certainly likely to be no less successful, in organising their lives according to their own cherished ideals than had been their Irish and Jewish predecessors. But these precedents were ignored. Instead, it was naïvely, and very patronisingly, assumed that the newcomers would inexorably be drawn into permanent membership of the indigenous working class. No one ever imagined that migrants from poverty-stricken corners of Britain's former empire could possibly sustain their 'backward' and 'primitive' traditions for long in the face of the wealth and sophistication of an 'advanced' industrial society. Still less was it envisaged that they might use those traditions to challenge, and at least in part to circumvent, the inequalities they faced. Assimilation was almost universally assumed to be the order of the day.

The 'colour-blind' approach

The established social work response to the growing black presence is best understood in the context of such assumptions. A few dissenting voices apart, a conventional wisdom soon developed. After a brief (but potentially traumatic) period of adjustment, 'immigrants'[3] would, it was assumed, rapidly incorporate themselves into the body of the indigenous population, presumably as members of an undifferentiated working class. And having done so it followed that their needs, at least in terms of social work, would thereafter be no different from those of anyone else. To be sure, some newcomers might go through a traumatic period of post-migratory adjustment; but such problems, it was assumed, would be self-limiting. Hence there seemed to be little need for any substantial revision of established policy and practice.

In so far as it wholly ignores the extent and the force of racial exclusionism, let alone the vigour of the processes of ethnic reaction that exposure to exclusionism has precipitated, such an assimilationistic perspective provides (as we shall see) a very unhelpful guide for good practice. But since cherished illusions are so much easier to live with than ugly and challenging realities, it is a perspective which remains influential. Even today most social workers still pride themselves on their alleged ability to maintain a colour-blind, and so, they would argue, unprejudiced approach to those of their clients who happen to be black. Clients, they assert, are clients, and needs are needs, whatever the colour of a person's skin. And on this basis they argue that as a matter of good professional practice every effort should be made *not* to notice any difference. Indeed, the very suggestion that they might have a special agenda for black people appears, to them, to be completely misguided. That, they argue, would introduce *apartheid* into social work, and is therefore quite unacceptable.

Yet, however comforting the colour-blind approach may seem in principle, it is becoming ever harder to sustain in practice. If only for demographic reasons, black people now form an ever-increasing proportion of social workers' clientele; and like it or not, most *do* find their Asian and Afro-Caribbean clients different, and often in extremely problematic ways. Yet rarely – as far as most white professionals are concerned – are these difficulties perceived as have anything to do with race or racism: instead, it is black people's *behaviour* which is perceived as causing problems. And these are often so serious that many begin to feel way out of their depth.

That this should be their experience is hardly surprising. In most Social Services Departments – and indeed throughout the health, education and welfare services – virtually everyone of any professional standing is white. Few, even amongst the recently qualified, will have received any training on how to work in multi-racial and poly-ethnic contexts; nor will their personal experience be of much use either. Not only are the great majority of social workers of middle class, or at least suburban, origins; even those few who did grow up in inner-city areas will in all probability have done so either well before the arrival of non-European settlers or in areas quite distant from the new ethnic colonies. And even today personal friendships across the racial and ethnic boundary – especially those which give white people access to a minority world, rather than vice versa – remain rare. Lacking an easy familiarity with the communities to which an ever-increasing proportion of their clients belong, and so a comprehension of their experiences and lifestyles, most white professionals still approach their black clients as strangers. No wonder they often find the going tough.

Problems ... problems

While just which dimensions of strangeness they experience as being most acutely problematic can vary enormously, some broad patterns are readily discernible. Linguistic differences, not surprisingly, are amongst the most frequently cited sources of difficulty: without a common medium of communication it is virtually impossible to carry out even the most basic social work tasks. But although lack of a common language is undoubtedly a problem, just whose problem is it? Do clients for whom English is not their first language suffer from a linguistic deficit of some sort? Or is it, on the contrary, the professionals – and the system which employs them – who are deficient, because of their inability to communicate with clients on their own terms and in their own tongue?

The issues can be further illuminated by considering how such difficulties might be overcome. Are interpreters, for example, the answer? Quite apart from the fact that properly trained and paid interpreters are rarely, if ever, available, and that to use English-speaking children to obtain intimate information from their parents is sheer bad practice, many social workers are now beginning to realise that their lack of linguistic skills is but the first of their problems. For even when they do manage to break through the language barrier – either by increasing their own linguistic competence, or by using a proper interpreter, or, most strikingly of all, when they are working with families whose English is fluent – most still find many aspects of their minority clients' behaviour exceedingly mysterious. Linguistic differences are only the most overt manifestation of more fundamental cultural differences.

The list of differences which cause confusion is almost endless – but includes, at the very least, confusion about names and naming systems, about how families and role relations within them are organised, about the conventional expression of respect and deference, about patterns of child-rearing and the organisation of discipline and authority, about religious belief and practice, about dietary conventions, about dress and modesty, about the use of personal space and the taking of leisure, about reactions to death and bereavement as well as mental illness and physical handicap, and much else besides. Faced with an ever-increasing number of clients whose behaviour appears, as a result of these differences, to range from the unexpected and inexplicable to the bizarre and rudely obstructive, many social workers are growing steadily more alarmed, puzzled, frightened, and confused. If they are prepared to be honest, many would admit that their confusion is often so severe as to make it difficult, if not impossible, for them to carry out their assigned professional tasks.

This is indeed a problem. But just whose? Are black clients, in and of themselves, a problem? Or is it that social workers who, lacking the appropriate skills and understandings, have problems? Just as linguistic incompetence inhibits verbal communication, so a lack of cultural competence[4] – that is, the capacity to assess and respond to behaviour in terms of the meanings and conventions which the other person has used – will necessarily render transactions across ethnic boundaries problematic. But power is just as important as the capacity to communicate, especially since social workers, like the employees of most other statutory agencies, are in a position to pathologise behaviour which they do not understand. So whenever they find themselves out of their depth, it is both easy and tempting for them to identify their clients' 'deviance' – rather than their own incompetence, cultural or otherwise – as being the root problem. And so it is that in working with black people, white professionals all too often perceive, and so create, problems where none exist, while simultaneously overlooking those that do. And even when they do correctly identify real problems, solutions pose similar difficulties. Assistance which fails to mesh with clients' own conventions, expectations, and resources, such that it cuts across, rather than working with, the cultural grain, is much more likely to be a hindrance than a help.

So, however uneasy white professionals may now have begun to feel about their encounters with black people, they should never forget that it is their clients who suffer most from their mistakes, and that the disadvantages thus precipitated are often just as grievous as those arising from more blatant kinds of racial exclusionism. Not only are black people's problems routinely overlooked; if behaviour is mistakenly interpreted as 'deviant', draconian 'solutions' to largely imaginary problems are likely to be imposed. And this, far more than most white professionals ever imagine, has become the routine experience of black people in Britain, Asian no less than Afro-Caribbean.[5] They are deeply disillusioned. Thanks to bitter experience, many have long since ceased to expect that white people in positions of power – be they judges, policemen, teachers, probation officers, or social workers – will ever have much understanding of or sympathy for their lifestyles and experiences. Most now approach all such persons with as much caution as they do with scepticsm.

By now the gross insufficiency of the 'colour-blind' perspective should be only too obvious. Not only does it leave white professionals floundering; it also fails their clients. And black people, who know full well that they are badly treated, are less and less prepared to stay quiet. Instead, they are making ever louder demands that public services should not only be made more accessible, but also much more relevant to their specific needs. And they are expressing those demands physically as well as verbally. Not only were the uprisings of the early eighties in large part reactions to just such misjudgements and misinterpretations; but their very power has also, at long last, promoted a realisation amongst policy makers that racial and ethnic issues can no longer be ignored. Radical improvements in the quality of public services, from social work through education to health care, are now imperative. How, though, can they be achieved?

Strategies for improving service delivery

So deep-rooted are the problems that simple answers will not suffice. For instance, one obvious deficiency is the paucity of black people in the public services; hence the recruitment of many more Asian and Afro-Caribbean people into main-line professional and managerial positions is undoubtedly an urgent priority. But how is this to be achieved? If changes are to be real, rather than merely tokenistic, the policies and practices which have so far prevented black people from reaching those positions must be identified and smashed. But doing so is far from straightforward, and has far-reaching ramifications.

Only very recently have local authority personnel departments and CQSW admissions tutors begun to acknowledge the need to ensure that recruitment reflects the racial and ethnic mix of the population at large. Yet, despite a belated recognition that they *must* do so, a huge backlog remains: trained and experienced black social workers cannot be created overnight. And although priorities have changed, careful thought must still be given to the *criteria* to be used in recruiting and training them. It is easy to make mistakes. Most organisations were (and many still are) quite unaware of the extent of their own internal racism. Not only are the skills and capabilities of existing black employees as regularly undervalued as they are overlooked, but the criteria used to assess them rarely pay any attention to who they really are, or to the complexities of their reactions to the racial and ethnic disjunctions which surround them.

White managers and tutors still almost always use conformity to English expectations as the yardstick of both competence and acceptability. But how relevant is this? While the younger generation of black Britons certainly have the capacity to conform to English expectations as and when they choose, many – having realised that white people continue to react negatively to their skin colour however much they may conform in behavioural terms – now maintain a strong sense of ethnic and cultural distinctiveness. Hence they often choose to differ, especially when placed in situations where they are expected to act in ways which they find personally demeaning, or which force them to collude in processes which disadvantage black clients. Yet, whenever they do begin to express their real opinions – as they must if they are to be anything more than tokens – black professionals routinely find themselves accused by their colleagues of being over-aggressive, over-sensitive, and as having 'a chip on their shoulder'. White people find it just as hard to establish good working relationships with their black colleagues as they do with black clients.

Yet, if it is inappropriate to evaluate black professionals by conventional standards, just what criteria *should* be used? Over-reaction is no less dangerous. What must certainly be avoided is a policy of 'anything goes', in the mistaken belief that it is always illegitimate for whites to subject black people to any kind of scrutiny. The adoption of such a policy – indeed, the very suspicion that such a policy *might* be in force – does black people a great disservice. On the one hand, all achievement is devalued by every whispered allegation that degrees are being awarded or jobs obtained only because the person involved was black; and on the other, it exposes black clients to the prospect of exchanging incompetent white workers for less than fully competent black ones. Since black people have no less of a right, as rate- and tax-payers to professionally effective services than anyone else, overcoming present staffing inadequacies by recruiting more black people willy-nilly and then calling them social workers is no real solution. To be sure, hiring more black staff must remain an urgent priority: but if those who are recruited are to have the professional standing they both demand and deserve, they must be recruited, trained, and promoted because they are *good,* not just because they are black. To achieve this very great care has to be given to such questions as just *why* they are recruited and for what tasks, for it is quite wrong always to expect them to be specialists; but when they are hired to improve service delivery, attention must also be focused on just *how* they are expected to achieve this. Will they be given for example, the freedom, the training, and the support which will enable them both to challenge existing policy and practice, and to devise more relevant and effective professional alternatives?

Rarely, if ever, does this occur. Stopgap measures are preferred instead – as is clear from the way in which black people are currently being recruited into most Social Services Departments. Hardly any arrive through normal procedures, or are recruited into main-line jobs: most are in 'specialist' positions of one kind or another, which are invariably Section 11 funded.[6] This is both a blessing and a bane. Since local authorities can reclaim 75 per cent of the cost of such posts, some extra jobs may well have been created; but on the other hand it is now taken for granted in most authorities that 'race' posts will *only* be created when Home Office funding is available. And in keeping with this, such posts are rarely integral to the organisation's routine operations: instead they are tacked on, anomalously, to the outside. So although Section 11 has substantially increased the number of black employees, most find the experience deeply frustrating. Ostensibly hired as 'experts' and 'advisers', most find themselves in positions marginal to mainstream operations. Lacking professional and organisational standing, they are largely excluded from substantial decision making, especially when their intervention might result in challenges to established policy and practice. Such tokenism is of little benefit to anyone.

Consequently, vital though it may be to recruit more black professionals, this is in no way a sufficient solution to the problem. On the one hand, it will take many years before the number of fully trained black professionals begins to come anywhere near matching the minority presence in the population at large. And on the other, it is quite wrong to assume that even if many more black social workers were available, they would then take over *all* black cases from their white colleagues: that would indeed introduce *apartheid* into social work. For as black professionals – who are invariably expected to act in just this way – are now realising, this not only leaves them with a heavier than average caseload; it also confines them to a specialist ghetto from which it is hard to escape, since their experience is invariably perceived as 'limited'. Meanwhile, their white colleagues, still monopolising all the senior jobs, can quietly absolve themselves of any responsibility for dealing with racial and ethnic issues.[7]

More training?

However, it would be wrong to suggest that no attempts at all have been made to promote an understanding of the issues of racism. On the contrary, Racism Awareness Training (RAT) programmes have recently been introduced by a wide range of local authorities. While this is progress of a sort, the whole philosophy of RAT is now being severely criticised, not least by black people themselves. As both Gurnah (1984) and Sivanandan (1985) have argued, because RAT's analytical foundations are essentially psychologistic, its perspectives and prescriptions are both sociologically and politically naïve. Moreover, since RAT tends to be almost exclusively concerned with what Sivanandan describes as 'racialism' – the tendency of individual white people (and particularly the trainees themselves!) to devalue and disparage black people – it both overlooks and diverts attention from the significance of racism: the structural, historical, and administrative processes which have given rise to these inequalities. Failing, as it does, to explore the structural foundations of individual attitudes, RAT tends to offer only moralistic explanations of how these arose and why they persist.

While exposure to RAT can produce strong guilt feelings amongst those prepared to be converted, by no means everyone is prepared to buy that line. What most trainees acquire is little more than a *vocabulary* of anti-racism, which – to widespread black alarm – they can then use to deflect and disarm all criticism of their usually still-unchanged practices. And precisely because their approach is so moralistic, enthusiasts of RAT have also found it hard to challenge those who – with the vigorous support of the new right and the tabloid press – have simply mocked the whole exercise, dismissing it as biased and ideologically motivated.

Further, and even more substantial, problems arise as a result of the narrowness of RAT's agenda. Given its almost exclusive concern with overt discrimination, and especially with the way in which racist attitudes lead to black people being denied access to scarce material resources, in most RAT programmes little or no attention gets paid to the more subtle, but equally devastating, patterns of disadvantage which are precipitated by the provision of inadequately and insensitively organised public services. This lack of engagement with service delivery is further reinforced by the immense reluctance of most RAT enthusiasts to address any of the cultural issues. Largely as a result of the influence of RAT, it is now often argued that the allegedly discredited multi-culturalist approach should be now replaced with a more progressive anti-racist stance (Stubbs 1985).

To be sure, multi-culturalism has its pitfalls. If, for example, it is assumed that cultural difference is the only issue at stake, race and racism can be, indeed regularly are, wrongly excluded from the agenda. Even larger problems arise when, as is again all too often the case, the very idea of culture is inadequately conceptualised.[8] So, for example, simplistic accounts of 'other cultures' which unreflexively highlight all that is apparently odd and bizarre in minority lifestyles may satisfy the thirst for more information; but if they fail, as they so often do, to emphasise the dynamic, creative, and reactive foundations of these lifestyles, and instead misrepresent them as static, inhibiting and so potentially pathogenic, all that will be achieved is an elaboration and reinforcement of existing stereotypes. Moreover, the very focus on 'otherness' introduces an even worse distortion. It fails to focus attention on the extent to which the taken-for-granted norms of the native English are no less culturally conditioned, and thus no less bizarre and artificial, than those of anyone else. It is not that the minorities are culturally different; rather, we all differ culturally.

The adoption of such a relativistic position allows us to gain a much more illuminating perspective on just what racial and ethnic diversity is all about, as well as on the role of ethno-centrism in reinforcing and legitimising racism. For it should by now be clear that black people do not differ from white only because they are constantly disadvantaged by white racism; in devising survival strategies with which to cope with that pressure, black settlers in Britain, as well as their locally born offspring, are drawing upon, and so constantly reinventing and reinterpreting, the resources of their cultural traditions. Black people in Britain are consequently far more than an excluded *racial* minority. Their response to exclusion has been to form themselves into a myriad of vigorously organised *ethnic* communities, whose internal networks, based as they are on mutual reciprocity, are the key to their survival. Their ethnicity is quintessentially a solution, not a problem. But precisely because the moral and cultural conventions around which ethnic colonies have been constructed differ so sharply from those of the native English, it is all too easy for outsiders to come to precisely the opposite conclusion.

For, however problematic they may seem to be to work with, there is no evidence that black people are referred to Social Services Departments more frequently than are whites, nor that such referrals involve problems which are intrinsically more serious or intractable than most. On the contrary, given their adverse social and material circumstances, black people generally manage to cope far better with adversity than do many whites: indeed, they remind us how wrong it is to assume that there is any direct relationship between personal and familial distress and high levels of material deprivation. For although poverty undoubtedly increases vulnerability to distress, those fortunate enough to belong to communities which still sustain extended family structures – with their attendant norms of discipline, frugality, mutuality, and an abhorrence of dependency on outsiders – are much better protected than those who do not, however adverse their material circumstances.

For it is in *cultural* terms that the life experience of black people contrasts most strongly with those of white people – and nowhere more clearly than in the case of the white 'problem families' which clog up so many social workers' long-term caseloads. Many of these families are composed of working-class people whose kinship networks have been terminally disrupted by the vagaries of re-housing policies, and whose sense of personal dignity and autonomy has been eroded virtually out of existence, thanks largely to years of exposure to the blandishments of consumer capitalism. For despite the additional disadvantages of racism, remarkably few black people have fallen into that kind of downward spiral. And they have avoided doing so precisely because they have largely resisted assimilation into the working-class statuses to which they 'objectively' belonged, and so into a world where reciprocities of family and kinship have broken down, and beyond that values such as morality, spirituality, and personal dignity, which continue to mean so much to them, now count for little or nothing.

Problems and potentialities in South Asian families

Does this then mean, as is sometimes suggested, that because well-organised groups, such as the South Asians, are so adept at looking after their own, they therefore require very little in the way of social work support? I do not think so. To be sure, extended family structures do, by their very nature, provide their members with much more support than do individualised and atomised nuclear families. But having said that, it does not follow that all extended families are idylls of perfect harmony. Far from it. Rather, they are much better conceived of as intensely dynamic social arenas, within which everyone constantly jostles to advance their own interests and to curb the advances of others. So even though mutual loyalties bind everyone together, internal tensions constantly threaten to drive everyone apart. For just like all other tight-knit networks, extended families have a decidedly double-edged character, especially when internal tensions get out of hand. Then the group's weakest and most vulnerable member may find him (or more usually her) self subjected to quite intolerable pressures. Hence cases of acute personal distress still occur even in – and in certain senses most especially in – the most tightly organised communities. And despite strong traditions of internal self-help, external assistance is often essential to their resolution.[9]

Yet, even though most of the (relatively few) South Asian cases which come to the attention of social workers are of just such a kind, this is not the only reason why support from external welfare agencies might be needed. Every so often Asian families, no less than anyone else, find themselves perplexed by such issues as caring for severely handicapped children, or over how best to support elders who have grown infirm, or how to cope with marital breakdown or with the grief and confusion that follows a sudden and unexpected bereavement. In other words, they sometimes need routine social work assistance. But do they get it? Even when social workers do take on such cases – and they are quite markedly reluctant to do so – they are rarely able to offer much in the way of useful assistance, at least from their clients' perspective. They lack the necessary cultural competence.

Yet just how can they acquire such competence? While it is obviously essential for them to be better informed, that, once again, is only the first step. For what inter-ethnic encounters always highlight are the radical contradictions between the cultural and ideological assumptions which members of the minorities use to organise their lives, and those which underpin the social workers' own preferences and practices, and at a personal as well as a professional level. For instance, it is a fundamental principle of South Asian family life that the interests of the group must always have primacy over those of the individual. Thus the fulfilment of obligations to others is always expected to have priority over the pursuit of self-interest. Yet even though they acknowledge that this leads to the formation of close-knit and strongly mutually supportive kinship networks, most white social workers – schooled as they are in both a personal and professional tradition which instead gives primacy to concepts of freedom, individualism, personal autonomy, and choice – invariably find it hard to cope with families in which there is such an explicit and positive emphasis on personal self-denial: they regularly perceive them as oppressive.

136

Knowledge of other people's lifestyles does not, in itself, lead to cultural competence. What is far more important is the recognition that other people's premises *will* differ from one's own, and to have developed the capacity to work with and through those alternative premises – whatever their content, and however much they may contradict one's own most cherished values. For it is here that most white professionals come unstuck. Because of their deep reluctance to transcend their own ethnocentrism, and the consequent inability even of the most liberal to step beyond the limits of the culture of dominance, most find it hard to avoid coming to negative conclusions about the value of non-standard lifestyles. And so it is that despite their obvious strengths, social workers still regularly come to the conclusion that their Asian clients' families are over-protective, over-authoritarian, and generally oppressive.

Problems and potentialities in Afro-Caribbean families

Whereas Asian families are regularly perceived as being oppressively over-organised, those of Afro-Caribbeans are, by contrast, routinely perceived as suffering from an opposite set of defects. To an uncritical eye, they certainly seem to be in a mess. Illegitimacy rates are high, for more than 50 per cent of children of Afro-Caribbean parentage are born outside marriage; meanwhile no less than 29 per cent of households are headed by a lone mother, as compared with only 8 per cent amongst the native English.[10] Just how are such figures explained? Can anything positive be said about such apparent chaos? Fearing they cannot, many commentators take refuge in determinism, and suggest that these patterns are the outcome of Afro-Caribbean people's disproportionate exposure to poverty and deprivation. Yet, although the inequalities which they encounter are beyond dispute, a crucial question remains. Is it really the case that everything distinctive about Afro-Caribbean behaviour is nothing more than an unfortunate – and so inevitably pathological – consequence of their undoubted deprivation? That may indeed be the commonplace view; but it is profoundly misguided. What it obscures is the extent to which Afro-Caribbeans – no less than members of all the other minorities – have access to a cultural tradition of their own, and from which they, too, are drawing creative inspiration as they seek to survive and resist a hostile environment.

But given its roots in four centuries' exposure to an extreme form of inequality and injustice, that tradition, and the strategies of resistance devised within it, have a very distinctive character. For although, as a result of the severity of their servitude, Afro-Caribbeans, like Afro-Americans, may have lost coherent contact with their roots in Africa, this did not mean, as naïve observers have sometimes assumed, that they consequently lacked a distinctive culture. On the contrary, as Genovese (1974) and many others have shown, slaves were by no means helpless victims of their undoubtedly horrendous circumstances. Minimal though the resources available to them may have been, they everywhere succeeded in carving out a substantial degree of cultural, linguistic, and moral autonomy for themselves, no matter how great the pressures to which they were subjected. That was the key to their survival, and to their ability to create and preserve both mutual security and a sense of personal dignity, no matter what. And even though now deployed in contexts very different from those where they were originally generated, these skills and capabilities remain inspirational to British Afro-Caribbeans.

The family provides an excellent illustration of how this has occurred. In the face of the profound domestic insecurity (especially for men) which slavery entailed, a distinctive form of family organisation emerged. The core of domestic stability came to rest not on the conjugal partnerships, but rather (echoing some West African traditions) on reciprocities amongst consanguineal kin, and most especially between mothers, daughters, and grand-daughters. Women might have a succession of male partners, but there was no expectation that such partnerships would be permanent, nor that by entering into them men were *necessarily* obliged to provide for the material needs of either his partner or her offspring. Indeed, there was no way in which a male slave could reliably undertake to do so. But the resultant fragility of conjugal partnerships does not mean that slaves and their descendants have been unable to construct stable family relation-ships. Rather, their families are often founded on premises which differ strongly from the 'English' norm, for matri-focal ties, rather than those of conjugality, can instead provide their core. For although they may have originated as a response to slavery, many black people have continued to find these strate-gies highly adaptive in the contemporary world, most especially in conditions of severe material deprivation. This is now well established in the case of Afro-American migrants from the rural South to the urban North (Aschenbrenner 1975, Lardner 1971); hence no one should be surprised that migrants from the Caribbean – where matri-focal tendencies were far more firmly established amongst the rural poor than they ever were in the southern USA (see Clarke 1957) – are now moving in exactly the same direction on this side of the Atlantic (Barrow 1981, Driver 1981). In other words, high levels of illegitimacy and single parenthood amongst British Afro-Caribbeans should not be taken as evidence of either social pathology or of family breakdown; what they illustrate instead is the extent to which Afro-Caribbean settlers and their offspring are continuing to find matri-focal strategies adaptive to their current condition.

This does not mean, of course, that those who now choose to organise their families in this way – for it should be emphasised that by no means all are following a matri-focal course, although many are influenced by it – have no problems. Far from it; the women holding such networks together have to cope with gender inequalities which ensure, for example, that their wages are substantially lower than those of men; meanwhile men who are *not* members of such units may, particularly in adolescence, find themselves critically exposed. In other words, not only do Afro-Caribbeans undoubtedly possess a cultural system of their own, but it has, like any other, its own characteristic strengths and weaknesses. Not only do they consequently require services which respond positively to those strengths, but in seeking to work with such clients it is no less essential, and no less of a challenge, for social workers to seek to develop the relevant degree of cultural competence.

Racism and its impact

But although cultural and ethnic issues loom no less large in Afro-Caribbean contexts than any other, it is not the case that culture exhausts the agenda of difference. The impact of racism – not just as a source of material disadvantage, but also in much more immediate personal and psychological terms – must also constantly be borne in mind. For one of the central consequences of living in Britain, and so of being in routine contact with white people and their world, is that black people are constantly exposed to suggestions that to be black, in both the physical and the cultural sense, is to be socially inferior. Those born and raised overseas usually have little difficulty in keeping such demeaning ascriptions at arm's length; they know who they are, and that such ideas are both illegitimate and absurd. But the British-raised are often not so confident; and to the extent they take these ideas aboard, it follows that the whiter they are – or at least can think themselves to be – the more personally and socially acceptable they might become.

So strong are these pressures that even children raised within the security of a black family and community can find themselves seduced, at least temporarily, by such ideas. But those unfortunate enough to have been raised in a wholly white world – as, for instance, when they have been adopted into a white family, or have been in long-term care in a children's home – not only receive a particularly large dose of such ideas, but have no immediate access to the antidote. Isolated from the mutually supportive networks and the alternative visions of an ethnic colony, many such children go through a phase of actually *believing* themselves to be white. Indeed, in cultural terms they may well be wholly English: they know no other world. And to the extent that they are, they also take aboard the racism which is integral to English culture. That is why so many set out on the impossible task of bringing their own bodies into conformity with what England says is best: trying, for example, to scrub the very colour from their skins.

Such a condition of self-disparagement is disastrous. As such children slowly and painfully discover, not only is it impossible to obliterate their physical selves; social identification as *black* is equally unavoidable, however English they may believe themselves to be, and no matter how often their carers – priding themselves, no doubt, on their colour-blindness – tell them they never notice any difference. For the plain fact is that their skin colour *is* always noticed, and invariably in a perjorative way. Thus in the long run most find they have no alternative but to try to come to terms with the fact that, because of the pervasiveness of white racism, they are black, even if, in genetic terms, they are half white. This can be an exceedingly traumatic experience, especially for those who have comprehensively absorbed themselves into a white world. And although such traumas are a direct consequence of inappropriate and insensitive care, and could have been avoided if those who took responsibility for them had been more aware of the racial and ethnic issues, such kids' now deep-seated problems will not necessarily be resolved by shipping them straight off to black foster parents. When black children are still at the stage of identifying themselves as white, a lengthy process of psychological rebuilding, quite possibly involving white inputs as well as black, is needed before that becomes possible.

But since sympathetic support is hardly ever available, most black kids have to find their own way out of these dilemmas, as most eventually do, by re-identifying themselves with a black community and its lifestyle. But since making that switch is both difficult and exceedingly traumatic, no one should be surprised if it is accompanied by an upsurge of bitter hatred towards white people. Yet white carers invariably find the eruption of such feelings exceedingly hard to handle. To be sure, black kids may be disturbed. But how did they get that way? If anyone is responsible for their agony and anger it is precisely those who put them on the rack in the first place. To criticise them now for having 'chips on their shoulders' only adds insult to injury.

'Rebellious black youth'

Although black children in white care undoubtedly feel these contradictions most painfully, they also figure, if rather less acutely, in the experience of all young black Britons. Every contact with white people and their society implicitly exposes them to just the same pressures. How, then, do they respond? Many certainly toy, especially during adolescence, with the fantasy of crossing the racial divide. Not only does English society constantly invite them to do so, but seems a good way of distancing themselves from their parents – with whom, of course, adolescents are likely to be in conflict anyway. This sets all sorts of traps for unwary social workers, especially if, on the basis of a vision of minority lifestyles as being inherently pathogenic and oppressive, they wheel out a theory of 'culture conflict' to explain what is going on (Ballard 1979, Ahmed 1978).

A more careful examination of the issues in such cases invariably reveals that these have quite as large a racial as a cultural dimension. For although young black people will invariably have the cultural competence to behave *as if* they were English – and thus the capacity to gain the instant sympathy of most social workers by alleging that their parents are about to arrange their marriage – their close contact with the English means that they experience just the same contradictions as children in care, albeit with a rather lesser degree of intensity. They, too, must go through a period of turmoil, and with similar outcomes: not only do they start to take an explicit pride in their own distinctiveness, they also begin to adopt a much more uncompromising stance towards the English, especially when they feel themselves to have been put down, than their immigrant parents would ever have dared. Rather than turning the other cheek, most now see resistance and retaliation are the only answers. And in devising strategies by means of which to do so, they are finding, no less than their parents, that their own traditions are a rich source of moral and strategic inspiration. Hence they, too, are sustaining ethnic loyalties: in that lies their strength.

For it is not just black children in care who regularly get labelled as 'unruly' and 'over-aggressive', and who are constantly criticised for having 'chips on their shoulders'. *All* young black Britons – Asian no less than Afro-Caribbean – now regularly find themselves subjected to such charges. And although the protests which lead to charges being laid may have entirely legitimate foundations, those who lay them refuse, by that very token, to recognise such a possibility: they pathologise instead. This is leading to ever-more disastrous consequences. Young black people, and especially young Afro-Caribbeans, are hugely over-represented in custodial facilities of all kinds – in exclusion classes in schools, in locked wards in psychiatric hospitals, and most particularly in Youth Custody Centres, Borstals and prisons: over 13 per cent of prisoners are now black. But why is this? Is it that black people are 'madder and badder' than their white counterparts? Or is it that black behaviour seems, to the holders of institutional power, to be so disturbingly unacceptable that the most vigorous steps are being taken to contain and suppress it?

The dynamics of these processes can only be fully understood when we examine them from a black perspective. To be sure, minority values, interests, and concerns are routinely overlooked by white people and their institutions. But black people, and most especially the younger generation of black Britons, are no longer prepared to remain passive victims: instead, many now seek actively to challenge those who put them down. And they are doing so with great success. For what most disturbs those in power is black people's *strength*. And they have that strength because they have developed a capacity to make their challenges collectively as well as individually, not least because they have succeeded in generating a powerful sense of *moral* solidarity amongst themselves, which is in turn based on their own cultural specificity.

Consider, for example, the kinds of confrontation which often occur when a white authority figure encounters a group of Afro-Caribbean youths. While all sorts of sparks can set them off, they most usually arise because someone feels (usually with some justice) unreasonably treated, and/or that his or her dignity has been disparaged. Not only do most young Afro-Caribbeans respond vigorously in such circumstances, but their response is couched in a style which most whites find hard to handle. For example, they may well explode into *patwa* speech. Much rests on this. Firstly, *patwa* is a particularly rich and graphic form of expression; secondly, much of its vocabulary highlights the moral inferiority and the oppressive propensities of white people; finally, and perhaps most importantly, it is a form of expression which is incomprehensible to white authority figures, even though all the other black people in earshot can understand precisely what is being said. Nothing could be a more calculated challenge to established authority. What the switch of linguistic (and moral) codes implicitly signifies is a refusal to respect the moral foundations of, and therefore the legitimacy of, established authority. But faced with such a comprehensive revolt, how is order to be restored? By far the easiest way of doing is using, or threatening the use of, force – be that arrest, exclusion, assault, confinement, a section, or whatever. Order is consequently restored, but as those who have been pressed into using such tactics will uncomfortably confirm, the *moral* victory seems to remain with their victims, and moreover the intensity of their resistance is redoubled. They refuse to lie down. Hence there is intense hostility towards 'cocky bastards' who not only refuse to recognise legitimate authority, but have constructed a vision which allows them to assert confidently that such authority has nakedly delegitimised itself by its own unjust actions.

While any subordinated group with an alternative linguistic, conceptual, and moral code is in a position to use such tactics, Afro-Caribbean settlers and their offspring are undoubtedly particularly adept exponents of them. This should come as no surprise. With nearly four centuries' experience of resistance behind them, they are acutely aware of the critical importance of maintaining a sense of personal dignity, come what may. Even when, and indeed particularly when, they have been stripped of all else, they know that a sense of righteousness is the most powerful weapon of all. For although those with the courage and the moral strength to challenge and expose hypocrisy will always have a hard time, they can at least avoid the indignity of bowing constantly to injustice; and by keeping faith, they can hope for change.[11]

However, as white authority figures find themselves increasingly confronted by determined black resistance, all they generally manage to perceive is uncalled for and unmanageable aggressiveness and disrespect, for which explanations and solutions are now hurriedly being sought. Hence, if not pushed straight into custody, they may well find plans being made to 'treat' their misguided deviance. No wonder some feel that even custody is preferable to that!

Conclusion

We are back, once again, with the question of where the problems really lie. Black people face some additional stresses as a result of the impact of white racism; but most also have access to the resources of elaborately and securely organised ethnic networks on which to rely when the going gets tough. So although the frequency with which they encounter severe personal problems may consequently be no greater than amongst the native English, the context within which those problems occur is often very different. Not only will the shoe pinch in different places, but solutions which are quite appropriate in a majority context may not work at all for the minorities. Thus systems and structures of service delivery which are implicitly based on English norms, experiences, and expectations (for that is what the colour-blind approach really means) will necessarily set those who differ at a disadvantage. Worse still, it almost always renders problematic black people's very strengths. What is required to reverse this disastrous trend is the adoption of a strategy which accepts, and therefore responds positively to, black people's distinctive interests and concerns – whatever they may be.

However, this is far more easily proposed than achieved, for the entrenched prejudices of the white natives (prejudices which, it must not be forgotten, defend and stabilise the established social order) stand firmly in the way. Most English people find it hard to accept that their own cultural tradition is pervaded by negative visions of non-European people and their cultures: and they do not thank black people for telling them so. Most find it even harder to acknowledge that their own cherished personal and professional ideals are not universally valid either, but are cultural products too – and that in putting their own lives together others may use – and indeed will and do use, an entirely different set of premises from their own. And most confusingly of all to those schooled in the culture of dominance, in choosing to differ, many members of the despised new minorities are managing to sustain lifestyles which have a much richer moral and spiritual texture than those now characteristic of the ever more individualistic, materialistic, and indignity-tolerant white natives. That is the paradoxical secret of black success; and it also highlights a further dynamic of ever-increasing levels of hostility towards them.

'Just whose problem is it?' is the question which must be repeatedly and insistently asked. Precisely because the answers which black Britons give are so unexpected, so counter-intuitive, and indeed so deeply disturbing to received opinions, white people, even the most ostensibly liberal, rarely find them welcome. No wonder black people – professional and client alike – are so regularly sidelined when they refuse to play the white man's game.

But the lessons flowing from this illuminate a much wider range of issues than those of race. Amongst Britain's white natives, the experiences and lifestyles of working-class people differ substantially from those of the dominant middle class. Yet how much account of such disjunctions is taken in the provision of social and welfare services? Or are they organised, once again, in terms of premises which are largely alien to most of their recipients? If so, black people are, through their resistance, highlighting some critical, but largely unexamined, questions about equality and justice which affect us all. If only Britain's white natives could manage to hold back from mindless dismissals of the strength of their black fellow citizens, and from jealous condemnations of their capacity to 'get away with it', they might find themselves learning a very great deal. The difference is quite unexpected!

© 1989 Roger Ballard

Notes

1. A definition is appropriate here. I use the term 'black' to refer to those people who find themselves, as a result of their physical characteristics, subjected to racial exclusionism by Britain's white natives. But although all black people therefore share a common experience, they do not form a single homogeneous group; since all are using the resources of their cultural traditions to generate survival strategies, the communities to which they belong are essentially *ethnic* in character. Cashmore (1986) provides a very illuminating study of the logic of white responses to the growth of racial and ethnic diversity, while Watson (1977) provides an equally useful basic compendium of developments amongst the minorities.
2. Although black people only make up just under 5% of the population as a whole, thanks to a marked demographic skew towards the younger end of the age scale, as well as higher fertility rates, nearly 10% of all babies born in Britain are now of non-European descent. The black population is further concentrated in the major conurbations: in Birmingham, Bradford, Leicester, Luton, Slough, and Wolverhampton where for example, more than a quarter of births are now black, while the figure rises to nearly 50% in some inner-London boroughs. These figures give a good indication of the likely future scale of the black presence in Britain.

3. Both the earliest textbooks, by Cheetham (1972) and Triseliotis (1972) refer to 'immigrants' in their titles, and both take a broadly assimilationist stance.

4. I am indebted to Driver (1977, 1979) for this concept.

5. Britain's ethnic minority population is nothing if not diverse, including Chinese, Yemenis, and Cypriots, for example, as well as South Asians and Afro-Caribbeans. But given limitations of space, as well as that the two latter groups are by far the largest, this chapter is written *as if* these two were the only ones that counted. But all of what I have to say is equally applicable to the other smaller groups.

6. Section 11 of the Local Government Act of 1966 allows local authorities to reclaim from the Home Office 75% of the cost of any additional services they provide to hasten the assimilation of New Commonwealth immigrants. For many years it was used primarily to cover the cost of additional language teaching in schools. Only since the riots of the early eighties has it been used for a wider range of purposes, and been seen as a means of hiring more black staff.

7. This section, and indeed the chapter as a whole, is heavily based on my observations of developments in Leeds' and Bradford's Social Services Departments. For extended analyses of the same issues, see Rooney (1987) and Ousley (1981).

8. Another definition might be useful here, since there is much confusion about how the concept of culture is best understood. My own view, which underpins my whole analysis, is that culture is essentially the system of ideas, values, and understandings which people in any given network of social relations use to order their interactions with one another, thus to give meaning and purpose to their lives.

9. A detailed review of the dynamics of South Asian families can be found in Ballard (1981) and Ballard (1979).

10. Labour Force Survey, 1986.

11. It is precisely this kind of morality that lies at the core of Rastafari (see Cashmore 1979), which in turn provided Afro-Caribbean youth so much of their strength. But it should not be thought that this is to be found *only* amongst the Rastas: the black churches, although little studied because so much less 'exotic', do much the same for their much more respectable congregations.

References

Ahmed, S. (1978) 'Asian girls and culture conflict', in *Social Work Today* 9.

Aschenbrenner, J. (1975) *Lifelines: Black Families in Chicago*, New York: Holt, Rinehart & Winston.

Ballard, C. (1979) 'Conflict, continuity and change', in V.S. Khan, (ed.) *Minority Families in Britain*, London: Macmillan.

Ballard, R. (1979) 'Ethnic minorities and the social services', in V.S. Khan (ed.) (1979) *Minority Families in Britain*, London: Macmillan.

Ballard, R. (1981) 'South Asian families', in R. Rapaport *et al.*(eds) *Families in Britain*, London: Routledge.

Barrow, J. (1981) 'West Indian families – an insider's perspective', in R. Rapaport *et al.* (eds) *Families in Britain*, London: Routledge.

Cashmore, E. (1979) *Rastaman*, London: Allen & Unwin.

Cashmore, E. (1986) *The Logic of Racism,* London: Allen & Unwin.

Cheetham, J. (1972) *Social Work with Immigrants,* London: Routledge & Kegan Paul.

Cheetham, J. (ed.) (1982) *Social Work and Ethnicity,* London: Allen & Unwin.

Cheetham, J., *et al* (eds) (1981) *Social and Community Work in a Multi-racial Society,* London: Harper & Row.

Clarke, E. (1957) *My Mother who Fathered Me,* London: Allen & Unwin.

Corrigan, P. (1979) *Schooling the Smash Street Kids,* London: Macmillan.

Driver, G. (1977) 'Cultural competence, social power and school achievement', in *New Community* 5.

Driver, G. (1979) 'Classroom stress and school achievement', in V.S. Khan (ed.) (1979) *Minority Families in Britain,* London: Macmillan.

Driver, G. (1981) 'West Indian families – an anthropological perspective', in R. Rapaport, *et al.* (eds) *Families in Britain,* London: Routledge.

Genovese, E. (1974) *The World the Slaves Made,* New York: NAYPIC.

Gurnah, Ahmed (1984) 'The politics of racism awareness training', in *Critical Social Policy* 4.

Lardner, J. (1971) *Tomorrow's Tomorrow,* New York: Garden City Press.

Ousley, H. (1981) *The System,* London: The Runnymede Trust.

Rooney, B. (1987) *Racism and Resistance to Change,* Liverpool: Merseyside Area Profile Group.

Seabrook, J. (1967) *The Unprivileged,* London: Longman.

Sivanandan, A. (1985) 'RAT and the degradation of black struggle', in *Race and Class* 26.

Stubbs, Paul (1985) 'The employment of black social workers: from "ethnic sensitivity" to anti-racism', in *Critical Social Policy* 4.

Triseliotis, J. (1972) *Social Work with Coloured Immigrants and their Families,* Oxford: Oxford University Press.

Watson, J. (ed.) (1977) *Between Two Cultures,* Oxford: Blackwell.

Willis, P. (1977) *Learning to Labour,* Farnborough: Saxon House.

7

Mental or experimental?
Social workers, clients, and psychiatry

Stewart Collins

> There is no shortage of 'received wisdom' about the quality
> and quantity of mental health social work currently under-
> taken.
>
> (Fisher, Newton, and Sainsbury 1984: 1)

This statement at the beginning of the first major study of mental
health social work for over fifteen years indicates the considerable amount of diverse opinion which has been expressed in the
United Kingdom on this topic. In fact, since 1971 there has been
criticism by some psychiatrists of the services provided by social
workers following the reorganisation of specialist provision for
mental health under the generic wing of Social Services
Departments. Before the Seebohm reorganisation, many psychiatrists claimed to enjoy close working relationships with mental
welfare officers in the community and with psychiatric social
workers in hospital and child guidance settings. These groups
were perceived as having special skills and knowledge in the mental health field and a particular commitment to that work. Since
reorganisation it has been suggested that these special skills and
knowledge have been diluted, on account of the lack of preparation available for social workers to enable them to function com-
petently to undertake tasks in the field of mental health.

'There have been complaints, particularly from psychiatrists,
that as a consequence of the abolition of the specialist social
worker . . . the level of psychiatric expertise possessed by social
workers in this field is lamentably low' (Clare 1976: 408). This
statement was made over ten years ago, and there is less reason to
suggest that the full weight of this comment applies today, as
there have been some improvements which have occurred following the Mental Health Act of 1983, the required in-service
training which accompanied it, and the appointment of

approved social workers. However, there is little room for complacency in view of the relatively small numbers that have received additional specialist training.

Social workers, individual clients and mental health

It is now appropriate to move on to examine contacts between social workers and clients with mental health problems. This is acknowledged as an area of difficulty for some social workers. Hence the quote from a social worker in reply to an enquiry about mental health social work: 'I don't know why you're bothering to study that – we don't do any' (Fisher, Newton, and Sainsbury 1984: 191). In fact, Fisher, Newton, and Sainsbury approached their survey of social work opinion with some trepidation: 'We were aware that social workers might not generally feel confident about their knowledge of mental health issues and we did not want to initiate discussions with an intimidating question' (Fisher, Newton, and Sainsbury 1984: 32).

Why is social work with mental health problems seen to be intimidating? Why do social workers lack confidence in this area? After all, it has been claimed that social workers are competent to work with mental health problems, to intervene with all client groups, to transfer existing skills and knowledge across client groups. Some have gone as far as to claim that the social worker is in a 'unique position' at the interface of client, family, and community interaction (Prins 1976). The role is said to involve history taking and the provision of personalised help, support and resources, with the social worker acting as an interpreter of client need to the community and to his/her family and vice versa in each case. *Better Services for the Mentally Ill* (1975) saw the place of the social worker as being one of fundamental importance to the client, while the DHSS Working Party on Social Work Support for the Health Service (1974) stressed the significance of the social worker to the client at any and every stage in the process of hospitalisation and in subsequent followup. Hudson (1982) went so far as to state that the social worker 'Can do casework and group work according to a variety of different models; he is an administrator and planner . . . a political campaigner . . . he is knowledgable about psychology, sociology and social policy . . . and he can develop specialised skills for work in the psychiatric services' (Hudson 1982: xi).

However, it should be noted that social workers have gone through early developmental processes like other human beings.

Although their courses of education and training enable them to expand their skills and knowledge, and there is also evidence that they evolve more understanding, liberal and tolerant attitudes during their courses, attitudes to mental health problems may well be firmly established at earlier stages of their development. Language and culture is highly influential here. The mass media, newspapers, TV, family and friends, and local culture all provide guides, patterns, and pointers about mental health problems which inculcate particular thoughts, ideas, and fears. The neophyte social worker is exposed to the 'ordinary language', the day-to-day labels and descriptions which are handed down and passed on to the infant, the adolescent, the 'pre'-social worker. Societal threats are deeply and darkly embedded in youthful minds. The psychiatric hospital is known as the 'nut house' or the 'loony bin', the psychiatrist as a 'shrink' or 'trick cyclist'. Threats are delivered which convey deep-seated fears, declaring that the youngster will be 'taken away in a green van' (for older readers); 'You should be in ——' (insert the name of the local psychiatric hospital); 'You'll end up like ——' (insert the name of the man or woman in the neighbourhood who has most recently received psychiatric help). Similar comments are made about disturbed or bizarre behaviour. At its mildest this is seen in suggestions of 'nervous trouble' or being 'highly strung'. In its more extreme forms, it escalates to 'having a screw loose', to someone being 'off their head', 'round the bend', or a 'nutter' and a 'head case'. These day-to-day, 'common-sense' phrases all generate a primitive fear of mental health problems; they generate uncertainty, worry, restlessness, ambiguity, even foreboding. As Butler and Pritchard have clearly stated:

> Social workers are not immune from the widely held stereotypes of the mentally ill. They must be just as fearful and uneasy about dealing with mental illness as are many of the general public. And yet, in the course of their work, they will be so called upon to talk with and assist many people who are either formally diagnosed as mentally ill or who show some signs of mental distress as part of some other problem. . . reasonable apprehensions about professional competence can so easily be amplified into unmanageable proportions if the worker has not learned to recognise and come to terms with his own culturally induced fears and prejudices about the mentally ill.
>
> (Butler and Pritchard 1983: 40)

One of my arguments is that many social workers do not find it easy to escape from the 'culturally induced fears and prejudices about the mentally ill', that these are deep-rooted and complex, established over many years. The result is that often social workers feel uncomfortable about working with mental health problems, continue to be influenced by the dark threats of childhood, the language of fear and apprehension and breakdown:

> Everybody holds within themselves a potential for disintegration; this is a necessary consequence of the formation of an individual through a process of splitting and reintegration of mental elements. Because of this underlying potential for disintegration, certain activities or ideas will be experienced as frightening, breaking down into a state of chaotic lack of structure being the feared consequence.
>
> (Banton *et al.* 1985: 158)

So, social workers find it hard to come to terms with the 'potential for disintegration' that is sparked off by some clients with mental health problems; they often feel inadequately prepared for this work, their 'competence [being seen] . . . at the level of a well motivated and personally resourceful layman' (Fisher, Newton, and Sainsbury 1984: 39).

Over half of the social workers interviewed in a recent survey in Strathclyde believed they were either only partially equipped or not equipped to work with mental health problems (Strathclyde Regional Council Social Work Department 1985). However, it is wise to issue a word of caution at this point. To question the validity of social work to operate effectively in *any* mental health situation would be wrong. The available evidence suggests that following the traditional 'neurosis . . . psychosis' continuum, it is the latter end of the spectrum which poses most problems for social workers. Bizarre behaviour, disturbed thought patterns, hallucinations, and delusions are phenomena with which social workers have problems in finding a strong sense of identification. Social workers in the Fisher, Newton, and Sainsbury study commented about

> mental states which are comprehensible and with which they can achieve a certain degree of empathy and those mental states which are characterised by bizarre thought processes where empathy seems impossible . . . . The achievement of empathy in the former situation was facilitated in the eyes of some social workers because of their personal

experiences of the emotions involved, especially depression.
(Fisher, Newton, and Sainsbury 1984: 34)

In fact, there is some indication that social workers may not classify, categorise or pigeonhole depression, anxiety states, and mild phobias as mental health problems but prefer to perceive them as environmental or social problems and focus upon the client's own experiences and definitions. Therefore it is not surprising that social workers then deny that they have any special knowledge or skills in working with mental health problems when they argue that they have generic skills in counselling, in respecting people and their rights, in valuing people, in understanding people, in advocating for clients. This, of course, reflects some of the controversies surrounding the genericism versus specialism debate; differences which have been reflected in the arguments about whether mental health social work requires either generalist or specialist skills (Barter 1976; Pritchard and Butler 1976). Most recently, we saw clear evidence of an intended re-emphasis on specialisation in social work education generally, in the CCETSW proposals for reformulated courses, with a 'specialism' in the 'extra year' (Central Council for Education and Training in Social Work 1987).

Some of the most recent literature in the social work journals has encouraged social workers to take a negative view of their skills. For example, Horder comments about psychiatry's 'scientific approach to assessments', which are 'rigorous and comprehensive' and, in comparison to social work, 'psychiatrists' assessments are, there is no doubt, more rigorous' (Horder 1987). In fact, this flies in the face of considerable evidence which questions the ability of psychiatrists to make sound assessments, Rosenhan's well-known work on the erroneous assessment of 'normal' subjects as 'psychotic' and the considerable variations in their stay in hospital being but one example (Rosenhan 1973). Furthermore, there is evidence, based on work with sixty para-suicide patients admitted to medical wards, that social workers can assess para-suicides both as safely and as reliably as junior psychiatrists (Newton, Smith, and Hirsch 1979). However, social workers in the Fisher, Newton, and Sainsbury study apparently lacked confidence in both the relevance and transferability of their existing skills. This was seen to be

related to a widespread belief that mental health problems were qualitatively different from the other personal and relationship difficulties which social workers commonly encounter. This belief has become part of the 'received wisdom' about work with the 'mentally ill' and is reinforced by occasional references to the danger of damaging people by 'unskilled' therapeutic intervention and to the fear of trespassing on areas of work seen as belonging to the psychiatric profession.

(Fisher, Newton, and Sainsbury 1984: 194)

This is an unfortunate situation because, during the postwar years, a considerable amount of social work literature developed; this made clear the difficulties which workers may encounter in facing bizarre thought processes and deluded behaviour; clarifying what the social worker's contribution might be; and culminating in the works of Nursten (1972) and Prins (1976). However, much of this effort has been lost as psychodynamic approaches have lost favour and have been largely replaced by systems thinking, which places an emphasis on the importance of community resources and the role of other agencies and networks, and does not claim to contribute to an understanding of an individual's internal dynamics and problems of family interaction. It is significant that some of the more recent literature on psychiatry (Ingleby 1981), social work (Jones 1983; Pearson, Treseder, and Yelloly 1988), and psychiatry and social work (Banton *et al.* 1985) has argued in favour of re-emphasising the significance of the psychodynamic approach and its contribution to mental health problems.

Therefore, at present, the perceptions of some social workers about mental health problems tend to be negative; a lack of hope, a lack of enthusiasm characterise much work. Low expectations, feelings of inadequacy and a perceived inability to help are bound to affect the help offered and its outcome (Smale 1977). The lack of opportunity for supportive, informed supervision reinforces the negative spiral. In many ways there are parallels here to social workers' attempts to help problem drinkers, where stereotyping, inadequate knowledge, a perceived lack of transferable skills, and ill-informed supervision all lead to poor-quality service to clients (Robinson 1976; Shaw, Cartwright, Spratley, and Harwin 1978; Isaacs and Moon 1985).

Social workers, families, and mental health

If individual clients have received a limited service, then what is the position of families where a member has been experiencing a mental health problem? The claims for social work in this area are impressive and have been made over a number of years. For example, the 1974 DHSS *Working Party on Social Work Support for the Health Service* noted the significance of the social worker in the family setting (DHSS 1974), while the 1975 *White Paper on Better Services for the Mentally Ill* stressed the importance of practical and psychotherapeutic support which should be given to families by social workers (DHSS 1975) as did the Short Report more recently.

Social work *literature* has presented a picture of the social work role with families in a comprehensive and positive manner (Prins 1976) – while the reality of *practice* is somewhat different! I have already noted the problems which social workers experience in working with individuals with mental health problems. If knowledge, skills, and experience are uncertain there, then it will be difficult to convey confidence in a family setting. It is often a frightening and bewildering experience for a family to discover over the years that one of its members has a mental health problem. For instance, in relation to schizophrenia, the initial tendency is to reject the idea, to try and disregard developing symptoms, to try to accommodate the problem as the family try to 'do their duty' (Miles 1987). The fears of family members, the uncertainties, and the stigma of having a mentally ill relative are all likely to be evident. Self-criticism is frequent, isolation grows, stress develops, relatives and friends make less frequent visits (Creer and Wing 1974; Miles 1987). There may be a tendency to put the family member with a mental health problem into a 'sick role' which can tend to absolve both the individual and cut off the family from responsibilities for moving on to attempts to remedy the situation (Parsons and Fox 1968; Mechanic 1968). Most important, often the family lacks relevant support and appropriate information; social workers have often proved inadequate and unreliable in this respect (Creer and Wing 1974; Olsen 1976).

Yet social workers *do* have an important role to play in providing information and support. Families will try to make sense of the mental health problem by recourse to 'common-sense' language. One husband described this most graphically: 'I don't know what happened – a cog inside her head got knocked out of place'. The social worker can provide knowledge and information, but, of course, this may be difficult if the worker lacks confidence in these areas. In turn, many workers have been influenced by some of Laing's earlier writings from the mid-sixties which placed the 'causation' of mental health problems firmly at the door of the family, and encouraged the latter to use the individual as scapegoat and victim (Laing 1961; Laing and Esterson 1964). Such writings, or partial understanding of such writings, backed up by films such as *Family Life*, percolate many social workers' thoughts and have been escalated beyond the plight of 'schizophrenics' into more generalised applicability to other mental health problems as well. Therefore, there is a danger of social workers concentrating too heavily upon the 'identified patient' as a result of received wisdom inherited from partially digested Laingian thinking. In no way would I wish to minimise Laing's considerable contribution in highlighting the importance and significance of the schizophrenic experience, rather to urge caution when considering the part played by family members. Although it is acknowledged that 50 per cent of schizophrenic situations may be genetically linked (Kety *et al.* 1968), at the same time there is evidence that family situations where there is 'high expressed emotion' can exacerbate existing schizophrenic states (Brown *et al.* 1972; Vaughn and Leff 1976). This brings us back to the importance of assessment skills and a willingness to see and acknowledge multiple causation when social workers are considering mental health questions.

Families can easily react with hostility, defensiveness, and guilt feelings when difficulties emerge. 'What did I do wrong?' is the reaction of one mother whose son was going through a schizophrenic experience. 'What can you do about it?' is the cry frequently aimed at the social worker. 'He (or she) is driving us mad' is often heard as the breakdown of one family member triggers off the doubts of other family members about their own mental state – 'What will happen to us?' Social workers require 'stickability' in these situations, a willingness not to be frightened off, a willingness to explain, and a willingness to understand. It can mean exposure to fear, aggression, and insults based on the inadequacy of previous offers of help; it can mean dealing with disputes, hidden tensions, and 'skeletons in the cupboard' which emerge as the stress of coping begins to increase and cracks in family functioning emerge which have been papered over for years. Difficult, bizarre behaviour such as aggressive outbursts, withdrawal from family contact, and problematic hygiene habits all impose enormous stress on families.

The social worker can offer an opportunity to enable a family to express much of their own aggression and act as an advocate and attempt to link in families to the limited social facilities which are available, such as day centres. Working with families in such situations is not easy, without the rewards of easy success, with the social worker sometimes acting as a 'long-term addition', a 'permanent palliative' (Fisher, Newton, and Sainsbury 1984: 117). In the latter study it was significant that in eleven stressful situations, where children were the 'identified' client the mental state of mothers was neglected in half of these cases, with the care and development of children being given priority. The mothers in these situations were sometimes subject to moral censure on account of their passivity, and the social workers generally found their work to be unrewarding and demoralising. This is a far cry from the ambitions outlined in the social work literature and policy documents.

The intentions of recent years: multi-disciplinary work

Much has been written about the importance of multi-disciplinary work in the mental health field, stressing the importance of the contributions to be made by all the professions involved, including social work. For example, the DHSS *Working Party on Social Work Support for the Health Service* talked about the importance of the social worker taking on a significant position in the clinical team, highlighting ideas of mutual understanding, co-operation, and support 'between equal partners with distinct contributions to make to a common purpose' (DHSS 1974: introduction). The report stressed the idea of personal contact between trusting individuals as frequently as possible in a team situation which

> in a clinical situation means that all members of the team accept that each has a professional contribution to make in his own right; and that it is both the right and equally the responsibility of each member of the team to make that contribution if the patient needs it. Such a responsibility derives not from the prescription of the head of the team, but from the right of the patient to have the benefit of all the team's skills as he needs them.
>
> (DHSS 1974: 22)

In 1975, *Better Services for the Mentally Ill* (DHSS) repeated the emphasis given to the importance of multi-disciplinary teams, with the social work role being seen as of fundamental importance; also an emphasis was given to joint work with other professionals in making assessments and in providing help to families. Furthermore, psychiatrists were asked to devote time to consultative and supportive work for Social Services. Thus the message of these and other policy documents has been clear: 'A comprehensive and effective mental health service depends on multi-disciplinary working' (Davis in Olsen 1984: 177).

I would suggest that no individual worker is able to possess all the knowledge and skills needed to help a person with a mental health problem, that understanding of physical problems is essential, that drug treatment and other physical treatments may be necessary, that the social and environmental context should not be forgotten, and that talking through problems may be helpful. However, Davis has expressed some considerable doubts about hopes for this multi-disciplinary heaven: 'Debate about the strengths and limitations of a multi-disciplinary approach remain largely academic. For, in reality, most social workers work in a world in which there are considerable problems communicating with other professionals and engaging in joint practice' (Davis in Olsen 1984: 178).

June Huntington has explored some of the differences between social workers and general practitioners that inhibit collaboration, seeing considerable differences in knowledge, values, technology, and language which are grounded in the different structural characteristics of the two occupations (Huntington 1981). While it is recognised that many of the contacts made by social workers in 'mental health' situations will be with general practitioners (Goldberg and Huxley 1980) and many so-called 'mental health' problems may not even reach a psychiatrist, nevertheless, it is my feeling that the relationship between psychiatry and social work is a neglected one.

Social work and psychiatry

In this section, therefore, I intend to examine relationships between social workers and psychiatrists and the attitudes of these groups towards each other. What, then, should we be seeking in order to improve present difficulties? What can be done to break down the barriers between psychiatrists and social workers? What are the chances for the development of a common language, shared meanings, and mutual comprehension? Clearly, these are questions which have been posed many times before, and several attempts have been made to provide answers, dating back twenty-five years (Ashdown and Brown 1953) and beyond that.

From the outset it seems important to recognise that a basic distinction should be made between social workers who operate in teams based in a psychiatric hospital, in a psychiatric unit, or child guidance setting and teams based in area offices. It is the latter setting, where the vast majority of statutory social workers are employed, which is primarily our concern.

Education and training

The tremendous investment of both psychiatry and social work in maintaining their separateness, their status and power, has continued for more than a century. It has been, and is, supported by the massive institutional machinery of psychiatric training centres, hospital centres, professional associations, and professional journals 'whose separate enterprises seem to speak different languages entirely' (Kovel 1981: 72). Social work, having initially ridden upon the back of psychiatry, has striven to build up its own massive institutional machinery of training centres, helping agencies, professional associations, professional journals, and language. The institutions of psychiatry and social work have different cultures and languages; the psychiatrist and social worker develop within and as part of these different cultures; their behaviours begin to reflect the basic features of each of these cultures. I am not suggesting that the institutions of social work and psychiatry are monolithic, entirely consistent, or universal, but there are underpinning features which support, sustain, and bolster the identities of both psychiatrists and social workers – features which are inherently contradictory as knowledge, myths, and legends are created and transmitted through institutional culture, language, and 'professional values'.

Ultimately, our concern should be with action, as a commitment to shared strategies and operational collaboration between psychiatrists and social workers does not necessarily mean that the two groups should necessarily hold similar attitudes and values (Booth *et al.* 1985). However, all action depends to some degree upon mutual understanding, upon a common definition of meanings, and upon a shared language.

All professional and occupational groups develop their own particular jargon and language which outsiders have difficulty in understanding (Robinson 1978; Hudson 1978). The worlds of psychiatry and social work stand apart from one another. The psychiatrist is initially a medical undergraduate on a five-year course, which is followed up by several years' specialised training to become a psychiatrist. Most psychiatrists are known to have above average 'A' level grades and, in common with medical undergraduates, may well be perceived as the *crème de la crème* in terms of educational achievement. In fact, psychiatry does have problems in obtaining recruits to the fold. It is one of the more unpopular medical specialisms, and sources have suggested that only around 5 per cent of final year medical students opt for psychiatry as a first career preference (Parkhouse and McLaughlin 1975). Furthermore, there is a high drop-out rate during training, partly linked to disillusionment and limited motivation (Clare 1980). Social work trainees, half of whom are graduates, and the other half non-graduates, do not tend to see themselves as high educational achievers. The educational attainments of social workers tend to be inferior to those of psychiatrists; this fact is rarely acknowledged or spoken about by social workers. But it does set the groups apart from an early stage. Both know of this discrepancy, it is received wisdom, it reinforces that status of both 'professional' groups before, during, and after training, which, in turn, is reinforced by salary scales available after qualification.

The psychiatrist in training has completed a medical undergraduate course which concentrates on the physical and upon 'disease', 'illness', and 'cure'; it involves attachments to various medical specialisms. The amount of time devoted to the behavioural sciences is small, despite recent modifications to medical undergraduate curricula. The likely academic input about social work is minimal – only one two-hour session on one medical undergraduate course known to the author and a similar amount on a course leading to a diploma in psychiatric medicine. This contrasts with the social work training course and its present core components linked to social work theory and practice, sociology, social policy, and psychology. Often, limited attention is paid to physical illness (although the latter may vary from course to course), and there is usually only a short input on psychiatry. These points may be obvious to the *cognoscenti*, but they are less obvious to those outside the professional circles of psychiatry and social workers who specialise in psychiatry. Thus it is not surprising that there is considerable scope for misunderstanding, stereotyping, and labelling between psychiatrists and social workers.

The medical model

Psychiatry has developed received ideas somewhat different from the received wisdom of social work. Much has been written about psychiatry's adherence to a 'medical model' view of mental health, although there have been different interpretations of the meaning of the term 'medical model' (see Siegler and Osmond

1974; Clare 1980; Ingleby 1981; Sedgwick 1982). Clare, for example, prefers the term 'organic' to 'medical', as he has argued that the medical model 'takes into account not merely the syndrome, symptom or disease but the person who suffers, his personal and social situation, his biological, psychological and social status' (Clare 1980: 69). He goes on to describe psychotherapeutic, sociotherapeutic, and behavioural approaches in psychiatry. Others have dismissed this perception as extravagant and exaggerated, claiming that psychiatrists place their focus much more narrowly and squarely upon physical and biological elements in mental health problems (Kovel 1981; Treacher and Baruch 1981).

Of course, it is perhaps as difficult to categorise, label, or diagnose psychiatrists as it is to categorise, label, or diagnose those on the receiving end of mental health care! Psychiatry does not possess any greater 'professional solidarity' than social work, contrary to the belief of Horder (1987); several surveys have revealed that psychiatrists do have an interest in the variety and range of psychotherapeutic, sociotherapeutic, and behavioural approaches noted above. Some consultant psychiatrists do have an active interest in psychotherapeutic approaches and have championed developments in marital and family therapy (Skynner 1976). Also, many psychiatrists in training do see themselves as having been highly motivated in their career choice by an interest in human emotions and behaviour (Brook 1973).

At the same time, medical model thinking has been also highly influential in the training and experience of all psychiatrists. Firstly, it is suggested that physical causation of 'mental illness' is important; that physical cures have a real part to play. One eminent psychiatrist concedes that:

By virtue of the immense public demand for psychiatric care, as much as by reason of a particular faith in the efficacy of such treatments many psychiatrists do seem to rely quite heavily on physical methods of treatment such as antidepressant drugs and ECT and do stress the genetic and organic factors operating in psychiatric illness.

(Clare 1976: 64)

Therefore, much psychiatric research has aimed at searching for the biological causation of 'mental illness', especially in investigations of the schizophrenias.

A second feature of the medical model concerns the emphasis placed on genetic elements – mental health problems perceived as phenomena inherited from parents. Psychiatric research in these areas has tended to concentrate upon the incidence of mental health problems in twins and adoptive children.

Thus two central features of the medical model – the perception of the roots of mental health problems as located in organic causation and genetic components – have provoked some feelings of unrest amongst many social workers. While it should be pointed out that considerable research does, in fact, support the significant role played by these elements – for example in the 'causation' of schizophrenia – for many workers the emphasis on these factors tends to run counter to the psychotherapeutic or sociotherapeutic models to which they hold allegiance. Social workers have difficulty in accepting approaches to clients which focus upon physical and genetic causations, preferring instead to see the client's 'strengths' and potential for growth and development, with the client in the process of 'becoming' (Rogers 1978). Also, social workers tend to prefer to 'talk out' problems; they see counselling as a major arm of social work, they locate problems in an environmental context, search for community resources, and, unlike psychiatrists, do not possess any right or facility in mental health situations to prescribe or administer drugs to their charges. Furthermore, psychiatrists are said to have tendencies to perceive recipients of their services as 'suffering from illnesses', but such language is not part of the social worker's everyday discourse. Yet it has been, and is, highly influential during the training and in the thinking of most psychiatrists. Other components of medical model thinking in psychiatry include an emphasis on terms such as 'diagnosis' and 'treatment', which link in further with concepts of 'disease' and invoke parallels to working in the area of physical illness. Brian Sheldon, a social work educator, has clearly stated his own views and the opposition of some social workers to such thinking: 'We are left with the conclusion . . . that diagnosing mental disorder is not at all like diagnosing whooping cough. The problem is that some medical personnel have convinced themselves that it is' (Sheldon 1984: 92).

Social workers react negatively to such attitudes, preferring the term 'assessment' to 'diagnosis', preferring to see the recipient as a much more equal participant in the 'helping' process. A key element here is the different language used by the two groups. Consider this interesting example in a book review in a recent issue of *Social Work Today:* 'This is a text written from the medical point of view and as such has some of the limitations one would expect for a social work reader' (Hugman 1987: 8). This example is obviously interesting in that the 'medical point of view' is associated with 'limitations' for a 'social work reader'. What is less obvious is that the meaning of the language used is very important here; the various definitions of meaning that are possible. Eagleton has expressed this precisely:

Meaning [is] not natural, a question of just looking and seeing, or something eternally settled; the way you interpret your world [is] a function of the languages you [have] at your disposal. Meaning [is] not something that men and women intuitively shared, and then articulated in various tongues and scripts; what meaning you [are] able to articulate depend[s] on what script or speech you share in the first place.

(Eagleton 1983: 107)

Psychiatrists and social workers find it difficult to use the same 'script'; they do not share the same 'speech'; they have different languages. Indeed, the respective discourses of psychiatry and social work suggest that it will be difficult for psychiatrists and social workers to exist in anything other than a relationship of some tension. We are illustrating here not just a question of identification with models; but the linguistic implications and inheritances derived from these models. If social workers are intending to come to terms with their relationships with psychiatry, if they are to develop a deeper understanding of mental health problems, then it is suggested that the barriers associated with the medical model should be overcome.

As a social worker, one has to have a familiarity with the main concepts of the model and an ability to work within it at least to the extent of gaining the confidence of the medical team. This is particularly important when dealing with the more serious forms of disorder . . . outright rejection is likely to lead to a very light caseload and a resultant poor service to the client.

(Butler and Pritchard 1983: 9)

'Objectivity' and 'subjectivity'

There has been much criticism of psychiatry's supposed unwillingness to give adequate attention to the experience of an individual encountering mental health problems, to the extent of invalidating the individual's experience in an attempt to relate to the natural sciences, with their so-called emphasis on objective evaluation. The criticisms of alleged scientific positivism and reification – the designation of people as objects – has come from a variety of sources (such as Ingleby 1981; Sedgwick 1982; Banton *et al.* 1985). Sedgwick has been particularly hostile to the positivism of psychiatry which, he feels, emphasises a separation between facts and values, with only the former as a subject matter for the professional investigator. In addition, he argued that positivism suppresses the interactive relationship between the investigator and the facts he is working on, thus leading to a neglect of social and cultural elements when psychiatric assessments are made (Sedgwick 1982).

Thus, objectification, reification, and labelling all prove to have a bitter taste to the social work palate. Social workers do not find it easy to relate to the so-called labels of 'schizophrenia', 'neurosis', and 'personality disorder'. Further, in addition to the sociological insights of the labelling theorists (Becker 1963; Scheff 1966; Lemert 1967), as noted earlier, many social workers have been strongly influenced by the anti-psychiatry of Laing which held sway in the late 1960s, and in the 1970s had a considerable impact on social work courses. Although recently such views have been strongly questioned by socialists such as Sedgwick (1982), for many years

> anti-psychiatry . . . harmonized with quite widely prevalent values and aspirations of the time . . . defined the collusive psychiatrist as an agent of control and coercion [and was] dramatically congruent with the sharp questioning of established institutions [thus providing help] for social workers hungry for new professional ideologies and in particular for ideas which gave them some moral advantage in the unequal battle for status and independence with the most firmly established of professions.
>
> (Martin 1984: 34)

One particular value of Laing's work was to emphasise the significance of the individual's subjective experience (Laing 1959; Laing 1967). Social work has tended to emphasise the subjective perceptions of the client and contrast these to the objective emphasis of psychiatry, which perhaps places greater weight on the judgements and perceptions of the psychiatrist:

> The liberal, humanistic response to the extremes of psychiatric objectification is to oppose it by focusing on the subjective account that the individual gives of her/his experi-

ences, thus coming to understand and treat him/her as a full human being whose communications are meaningful and worthy of respect.

(Banton *et al.* 1985: 151)

There is a strong, well established tradition in social work which emphasises the importance of the individual's world view, the significance of the individual, respect for the individual, the meaning which an individual attaches to his life experiences. Phenomenological perspectives endorse this view and 'promise nothing less than a science of subjectivity itself where the individual "is to be seen as the source and origin of all meaning"' (Eagleton 1983: 58). I might not go so far as to endorse entirely the idea of a 'science' of subjectivity in social work. Nevertheless, the recent language of British social work is clearly one which has been influenced by phenomenology, by humanism, and by quasi-religious thinking.

The social context

Also, social work has traditionally placed great emphasis on the social situation of the client from its earliest days; Richmond's classic text of 1917 is an example of such thinking. The development of Marxist literature on the social work scene during the mid-1970s and early 1980s gave even stronger impetus to the location of client problems into the social context, while the supposed neglect of the social element in mental health problems has long been one of the major planks of criticisms of psychiatry. In fact, psychiatry is a two-time loser in the eyes of many social workers: because they criticise it for objectification and reification of the individual, while simultaneously attacking its neglect of the societal and cultural context. This inability to appreciate structural determinants of behaviour is used as another rod to beat the psychiatrist's back; the societal context is felt to 'have been overlooked because traditionally psychiatry lacks any way of doing justice to it' (Ingleby 1981: 59). Thus the social worker is brought in to provide background social histories, to discover what resources there are 'out there' in the community, to provide accommodation, and to help with financial problems.

Psychiatric institutions and social work

Social workers have also tended to condemn psychiatry along with the institutions in which psychiatrists were housed. The late 1960s and early 1970s were characterised by attacks on the institutional base of psychiatry by Thomas Szasz, R.D. Laing and Ivan Illich. The work of the British psychiatrist Russel Barton (1959) and that of Goffman (1961) were pungent polemics which severely criticised the regimes in psychiatric hospitals. Doubts have been cast on the objectivity and rigour of Goffman's study of 1000 mental-hospital patients in Washington in the United States but, on the other hand, the thorough research work of Wing and Brown (1970) appeared to confirm Barton's tentative hypotheses. In addition, episodic scandals in psychiatric hospitals during the 1970s, such as at Ely, Farleigh and Wittingham, all raised social work hackles against the tyranny of the institution, with psychiatry being bracketed alongside such establishments.

Institutions were perceived in negative terms; psychiatrists were thought to be guilty by association. Consequently, many social workers have been reluctant to work in psychiatric or penal establishments, and their negative feelings have influenced even their willingness to work closely with those located in such institutions – both social workers and psychiatrists! Fortunately, the moves towards psychiatric units and community care (inadequate though the latter may be) have perhaps helped reduce at least some of the stigma attached to the bracketing of psychiatrists with large institutions. At the same time, perhaps, social workers are now more appreciative of the need of some (albeit a small proportion) of their clients to receive asylum in the best sense of the word. This brings me on to a crucial element in the interaction between psychiatrist and social workers; the question of power and the language of power.

Social workers, psychiatry, and power

Social work as a profession has developed in the shadow of psychiatry. Although some authors have noted the relative youth of psychiatry (Clare 1980) and others have questioned its domination of the mental health field (Kovel 1981; Treacher and Baruch 1981), there is little doubt that professional social work in the mental health field has a somewhat shorter history.

Not all social workers criticise psychiatrists. In a recent survey of the social work personnel in three area teams, by Fisher,

Newton, and Sainsbury, whilst 'half of the respondents believed that psychiatrists offered only medication and containment, the other half referred to them in positive terms, seeing them as having therapeutic skills, being good at their work and understanding towards their patients' (Fisher *et al.* 1984). However, 'about one third of the respondents criticised psychiatrists for being too distanced, "superior" or too busy to talk to them and a few remarked that they seemed to have a poor understanding of social work' (ibid., 1984: 46). The situation becomes more gloomy as social workers in this survey were reluctant to liaise with psychiatrists, and would only do so when there was a marked deterioration in the mental health of a client or when they encountered a situation of some severity – in fact, as a last resort. Research work undertaken with three area teams in Strathclyde reached similar conclusions in that social workers did not enjoy good liaison with health service personnel, although 'social workers were not anti-psychiatry but did not necessarily accept medical diagnoses' (Strathclyde Regional Council Social Work Department 1985: 36). Fisher, Newton, and Sainsbury note that in the twenty-six cases in which 'liaison was maintained between social workers and psychiatrists, fifteen ran into difficulties in the view of the social workers' (Fisher *et al.* 1984: 51). These difficulties surrounded social workers' feeling that they were not involved in changes of plans, or had plans imposed upon them, or had patients written off and that their own views were received with scant respect. The same social workers believed there was considerable difficulty in finding a common base of understanding in their work with psychiatrists.

To be sure, psychiatrists themselves have widely varying perceptions of social workers, but sometimes see them as indecisive, uncertain, and lacking in an adequate preparation for mental health work, as 'talkers', 'jacks of all trades, masters of none', 'procrastinators', and 'vague'. At the same time, several authors have commented upon the reluctance of psychiatrists to relinquish their exclusive hold upon mental health problems (Miles 1977; Baruch and Treacher 1978; Martin 1984). Baruch and Treacher have talked about the 'major historical anachronism' which has 'allowed psychiatry to exert its hegemony in the field of therapy by effectively precluding other differently trained therapists from having primary responsibility for patient care' (Baruch and Treacher 1978: 201). Also, Agnes Miles interviewed six psychiatrists who all stated that the medical profession had exclusive competence in diagnosing illness, prescribing treatment, administering treatment, and in assessing patients' reactions (Miles 1977: 130).

Furthermore, it is the psychiatrist who is the leader of the hospital team or firm, who makes decisions to admit or discharge patients, who ultimately has responsibility in the team, and who directs the relationship with the social worker. The social worker is under pressure to comprehend the psychiatrist's comments (witness the remarks we quoted earlier from Butler and Pritchard), it is 'the social worker [who] has to have a familiarity with the main concepts of the [medical] model and an ability to work within it' (Butler and Pritchard 1983: 9) not the psychiatrist who should be familiar with the 'models' of the social worker. There are interesting perceptions in the literature about the use of power in teamwork. Some wish to endorse the power of psychiatry and glorify in it (Siegler and Osmond 1974). Others resent it – the view from a social policy perspective – 'it is difficult for doctors to join teams except in the role of captain' (Martin 1984: 138). Still others ruefully accept it – the view from a psychiatrist's perspective – '[the psychiatrist] is a member of a multi-disciplinary team, less its captain than its sweeper' (Clare 1976: 400). It is stating the obvious to note that psychiatrists have more power than social workers; it is not stating the obvious to consider how this power, once achieved, is maintained. In particular the received wisdom is that psychiatrist's definitions do have some meaning. After all, psychiatry is an established profession; some would argue that social work is not. Social work has its own jargon, its own literature, its own *modus operandi*. Yet it is psychiatry which dominates the relationship between the two; it is the discourse of psychiatry which dominates the discourse of social work. Banton *et al.* have expressed this most succinctly: 'The discourses that dominate, within as well as between people, are likely to be those that can be enforced by the power relations that characterise the social world' (Banton *et al.* 1985, 16). Therefore many social workers, like the lay public, defer to the definitions of mental health problems provided by psychiatry. Covertly, they may deny these definitions, secretly question their authenticity and value, debate their veracity with colleagues and, when in contact with psychiatrists' decisions, attempt avoidance and manipulation of their decision making (Goldie 1976).

It is interesting to consider the literature on mental health that considers the contribution of social work and psychiatry which are written by psychiatrists or social workers, as so often only limited attention is given to the role of the other profession. For example, in Clare's book *Psychiatry in Dissent* (1976) one notes in the index only three pages devoted to the role of social workers. Equally, in the recent text for social workers by Banton *et al.* entitled *The Politics of Mental Health* (1985), one notes that only three pages are devoted to the role of psychiatrists!

Several solutions have been suggested to improve contacts between psychiatrists and social workers. The idea of sharing interests and problems in seminars at various levels, both during training and in practice, has been advocated. So also has the idea of shared attachments, the breaking down of professional power and status barriers, as in some of the examples set in Italy under the impetus of *Psychiatrica Democratica*. These are just some of the solutions suggested. The discourse of psychiatry can then more effectively encounter the discourse of social work. Mutual trust, joint responsibility, and teamwork become more likely; without a focus for interaction the cause is lost. Openness, flexibility, and a sense of the unfinished are essential attributes for the pursuit of a joint enterprise between psychiatrists and social workers. Furthermore, such rhetoric will only be achievable in reality if the participating parties are willing to question and willing to examine some of their strongest beliefs, attitudes, and aspirations – a painful and difficult target.

Conclusion

I have contrasted some of the pronouncements and exhortations made about mental health social work with day-to-day practice. I have contrasted some of the intentions and recommendations of policy documents which have focused upon developing closer relationships between psychiatrists and social workers with some of the problems which underpin such intentions. Social workers are under considerable pressure in their relationships with psychiatrists, clients, and their families to provide competent, knowledgeable, and skilful services. They are also under pressure from within their own discipline, which is an arena for considerable conflict and difference. The role of the generic social worker is a demanding and difficult one; a role which has not been adequately clarified in the mental health field by the Barclay Report or the recent Mental Health Acts in England and Scotland. Furthermore, within many Social Services departments, the low priority given to mental health social work and the financial pressures imposed by government rate-capping and rate-support grant penalties have discouraged even the more positive-minded local authorities from taking more active steps in that area.

Social workers themselves seem to lack confidence and self-assurance when undertaking much mental health social work, being partly enmeshed in some of society's negative attitudes towards mental illness. The training linked to the new Acts may help to remedy some of these deficiencies, but it is sad that much of the helpful literature based on wide and in-depth experience of social workers in mental health situations should be now either undervalued or lost almost entirely. It is difficult for many social workers to face the pain, anguish, and distress which much mental health social work may involve, to 'break this silence, to make troubles speak again in the reality of their own language' (Banton *et al.* 1985: 193).

At a wider level, structural issues hinder the development of more constructive relationships between psychiatry and social work. No one group has been able to present collective leadership to change the national scene. Attempts to out-manoeuvre the other, to convince the other of the rightness of one's own definitions or to defer to the authority of the other have characterised the relationship between social work and psychiatry. A committed dialogue is necessary to break down these barriers, a perception of collaboration as being important for genuine, positive action on behalf of the recipient, rather than a nominal or convenient attempt which only pays lip-service to joint endeavours.

The establishment of an open dialogue at the training stage is very important; this should be continued in joint, national, and local forums – for example, local mental health development groups which can help to break down the divisions between health and local authority services, provide resources, agreed philosophies, and specific objectives. Personal, trusting relationships between social work and psychiatry mean a great deal when sharing the delivery of a service in the mental health field, but these can only be of wider significance if issues of policy, priorities, and resources are satisfactorily resolved at both national and local levels.

© 1989 Stewart Collins

References

Ashdown, M. and Brown, C. (1953) *Social Services and Mental Health,* London: Routledge & Kegan Paul.
Banton, R., Clifford, P., Frosh S., Lousada, J., Rosenhall, J. (1985) *The Politics of Mental Health,* London: Macmillan.
Barter, J. (1976) 'Mental health and social work training', *Social Work*

Today 7, 13: 367-70.

Barton, R. (1959) *Institutional Neurosis,* Bristol: John Wright.

Baruch, G. and Treacher, A. (1978) *Psychiatry Observed,* London: Routledge & Kegan Paul.

Becker, H.S. (1963) *Outsiders: Studies in the Sociology of Deviance,* New York: Free Press.

Booth, T., Melotte, C., Phillips, D., Pritlove, J., Barrit, A. and Lightup, R. (1985) 'Psychiatric crises in the community: collaboration and the 1983 Mental Health Act', in G. Harobin, (ed.) *Responding to Mental Illness, Research Highlights in Social Work,* London: Routledge & Kegan Paul.

Brook, P. (1973) 'Psychiatrists in Training', *British Journal of Psychiatry,* Special publication 7, Ashford: Headley Brothers.

Brown, G., Birley, J. and Wing, J.K. (1972) 'Influence of family life on the cause of schizophrenic disorders: a replication', *British Journal of Psychiatry* 121: 241-58.

Butler, A. and Pritchard, C. (1983) *Social Work and Mental Illness,* London: Macmillan.

Central Council for Education and Training in Social Work (1987) *Statement of Minimum Requirements of the Social Worker at the Point of Qualification,* London: CCETSW.

Clare, A. (1976 and 1980) *Psychiatry in Dissent,* London: Tavistock.

Creer, C. and Wing, J.K. (1974) *Schizophrenia at Home,* London: National Schizophrenia Fellowship.

Davis, A. (1984) 'Working with other professions', in R. Olsen (ed.) *Social Work and Mental Health,* London: Tavistock.

Department of Health and Social Security (1974) *Working Party on Social Work Support for the Health Services,* London: HMSO.

Department of Health and Social Security (1975) *Better Services for the Mentally Ill,* London: HMSO.

Eagleton, T. (1983) *Literary Theory,* Oxford: Blackwell.

Fisher, C., Newton, C., and Sainsbury, E. (1984) *Mental Health Social Work Observed,* London: George Allen & Unwin.

Goffman, E. (1961) *Asylums,* Harmondsworth: Penguin Books.

Goldberg, D. and Huxley, P. (1980) *Mental Illness in the Community,* London: Tavistock.

Goldie, N. (1976) 'The division of labour among the mental health professions – a negotiated or an imposed order', Paper presented to the BSA Conference (Manchester).

Horder, W. (1987) 'Working with psychiatrists', *Social Work Today* 18, 25: 10-11.

Hudson, B. (1982) *Social Work with Psychiatric Patients,* London: Macmillan.

Hudson, K. (1978) *The Jargon of the Professions,* London: Macmillan.

Hugman, R. (1987) 'Medical viewpoint of the behavioural sciences', *Social Work Today,* 9, 3.

Huntington, J. (1981) *Social Work and General Medical Practice: Collaboration or Conflict?* London: Allen & Unwin.

Illich, I. (1975) *Medical Neurosis,* London: Calder & Boyars.

Ingleby, D. (1981) *Critical Psychiatry,* Harmondsworth: Penguin Books.

Isaacs, J. and Moon, G. (1985) *Alcohol Problems – the Social Work Response,* Portsmouth: Social Services Research and Intelligence Unit.

Jones, C. (1983) *State Social Work and the Working Class*, London: Macmillan.

Kety, S.S., Rosenthal, D., Wender, P., and Shulsinger, T. (1968) 'The types and prevalence of mental illness in the biological and adoptive families of adopted schizophrenics', in D. Rosenthal and S.S. Kety (eds) *The Transmission of Schizophrenia*, Oxford: Pergamon.

Kovel, J. (1981) 'The American mental health industry', in D. Ingleby (ed.) *Critical Psychiatry*, Harmondsworth: Penguin Books.

Laing, R.D. (1959) *The Divided Self*, London: Tavistock.

Laing, R.D. (1961) *The Self and Others*, London: Tavistock.

Laing, R.D. (1967) *The Politics of Experience*, Harmondsworth: Penguin Books.

Laing, R.D. and Esterson, A. (1964) *Sanity, Madness and the Family*, Harmondsworth: Penguin Books.

Lemert, E. (1967) *Human Deviance, Social Problems and Social Control*, Englewood Cliffs, NJ: Prentice-Hall.

Martin, F. (1984) *Between the Acts: Community Mental Health Services 1959-1983*, London: Nuffield Trust.

Mechanic, D. (1968) *Medical Sociology*, New York: Free Press.

Miles, A. (1977) 'Staff relations in psychiatric hospitals', *British Journal of Psychiatry*, 130, 84-8.

Miles, A. (1981 and 1987) *The Mentally Ill in Contemporary Society*, Oxford: Blackwell.

Newton,C., Smith, J., and Hirsch, S. (1979) 'A comparison of social workers and psychiatrists in evaluating parasuicide', *British Journal of Psychiatry*, 134, 335-42.

Nursten, J. (1972) *Process of Casework*, London: Pitman.

Olsen, R. (1976) 'Boarding out the long stay psychiatric patient', in R. Olsen (ed.) *Differential Approaches in Social Work with the Mentally Disordered*, Birmingham: BASW.

Parkhouse, F. and McLaughlin, C. (1975) 'Career preferences of 1973 graduates', *Lancet* i, 1342.

Parsons, T. and Fox, R. 'Illness, therapy and the modern American family', in R. Bell and E.F. Vogel (eds) *A Modern Introduction to the Family*, New York: Free Press.

Pearson, G. Treseder, J., and Yelloly, M. (1988) *Social Work and the Legacy of Freud*, London: Macmillan.

Prins, H. (1976) 'The contribution of social work to the treatment of the mentally disordered', in R. Olsen (ed.) *Differential Approaches in Social Work with the Mentally Disordered*, Birmingham: BASW.

Pritchard, C. and Butler, A. (1976) 'Why specialism? The case for mental health social work', *Social Work Today* 7(6), 176-90.

Robinson, D. (1976) *From Drinking to Alcoholism*, Chichester: John Wiley.

Robinson, T. (1978) *In Worlds Apart*, London: Bedford Square Press.

Rogers, C. (1978) *On Becoming a Person*, BostonMass.: Houghton Mifflin.

Rosenhan, D.L. (1973) 'On being sane in insane places', *Science* 179, 250-8.

Scheff, T. (1966) *Being Mentally Ill*, Chicago: Aldine.

Sedgwick, P. (1982) *Psychopolitics*, London: Pluto Press.

Shaw, S., Cartwright, A., Spratley, T., and Harwin, J. (1978) *Responding to Drinking Problems*, London: Croom Helm.

Sheldon, B. (1984) 'A critical appraisal of the medical model in psychiatry', in R. Olsen (ed.) *Social Work and Mental Health*, London: Tavistock.

Siegler, M. and Osmond, H. (1974) *Models of Madness, Models of Medicine,* New York: Macmillan; London: Constable.

Skynner, R. (1976) *One Flesh: Separate Persons,* London: Constable.

Smale, G. (1977) *Prophecy, Behaviour and Change,* London: Routledge & Kegan Paul.

Strathclyde Regional Council Social Work Department (1985) *Are a Team Social Work Response to Mental Health Problems,* Glasgow: Strathclyde Regional Council.

Szasz, T. (1961) *The Manufacture of Madness,* London: Routledge & Kegan Paul.

Szasz, T. (1971) *The Myth of Mental Illness,* New York: Harper.

Treacher, A. and Baruch, G. (1981) 'Towards a critical history of the psychiatric profession', in D. Ingleby (ed.) *Critical Psychiatry,* Harmondsworth: Penguin Books.

Vaughn, C.E. and Leff, J.P. (1976) 'The influence of family and social factors on the course of psychotic illness', *British Journal of Psychiatry,* 129: 125-37.

Wing, T.K. and Brown, G. (1970) *Institutionalism and Schizophrenia,* Cambridge: Cambridge University Press.

8

Social work and self-management

Chris Rojek

Although social workers have written much about self-determination, they have written very little about self-management. This is regrettable, for a concept of self-determination which fails to specify how personal choice is organised is not worthy of the name. The purpose of this chapter is to explain why self-management is important to social workers and to consider examples of self-management that might be concretely applied to social work settings. However, before commencing with the main business of these pages, it is necessary to say a little about traditional and radical views of self-determination.

Self-determination: traditional and radical views

Traditional social workers identify self-determination as a core value of social work (for example, see Hollis 1964; Pincus and Minahan 1973; BASW 1975; NASW 1980). Biestek (1961: 103) provided one of the most influential and enduring definitions when he wrote:

> The principle of client self determination is the practical recognition of the right and need of clients to freedom in making their own choices and decisions . . . . The client's right to self-determination, however, is limited by the client's capacity for positive and constructive decision-making, by the framework of civil law, and by the function of the agency.

From the first, a degree of controversy has attended the meaning and use of the concept in social work. The tension is visible in Biestek's definition. It insists on the right of clients to be free, which is a voluntaristic proposition. Yet simultaneously, it posits a natural, social, legal, and political framework behind action, which is a deterministic proposition.

Radical circles have responded by detailing the structural constraints which limit the freedom of the individual; for example, class, sexual inequality, and racism. They continue by disparaging self-determination in social work as an ideological construct. Its alleged function is to deflect consciousness of the structural basis of personal problems and to mask the role of traditional social work in reproducing the existing state of inequality and repression: for examples of the radical case, see Galper 1975; Wilson 1977; Corrigan and Leonard 1978; Simpkin 1979; Bolger *et al.* 1981; Finch and Groves 1983; Brook and Davis 1985; Marchant and Waring 1986.

While radical social workers reject the traditional meaning and use of self-determination, they do not want to abandon the concept entirely. On the contrary, as Leonard (1984: 217) observes, a major aim of radical social work is to create 'a social order which no longer deforms and limits the potential of human personality'.

'The social order', 'the potential of human personality' – these are abstractions which maintain a wide berth for different interpretations. For example, Marxist social workers identify the social order with capitalism and conceive of realising human potentiality in terms of working-class revolution. As the *Case Con Manifesto* (1975: 147) puts it:

> *Case Con* believes that the problems of our 'clients' are rooted in the society in which we live, not in supposed individual inadequacies. Until this society, based on private ownership, profit and the needs of a minority ruling class, is replaced by a workers' state, based on the interests of the vast majority of the population, the fundamental causes of social problems will remain. It is therefore our aim to join the struggle for the workers' state.

However, many radical social workers in the present day scorn workers' revolution as the best hope for progressive change. For example, the Birmingham Women and Social Work Group (81) (1985: 122) state:

> The early radical social workers aligned themselves in unequivocal opposition to the monolithic state. They worked from 'outposts' such as advice and community centres, and

[were] only reluctantly admitted by whom they were paid. They talked of the interests of the working class, the Revolution, the Workers' State, and either failed to see or chose to ignore the fact that male revolutionary heroes in the privacy of their homes sometimes beat up their wives. Women simply cannot afford to hang on in the hope that the 'the Revolution' will liberate them, along with the working class.

There are deep tensions in radical social work, and we have written about them elsewhere (see Chapters 2 and 3 of Rojek, Peacock, and Collins 1988). Nevertheless, self-determination, conceived as the capacity to develop one's faculties and energies freely and fully, remains a major theme in radical writing. Yet surprisingly, hardly any social work text has seriously addressed the question of the organisational form necessary to realise this development in social work. I shall come to this question and take it up in detail later in the chapter. However, before reaching that point it is important to set out some of the ways in which society has changed since the 1960s and early seventies and to consider how these changes bear on current options for self-determination and self-management in social work.

From red to green?

Social work is indivisible from society. In order to understand the potential of self-management in social work it is necessary to see where the question of radical change stands in the critical discourse of recent times. My discussion is necessarily brief. However, the reader may be referred to a number of full-length studies which explore the issue in detail (see, in particular, Frankel 1987; Geoghegan 1987).

For most of the postwar period, critical discourse on social transformation has been dominated by the question of working-class revolution. The high hopes that Marx and Engels nourished for working-class action have not been realised. Some commentators speak of the exhaustion of the revolutionary potential of the working class (see for example, Gorz 1980; Nove 1983). Others point to the diffusion of radical energies from the task of gaining control of the economy to a variety of radical programmes based on feminism, ecological concerns, the peace movement, health campaigns, anti-racist sentiments, and so on (see, for example, Feher and Heller 1984; Galtung 1986). Several themes have emerged from radical considerations of this state of affairs.

Radical opposition to the established order is now understood to be represented through critical pluralism rather than a coherent, unified mass movement. Relations of consumption are identified as equivalent to relations of production in the organisation of radical consciousness. The home and the leisure-place have emerged as forums for radical organisation which are as important as the workplace. Thus CND, the Green movement, the Anti Nazi League, and so on are pre-eminently phenomena of the non-work environment: they depend on people meeting and acting together in hours after work, on the weekends, and during vacations. This development means that the politics of radicalism are more complicated than when radical opposition to the established order was concentrated in the workers' movement (for example, the trade unions and the Labour Party – although it should be noted that things were pretty complicated even then).

A rainbow coalition of radical interests cannot be discounted. For example, it is always possible that the threat of a major global catastrophe, such as world war, the collapse of the world economic order, nuclear disaster, or environmental hazard might force a coalition of radical interest. However, the prospects for this are currently remote.

Caring and helping remain fruitful areas for building bridges between groups and challenging the established order. This is because carers and helpers, whether they be formally or informally employed, directly confront the casualties of a system based on organised inequality and repression. Dorn and South's (1988) research on the drugalogue and self-help groups can serve to illustrate what can be achieved in this field. The drugalogue is that area of discussion regarding drug use and its social origins and effects which develop among support groups organised around the drug user. These support groups consist of close kith and kin of drug users, principally mothers and fathers. Dorn and South mention that the drugalogue invariably raises questions which have radical import beyond the matter of drug abuse. For example, commenting on the drugalogue and sexual stereotyping in society they report (1988: 186):

[The drugalogue] involves a questioning of those aspects of gender identity that previously under-pinned the hegemony of 'parenthood'. For mothers this means the giving-up of those aspects of 'femininity' that previously underpinned modes of motherly care, nurturance and support that have come to be seen as counter-productive. For fathers, it means (for the relative minority who stay the course) a degree of conscious 'feminisation' as they struggle with themselves to find ways of relating in other than authoritarian ways. Women, it is claimed learn to care for themselves for the first time; men learn to care for the first time.

The drugalogue teaches participants that one's own perspective is partial; and this is the first prerequisite of self-management, for the recognition of partial interests is nothing else than the acknowledgement that people have different interests. The efficiency of organisations is not served by the suppression of interests, as occurs under the present hierarchical system of management in social work. Nor is it served by allowing each interest to develop independently, since this leads to all sorts of social abuses and ultimately to chaos. The pursuit of one's own interest requires partnership, for the realisation of each of our interests depends upon the co-operation of others.

Self-help groups reveal the diversity of social interests and show what can be achieved in helping and caring through planned co-operation. Moreover, this example is available at a time when traditional, hierarchical systems of social work appear to be on the brink of collapse. There are two aspects to this point which need to be distinguished. In the first place traditional systems maintain individualistic models of client care which are inappropriate to the structural basis of current social problems. This perpetuates ways of speaking and acting in traditional social work which fail to satisfy felt needs. The result is a crisis of confidence in the validity and efficacy of traditional methods and practices. We take up this matter and examine it at length elsewhere (see Rojek, Peacock, and Collins 1988). The second point is that government economies are preventing traditional agencies from discharging an adequate service. The position is stated with passion by Jeremy Oppenheim (1987: 10-12):

Things are going wrong in social services. I am not discussing a local problem or a wrangle with a proposed change . . . . We are talking about whether departments can meet their legal commitments; whether they can provide a service to children in care, abused children, people who are old and in crisis, and to people with disabilities, etc. The stark conclusion I reach is that some cannot and some do not . . . . This Conservative Government and our employers have brought us close to reflecting our clients. They have brought us to our knees.

Unrest among social workers

Oppenheim's words convey anger in the face of a deteriorating resource situation and exasperation with employers. His anger and exasperation is shared by many social workers. There is, in fact, considerable unrest and frustration within the profession. Some of the main grievances and sources of tension can be listed as follows:

(1) The significant steps taken by line managers to simplify and standardise work tasks. This is in response to the freezing of posts and demands from the state for greater accountability in the social services. One concrete effect of this on the social worker's working day is the enormous growth in form filling and record keeping. The paperwork has a double-edged function. It supplies management with a written basis for monitoring the work rate of social workers; and it is also a means for disciplining workers who fail to meet budgeted work rates. These functions are, of course, carried further with the computerisation of services. The drawback of computerisation is the high initial cost. However, it is attractive to senior management not just as a symbol of high tech, but also as a means of reducing labour costs in the medium and long term; namely, through freezing posts and producing redundancies. More paperwork and computerisation is resented by staff as an onerous burden which takes them away from what they see as their main job: face-to-face work with clients.

(2) Job security for all levels of staff have diminished in recent years. Workers are liable to be redeployed at the discretion of management and they have few powers of redress. Job prospects in the profession are no longer very attractive. Basic grade pay scales have not kept pace with rising professional expectations or increases in the cost of living. Similarly, economies in staffing have greatly reduced job mobility at senior management levels. Not only is there less scope for experienced staff to move, but young basic grade staff have fewer promotion opportunities. On top of this, there are serious and long-standing anomalies in the distribution of senior management positions between the sexes. DHSS figures on staffing in Social Services departments for 1976 indicated that 91 per cent of all Directors of Social Services are men; 86 per cent of Deputy Directors are men. In contrast, 64 per cent of basic grade workers are women; and 83 per cent of social work assistants are women (cited in Brook and Davis 1985: 4). In addition, the racial imbalance among social work staff is a real cause for alarm. It is estimated that there are no more than

300 black social workers in Britain out of a total staff of 20,000. The number of senior posts is insignificant. Moreover, in 1986 only one black person sat on the twenty-six strong Central Council for Education and Training in Social Work (all figures, The *Guardian* 29 Dec. 1986).

(3) Many social workers feel that changes in the system of social security provision are increasingly pitching them even further into a policing role with clients. For example, the *Social Security Act* of 1986 introduced new income support and family credit schemes to replace supplementary benefit and family income supplement, changes in the payment of housing benefit, and the Social Fund. Some critics see this as a significant move towards a full-scale means-tested system of benefits. At all events, one of the probable effects of the legislation is for new demands on social workers to increase surveillance of their clients' living conditions and sources of income. Senior management are likely to be concerned that funds for claimants are not misallocated and that Social Services departments do not aid and abet abuses of the new benefit system.

(4) There is a lack of understanding of social work skills and knowledge in the highest levels of state administration. Scepticism overshadows support. According to Loney (1986: 142) social workers have been denigrated as the bearers of 'those very soft, liberal reform attitudes which are [held to be] responsible for undermining effort [and] weakening morality'. Furthermore, he alleges that social workers have been used as scapegoats, notably in respect of child abuse tragedies, to divert public attention from poverty, bad housing, unemployment, and inadequate state spending on the personal social services.

All of these factors are combining to perpetuate a low state of morale in the profession. In particular, the duty of senior management to ensure cost effectiveness in the agencies often comes into conflict with that of basic grade workers, who see their primary and most urgent duty in terms of the alleviation of client distress. For example, in the late 1970s social workers formed the Birmingham Children's Defence Campaign to oppose the council's decision to close several children's homes as part of the expenditure cuts. Similarly, basic grade staff have challenged the monopoly of senior management to set plans and priorities in social services. For example, at the turn of the last decade the Leeds Social Work Action Group criticised senior management over the planning of social services, and the provision of services for the mentally handicapped in particular. Dissatisfaction and militancy may not be evenly spread through the ranks of social workers up and down the country. Nevertheless, there is widespread unrest and misgivings regarding the trend of government policy. The time is right for a fundamental rethink about how social work agencies should be run.

Self-management: whys and wherefores

The main moral argument for self-management is that it is a fairer means of corporate decision making. By co-opting representatives from all levels of the workforce into the management process, self-management extends democracy and accountability. The main technical argument for self-management is that it utilises information, talents, and skills which are ignored or wasted under hierarchical systems of management.

Systems of self-management have made the greatest advances in industrial enterprises. The reconstruction of the West German economy in the postwar years made provision for institutions of industrial democracy. These provide for employee representation on the supervisory board and a say in major strategic decisions. Industrial democracy has gone further in Sweden. Here manual workers do not merely have a say in work control, they also have a stake in company equity through 'wage-earner funds' (see Korpi 1978: 327-30). Other countries in which co-operative schemes are well established include France, Italy, Holland, Israel and Spain. The Mondragon group of co-operatives in Spain is often singled out as the leading European industrial democracy.

In Britain the experience of industrial democracy has been mixed. There is a long tradition of paternalist co-operation in companies like Scott Bader and the John Lewis Partnership. Here workers are given representation on the management board and are usually entitled to a share of profits. Experience of direct workers' control is more limited. The Upper Clyde Shipbuilders work-in in 1971 achieved considerable publicity and raised many expectations. It heralded a series of full-scale experiments in workers' co-operatives in the seventies; for example, the Triumph motor-cycle works at Meriden, the Kirkby Manufacturing and Engineering Works, the *Scottish Daily News*, and the Lucas Aerospace plan at Bristol. Although each of these ventures gave workers valuable experience of real participation they were not, for the most part, economic successes. Indeed, most crashed within a few years of trading. It would be rash to see these economic failures as evidence that the principle of industrial democracy is bankrupt. For, in each case, the co-operatives sprang into life in adverse or rapidly declining markets.

The Yugoslav system of self-management

The most fully developed attempt to build and sustain a self-managing economy in Europe is in Yugoslavia. In this section I shall describe the basic features of the Yugoslav system. In the next section of my discussion I will try to show how these features can be exploited and developed by social workers interested in exploring possibilities for self-management in Britain.

Before describing the Yugoslav system, it is perhaps worth commenting that the lack of a comparative dimension has been a major defect in radical social work in Britain. The failure to examine systematically social work in other countries has left British radical social workers with a narrow and misleading picture of the potential and varieties of fundamental change. By looking at Yugoslavia, I hope not only to give a perspective on the most mature self-management system in Europe, but also to show why comparative analysis is theoretically important for radical social workers.

Most non-Yugoslavs who have not looked into the matter assume that Yugoslavia is part of the Soviet bloc. In fact, Tito broke with the USSR in 1948. Since then, the Yugoslavs have sought to pursue a foreign policy of non-alignment and an economic and social policy of market socialism.

The centrepiece of economic and social policy is the system of workers' self-management. This dates from 1950, when the ruling League of Communists passed the 'Basic Law on the Management of State Enterprises by Working Collectives'. This created workers' councils. In enterprises of fewer than thirty members, the members managed their affairs directly as a collective unit. In larger enterprises, a representative system of management was enforced. Workers were elected to the workers' council. The size of councils varied from 15 to 120, depending upon the size of the workforce. In order to ensure the regular participation of all of the workforce, no member was allowed to serve for more than two consecutive terms. What were the duties of the council?

Three main duties were noted. Firstly, councils were intended to approve financial accounts and change the constitution wherever necessary. Secondly, they disciplined workers and determined the distribution of income. Thirdly, the councils ensured that enterprise taxes were met and supervised the actions of the managerial board.

All organisations require a storehouse of technical and market knowledge. The managerial board was designed to act as this storehouse. The board sought to advise the council on the implications of policy decisions, and to translate the decisions of the council into action. Three-quarters of the board were to be drawn from the shop floor and only one-third were eligible for re-election. The term of office was fixed at three years.

Although councils were, by definition, collectively managed, provision was made for a head person to front the organisation. The Director was intended to be the public face of the organisation. He – and in most cases it was a man – had responsibility for guaranteeing the productive, harmonious, and efficient operation of the enterprise. However, a system of checks and balances was installed to prevent the Director from abusing his position. The immediate check was provided by the workers' council, which possessed the power to veto the Director's decisions. However, the supreme organ of self-management was designated as the workforce. By holding a general meeting, the workers had the capacity to overturn the decisions of both the Director and the workers' council.

The rider to self-management in Yugoslavia is the trade-union system. The Confederation of Trade Unions (CUTY) is assigned two important tasks in running self-management. The first task is to raise the consciousness of the workforce about the positive pay-offs of self-management. This educational task is designed to spread knowledge, expertise, and enthusiasm for the principles of self-management. The second task is to protect the rights of the associated producers from counter-revolutionary movements in the system.

The Yugoslav system does not exist in aspic. A series of reforms have been introduced since 1950. In 1965 reforms were introduced to increase the autonomy of enterprises. The move towards decentralisation was continued in the early seventies. A series of laws were passed to establish a new unit of self-management: the Basic Organisation of Associated Labour (BOAL). BOALs were introduced in all cases where work teams recognised the right to work together as associated producers. Each BOAL was required to be efficient, harmonious, and to show a profit on operations.

It would be wrong to assume that the Yugoslav system is without defects. On the contrary, the system has produced many anomalies. For example, although self-management is open to all, decision making is dominated by white, male, university-educated, white-collar, and skilled workers. Furthermore, there are worrying inequalities in the sophistication of the system between the economically developed north and the rural, underdeveloped south. In addition, the workings of the entire system are hamstrung by the indebtedness of the Yugoslav economy to foreign creditors. I have written about these defects at length elsewhere (see Rojek and Wilson 1987). Nevertheless, the Yugoslav system has probably gone further than any other industrial society in decentralising power and responsibility to the workers.

Self-management for British social work

Now, I do not want, or expect, British social workers to copy the Yugoslav experiment slavishly. The historical, economic, political, and social circumstances of the two countries differ considerably. To take only the most obvious point, the Yugoslav system emerged through workers' revolution which sought to overthrow the rule of capital and create fully fledged communism. In contrast, Britain remains a tenaciously capitalist country, and the prospect for workers' revolution here is remote.

However, there is widespread anxiety among British social workers that the hierarchical system of management is failing clients. Similarly, there are fears that the government's concern to tighten up welfare provision and increase central control will bounce the social worker into a stronger policing role. Furthermore, there is a powerful and vociferous demand from politicians, civil servants, the media, clients, and social workers themselves, for more relevant and efficient systems of welfare. In these circumstances, it would be foolish to ignore the experience of full-scale models of self-management, if only for the purposes of comparison.

It is true that the option of decentralisation has already been considered by some writers on welfare management. The work of Croft and Beresford (see, in particular, 1986) provides exciting and concrete ideas of what non-hierarchical, non-bureaucratic, and non-paternalistic systems of welfare can achieve. It clearly demonstrates the sheer waste of energies and talents which occurs routinely under hierarchical systems of welfare management. However, Croft and Beresford do not say very much about planned decentralisation *within* the profession of social work. Here the Yugoslav experience provides a useful counterpoint.

For the remainder of this section I want to consider what self-management in British social work would look like if it was organised according to Yugoslav principles of decentralisation. My aim is to stimulate debate on what is an urgent, important but neglected subject in British social work. The discussion is not intended to be prescriptive. I am offering a version of self-management for consideration. I am not seeking the last word. Indeed, I would be happiest if the discussion provoked others to think about systems of management in social work which produce more flexible, more democratic, and more relevant forms of welfare than my own ideas.

Details of self-management organisation will vary between residential and area team settings. Self-management should not seek to impose uniform systems of management upon work teams. Rather, the goal should be to liberate repressed talents and energies in order to produce more relevant and efficient systems of care. Allowance must therefore be made for local traditions of wage bargaining, establishing terms and conditions of work, and the ideas of managers, workers, and clients. Self-management should encourage flexibility and diversity. The social problems in different geographical areas vary in incidence and intensity. This variation must be recognised in the procedures and objectives of the immediate care teams. In this, the hands-on experience of workers in the locality is a key resource.

The Yugoslav system is based on the fundamental principle that workers should manage their own affairs directly. Workers are responsible for determining policy, income allocation, work tasks, and, crucially, the effects of their own decisions. This principle should also be the cornerstone of self-management in British social work. That is to say, area teams and residential staff should have the power to manage their own work affairs directly. Since they are in closest contact with the welfare needs of clients, they have the best resource for translating knowledge into relevant forms of service. Self-management should encourage innovation through co-operation. Obviously, since in all foreseeable circumstances resources will be scarce, workers will be required to vote on priorities of care in the immediate service area. However, these priorities should be subject to regular monitoring, and free and open discussion should be held to determine whether they should be changed or not in the light of experience.

Although self-management is non-hierarchical, all work units require a symbolic head. In area teams, therefore, the Area Manager's post should be retained. The Area Manager should act as the chairperson of the self-managers in consultation and negotiation with external bodies; setting out the legal, financial, and political implications of the decisions of the self-managers; officiating at public ceremonies on behalf of the self-management group; and signing legal and contractual documents. However, the post should be subject to regular, open, and free elections from within the office. No term should exceed four years, and no person should be permitted to serve for more than two consecutive terms. The self-managers represent the sovereign body of power. If an Area Manager is found to be deficient or dishonest, steps must be taken to expel the person from office. As for institutions of residential care, the same arrangement should apply to the Head of House or Officer in Charge.

Self-management means autonomy. The new self-managing bodies will be self-sufficient in planning and have statutory responsibilities for local services. They will be required to liaise with other self-managing groups in social work and the wider care services. Obviously, this requires a techno-structure charged with the task of amassing and processing technical information for administration and planning. Given the economies of scale, the techno-structure would require a central location, probably in a town hall or county hall. However, steps should be taken to safeguard against Michel's 'iron law of oligarchy' which states that in large democratic organisations power tends to aggregate to those who execute bureaucratic and technical functions. One way of ensuring this would be to construct a proportional representation system which would place representatives of social workers and client groups inside the techno-structure. Where representatives lack the technical knowledge to operate and assess the functions of the techno-structure, they should be given access to training courses. The proportional representation system should be based on regular, open, and free elections. Furthermore, it should ensure that no elected member could apply for re-election after having served two consecutive terms.

The main task of the self-management bodies should be to provide relevant services to the community. Each body would receive an annual grant from the state. It would be then left to the associated managers to determine the allocation of funds between wages, administration, support services, training, transport, and so on. Everything should be done to oppose what Fox (1974) terms the 'low trust' relations which currently prevail in social work settings – that is, relations in which basic-grade workers, social work assistants, home-makers, home helps, cleaning and maintenance staff, client collectives, and so on, are assigned negligible autonomy and responsibility. Under self-management, where the workers run their affairs directly, the prime source of discipline should be self-discipline.

However, it would be naïve to imagine that the actions of the self-managing bodies will be free from conflict or abuses. If disciplinary situations arise, the associated producers will examine the case and determine the appropriate response in accordance with the facts and the constitution of self-management. Here the professional associations and trade unions in social work, such as BASW and NALGO, may have an important role to play, as in Yugoslavia. These organisations should ensure that each case is treated fairly and that the self-management constitution is applied. They might also have an important role to play in administering elections.

So far, I have confined my remarks on management reorganisation to changes which involve the workers directly. However, let there be no doubt, that full-scale self-management must find a legitimate place for the direct participation of the client. There are several ways in which the arrangement might be made. Where workers deal directly with client collectives, representatives from the collectives might be elected on to self-managing bodies. Similarly, communities served by the workers have an interest in the management of the local care services. They should have the right to elect representatives on to the self-managing bodies. No representative should be permitted to service for more than two consecutive terms. In this way, clients and the community should have a direct say in producing relevant services. As for residential units, the residents form a ready-made constituency of interests. In some progressive establishments provision already exists for representatives of the resident group to be on the board of decision makers. However, under self-management this provision would be extended. If necessary, clients would be sent on training courses to accumulate the technical knowledge to play a full and meaningful part in the self-management process.

Conclusion

It would be foolish to claim that the move away from hierarchical systems of management will avoid friction and dissent. After all, the logic of self-management prevails upon senior line managers to relinquish their traditional authority and power. Similarly, social workers will find their professional judgements challenged and their comprehension of welfare needs and services questioned, often by people who have had no social work training. Equally, clients, basic grade staff, and ancillary workers will be required to support their demands for more services, more staff, or whatever, with solid arguments and clear evidence.

All of this will be unfamiliar, and perhaps, disturbing, for most of the actors involved. Social workers in particular may object to the idea that their decisions can be overturned by consumers or by unqualified personnel. Given the long and difficult struggle by social workers to gain recognition for their professionalism, this is understandable. However, when all is said and done, we have to ask ourselves who is social work for? If clients and unqualified staff feel that their talents, energies, and ideas are monotonously ignored, who can be said to be the gainer?

Very obviously, self-management is not a panacea for the many and complicated problems and dilemmas facing social workers. What it can do is to give more people direct responsibility for the planning and administration of care. By harnessing the knowledge and skills of consumers and workers on the spot, self-management can contribute to more flexible, relevant systems of welfare. Furthermore, the decentralisation of power increases the accountability of the self-managers. Self-management, therefore, has a tendency to increase not only the relevance of welfare services, but also the efficiency of social work.

Of course, self-management presupposes radical changes in the organisation of social work in Britain. Some readers may discount these changes as unlikely or impractical. However, let no one forget that social workers face huge challenges, and that established hierarchical systems of management seem unable to tackle them. Under the established system, we descant on the needs of our clients and unqualified co-workers without acknowledging the immense diversity of those needs. We struggle to treat clients as fellow citizens, in conditions of material, sexual and racial inequality which makes a mockery of our aspirations to fellowship. In our working lives, we remake a system which controls even as it cares, and represses what it constantly promises to set free: the faculties and energies of the mass of clients and co-workers. Self-management moves away from a donatory system of welfare administration to a participatory one. It offers social workers the best means of translating their words on liberation, justice, and relevant social work into lasting deeds.

References

BASW (1975) 'A Code of Ethics for Social Work', in D. Watson (ed.) *A Code of Ethics for Social Work: the Second Stage,* London: Routledge & Kegan Paul, 1985.
Biestek, F. (1961) *The Casework Relationship,* London: Allen & Unwin.

Birmingham Women and Social Work Group (81) (1985) 'Women and social work in Birmingham', in E. Brook and A. Davis (eds) *Women, the Family and Social Work*, London: Tavistock.

Bolger, S., Corrigan, P., Docking, J., and Frost, N. (1981) *Towards Socialist Welfare Work*, London: Macmillan.

Brook, E. and Davis, A. (eds) (1985) *Women, the Family and Social Work*, London: Tavistock.

Case Con Manifesto (1975) in R. Bailey and M. Brake, (eds) *Radical Social Work*, London: Edward Arnold, 144-7.

Corrigan, P. and Leonard, P. (1978) *Social Work Practice under Capitalism*, London: Macmillan.

Croft, S. and Beresford, P. (1986) *Whose Welfare: Private Care or Public Services?* Social Services and Community Action Research Project, London: Lewis Cohen Urban Studies Centre.

Dorn, N. and South, N. (1988) 'Drugs and leisure, prohibition and pleasure: from subculture to the drugalogue', in C. Rojek, (ed.) *Leisure for Leisure: Critical Essays*, London: Macmillan, 171-89.

Feher, F. and Heller, A. (1984) 'From red to green', *Telos*, 59: 35-44.

Finch, J. and Groves, D. (eds) (1983) *A Labour of Love: Women, Work and Caring*, London: Routledge & Kegan Paul.

Fox, A. (1974) *Beyond Contract*, London: Faber & Faber.

Frankel, B. (1987) *The Post-Industrial Utopias*, Oxford: Polity.

Galper, J. (1975) *The Politics of Social Service*, Englewood Cliffs, NJ: Prentice-Hall.

Galtung, J. (1986) 'The Green Movement: A Socio-historical Exploration', *International Sociology*, 1 (1): 75-90.

Geoghegan, V. (1987) *Utopianism and Marxism*, London: Methuen.

Gorz, A. (1980) *Farewell to the Working Class*, London: Pluto.

Hollis, F. (1964) *Casework, a Psychosocial Theory*, New York: Random House.

Korpi, W. (1978) *The Working Class in Welfare Capitalism*, London: Routledge & Kegan Paul.

Leonard, P. (1984) *Personality and Ideology*, London: Macmillan.

Loney, M. (1986) *The Politics of Greed*, London: Pluto.

Marchant, H. and Waring, B. (eds) (1986) *Gender Reclaimed: Women in Social Work*, Sydney: Hale and Ironmonger.

NASW (1980) *Code of Ethics of the National Association of Social Workers*, Washington DC: NASW.

Nove, A. (1983) *The Economics of Feasible Socialism*, London: Allen & Unwin.

Oppenheim, J. (1987) 'Falling Apart At The Seams', *Insight*, 20 Dec.: 10-11.

Pincus, A. and Minahan, A. (1973) *Social Work Practice: Model and Method*, Illinois: Peacock Press.

Rojek, C. and Collins, S. (1987) 'Contract or Con Trick?', *British Journal of Social Work*, 17: 199-211.

Rojek, C. and Wilson, D. (1987) 'Workers' Self Management in the World System: The Yugoslav Case', *Organization Studies*, 8 (4): 297-308.

Rojek, C., Peacock, G. and Collins, S. (1988) *Social Work and Received Ideas*, London: Routledge.

Simpkin, M. (1979) *Trapped Within Welfare*, London: Macmillan.

Wilson, E. (1977) *Women and the Welfare State*, London: Tavistock.

Name index

Subject index

adult literacy programmes 32
adult psychiatric services 75
Advisory Council on the Misuse of
　Drugs 73
Age Concern 119
ageism 109, 117, 118
AIDS and HIV infection 3, 42-62;
　and black people 42, 44, 45, 47;
　and children 46, 49, 60; and
　drug use 42, 45, 59, 65; govern-
　ment campaign against 48-9,
　50, 52, 55, 57, 62; and
　haemophilia 46; and joint fund-
　ing 55; and language 52-3, 54,
　57-9, 62; and the media 43, 44-
　50, 53-4, 57-9, 62; and medicine
　47-8, 51-4, 58, 60, 61, 62; and
　moral panics 50-2; and public
　image 42; and prisons 45;
　received ideas of 53, 54, 58; and
　social work 42, 53, 54, 56, 57,
　58, 59, 60, 61, 62; training 56,
　61; and unions 45; and volun-
　tary organisations *see* voluntary
　agencies
Alcoholics Anonymous 98
Alzheimers' Disease Society 98
anti-psychiatry 163
anti-racism 133, 134
Area Manager's post, under self-
　management 184-5
assessment in mental health 152,
　153, 161, 163
Association of Metropolitan
　Authorities 59, 88

Barclay Report (1984) 6, 31, 168
BASW Code of Ethics 2

bereavement counselling 116
Birmingham Children's Defence
　Campaign 179
Birmingham Women and Social
　Work Group 174
Black and in Care 103
black people 21, 24, 42, 44, 123-8;
　birth rate of, 145; cases of, 132;
　children of, 140-2; and church-
　es 146; as clients, 129, 131, 145;
　as colleagues, 131-2; and educa-
　tion, 130; as employees 131;
　and families, 135-9, 140; and
　linguistic differences 128-9; and
　order, 124, 125, 143, 144; and
　police, 130; and policy makers
　125, 130; population of, 125-6;
　and poverty 123-5; and power
　142; as prisoners, 142; and pro-
　fessionals 131-2; as settlers, 134;
　as social workers 146; and ser-
　vice delivery 127, 130-1; and
　sociologists 123-5; and teachers,
　130; and training for.work with,
　133-5; and uprisings, 123; as
　youths 141-3
Body Positive 58, 59
Brain Committee 67

Camden 44
'Can-U-Cope' 18
Carlile Inquiry (1987) 6
Case Con 18, 33, 174
casework 17, 18, 21, 91
CCETSW 152, 179
Charity Organisation Society 13,
　20
child care 81, 87, 90, 102

claimants union 21, 93, 97, 98
class 1, 2, 124, 126, 174
Cleveland Inquiry (1988) 6
CND 1, 176
collectives 84-108; action-oriented
practice in 97, 98 benefits of,
96-8; consciousness-oriented
practice 98-9; in practice 98-
107; problems of, 94; and
women 97
community care 31, 54-5, 110
Community Development Projects
84
Community Relations Commission
21
community work 116, 118
computerisation of services 178
consultation 89-90
consumerism, in social work 4
'Cooling Out' 20
culture 139; and counter-culture
20; definition of 146; dominance of 137, 144; products
144; systems 138; traditions 145

decentralisation 85, 89-91
dehumanised approaches to
unemployed people 25
Derbyshire Coalition of Disabled
People 92-3
deviants 11, 21, 124, 137
DHSS 59, 102
domestic science 32-3
drugalogue 176-7
drug use 64-83; and assessment
76-8; and child abuse 76; and
Dangerous Drugs Act (1920)
66; and Dangerous Drugs Act
(1967) 67; definitions of, 65,
and detoxification 77, 79; Drug
Dependency Units 67, 72, 73,
75; history of, 65; and ideology,
74-5; and media 69-73; prevalence of, 66-8; as recreation 67;
and rehabilitation 79; stereotypes 65, 69, 71, 76, 78-9; and
social work 64-83; therapeutic
ends 66; training 76; treatment
157

ecology Groups 1
Edinburgh Social Work
Department 58

elderly people 4-5, 87, 94-6
empathy 115-6
employment 3
enterprise culture 7-8
ethnicity 124, 134

failure 79, 80
family interaction 153; and social
work 14-17, 153-6; therapy 116,
160
feminism 110-1
Freudian thought 18
Front Liners 59
functionalism 20

general practitioners 49, 50, 77,
81, 115, 157
group work 31

Hammersmith and Fulham Social
Services Department 57, 58
Head of House, under self-
management system 185
heroin epidemics 27
hidden economy 35, 36
hierarchical systems of management 178-80, 183-5, 186-7
HIV infection *see* Aids and HIV
infection
hooligans 15
home helps 44, 113
Home Office 64, 67
Home Office licensed doctors 67
hopelessness 37
House of Commons Social
Services Committee 55
housing 110,118
housing benefit 110
humanism 26, 28, 164

immigration 123-6
informal carers 84
International Year of Disabled
People 119

Job security, of social workers 178-9

Kensington and Chelsea Social
Services Department 57, 58
Kilbrandon Report 74

labelling theory 18, 104, 163